More Coding in Delphi

Nick Hodges

More Coding in Delphi

Nick Hodges

This book is for sale at http://www.morecodingindelphi.com

This version was published on 2015-08-18

ISBN 978-1-941266-10-6

Leanpub

This is a Leanpub book. Leanpub empowers authors and publishers with the Lean Publishing process. Lean Publishing is the act of publishing an in-progress ebook using lightweight tools and many iterations to get reader feedback, pivot until you have the right book and build traction once you do.

Tweet This Book!

Please help Nick Hodges by spreading the word about this book on Twitter!

The suggested hashtag for this book is #morecodingindelphi.

Find out what other people are saying about the book by clicking on this link to search for this hashtag on Twitter:

https://twitter.com/search?q=#morecodingindelphi

Also By Nick Hodges

Coding In Delphi

Contents

Foreword

I first met Nick Hodges at a meeting of the Naval Postgraduate School's PC Computer Club the early 1990's. I drove down to the meeting from Scotts Valley to present Borland's developer tools (which included Turbo Pascal for Windows, Borland Pascal, Turbo C++ and Borland C++). In those early days we had the Turbo Vision and OWL class libraries for writing DOS and Windows applications. By the middle of the 1990's the VCL component architecture (Properties, Methods, Events) was added to move GUI programming to the next level for Pascal and C++ developers. Even with these extensive class and component libraries, developers still needed to focus a majority of their time on their code, the real business logic of an application.

I have had the privilege of working closely with Nick Hodges since those early days when he was a member of our developer community and also as a fellow employee. Nick has always had a passion for programming, developer tools and the community of developers who love what we can do with the tools and code. Nick has also shown the development world new tips, tricks and techniques at our live conferences, online events, technical articles, blog posts and videos.

In his first book, "Coding in Delphi", Nick shared even more of his coding experiences to the world showing developers the power and new innovations in the Object Pascal programming language including: interfaces, generics, attributes and anonymous methods. Beyond new language syntax, Nick went on to showcase best practices for exception handing, using the extended runtime type information system and exception handling. To finish the book, Nick documented his years of experience modernizing legacy applications while keeping them stable using dependency injection and unit testing.

In this new book, "More Coding in Delphi", Nick brings us all to an even higher level of programming expertise covering patterns, operator overloading, parallel programming, multi-threading, aspect oriented programming and component development.

It is my honor to call Nick Hodges my friend. More importantly, I am an avid Nick Hodges student of programming. Put together, these two books provide the largest amount of deep Delphi coding expertise covering the most important programming topics.

I know you will enjoy reading and learning about "More Coding in Delphi".

David Intersimone "David I"

Vice President of Developer Relations and Chief Evangelist

Embarcadero Technologies

August 1, 2015

Preface

Well, here we are again. This book is to follow my first book, *Coding in Delphi*. I was humbled and pleased by the reception it received, and so I decided to give book writing another shot.

The first book didn't have many screen shots of forms and such. The focus was on the code. Ultimately, that's what we developers produce, right? I thought it would be a good idea to write another book of the same ilk because, well, the first one worked out really well and because there was a lot more to write about. However, this one will have a few screen shots in it, as there are some coding principles – parallel programming comes to mind – where a simple console application won't quite illustrate things well. So this book will have some VCL applications in the demo code.

I've actually broken down and included an entire chapter on VCL component writing. My friend, Bob Dawson, suggested that it has been quite a while since anyone wrote about components, and I decided he was right. So we'll get a chapter covering the latest techniques on building the immortal TSmiley.

But the focus will remain, as always, on the code.

One of the reasons that I've written these books is that they force me to learn new things. I'll be honest: at the start of the first book, I didn't always know enough to write a complete chapter on the topic at hand (cough, parallel programming, cough, cough). But I used writing about the topic as an opportunity to learn all I could and share it with you. The same is true of this book – I've learned a lot in writing it. This seems to work well, as we both end up smarter. I love learning, and I assume you do, too, because you bought this book. They say that you never really know a topic until you have to teach it, and these books are my way of teaching to learn, in addition to giving back to the Delphi community that has given me so much.

Another aspect to this book is that it uses a number of open source frameworks to teach the principles and techniques within. One of the objections that I hear from developers about using some of the tools and frameworks included in these books is that they add "bloat" and make binaries bigger. While I might not agree with the characterization that comes with the term "bloat," I have no choice but to concede the point about binary size. However, I'm going to press forward with the assumption that binary size isn't an issue. You can't make an omelet without breaking a few eggs, and in this case, the broken eggs are an expansion of generated code. For instance, if you want to use Duck Typing in your application, you'll need to enable RTTI, and that is going to increase the size of your binary. But without that increase, you don't get Duck Typing. It's a price that must be paid for cleaner, more powerful code.

The same thing could be said for performance. Much of what is discussed here won't make for the most blazingly fast code ever written, but blazingly fast code isn't always the goal. If speed is your deal, you've likely come to the wrong place. My friend, Bob Dawson, refers to the battle between two types of developers: those that want speed and performance and would have Delphi be more like C++, and those that want Delphi to be more like C#, with more powerful language features and libraries as part of the system. I fall in the second camp, and this book, as did my previous book, will reflect that. Speed is nice, but clear, powerful code is what I'm interested in.

Some things to note:

- I'm going to assume in this book that you have read my first book, *Coding in Delphi.* If you haven't done so, I very strongly recommend that you head over to the book's website[1], buy a copy and read it first. There will be things I talk about here that assume you know the ideas and principles found in the first book. In addition, my demo code may make use of things like the the Spring4D[2] collections and other frameworks discussed in *Coding in Delphi.*
- All of the code and this entire book is written about the Windows compiler. We won't be covering any of the newer features added to the mobile compilers in more recent versions of Delphi.
- This book was written with Delphi XE8 as the main development platform – most of the code will very likely work with earlier versions, but some of it won't. Specifically, the Parallel library is found only in Delphi XE7 and above, so for that chapter you'll have to have at least XE7.

There's a further point that I want to emphasize that I don't think I made clear enough in my previous book. The techniques that I describe here and in my previous book should generally be applied to green-field code. By that, I mean "code that you write from scratch." I'm pleased that I've helped some people "see the light" on writing clean, decoupled code, but you can only take these principles so far.

For instance, I urge you to code against interfaces and not implementations. But I wouldn't argue that you should wrap every component in an interface. I would argue that when you start writing your domain objects and business classes, you should write against interfaces, but for things like already existing code or components, you can use those as is. There's no need to try to put your datamodules into the Spring4D Container. The bottom line – if it seems hard to do, then maybe you shouldn't be doing it. Writing clean code should flow naturally, and if you find yourself fighting to do it, then perhaps you need to rethink your approach.

In any event, the goal here is as before: to help you write clean, uncoupled code with your concerns neatly separated and your code highly maintainable and testable. I hope that this book does that for you like the last one did.

[1]http://www.codingindelphi.com
[2]http://www.spring4d.org

Acknowledgments

First of all, I'd like to acknowledge and thank my beautiful wife, Pamela, who put up with me sitting at Burger King getting jacked up on caffeine via iced tea and working on this book. She's a marvelous woman, and I love her with all my heart. I'm grateful to her. I'd also like to thank my three kids who didn't see their dad for all the time I was working on this book. I love you more than you can know until you have kids of your own.

I'd like to thank all the people who bought my first book. Its success inspired me to keep writing and produce this book. I hope it is as well received as the first one was. Thank you.

I'd like to thank the fine people at the Burger King on North Charlotte Avenue in Pottstown, PA, for their kind service and patience with that strange guy who came in on Saturday and Sunday mornings and sat there at the computer station with his laptop and typed away. You guys were all great.

Many people – mostly members of the Google Group for *Coding in Delphi* – read drafts of this book and helped make it better. Some folks went above and beyond, and I'd like to make note of them here:

- Andris Klaipins
- Asbjørn Heid
- Andrea Raimondi
- David Milllington
- Stefan Glienke

Some specific shout-outs:

Thanks very much to David Heffernan for his help in fleshing out the `TFraction` example in the Operator Overloading chapter. I'm grateful for his help.

RemyLebeau(the guy from TeamB, not the guy from the X-Men) helped me immensely in writing the chapter on the Parallel Programming Library. I'm grateful for his help, too.

Thank you to Danny Wind for letting me use his demo in the `TParallel.For` chapter. I'm grateful.

The parallelism chapters were made much better by the careful and thorough reading of Andrea Raimondi and Asbjørn Heid. I'm grateful.

David Millington and Asbjørn Heid went over the `TThread` chapter with a fine tooth comb, improving it immensely. I can't say enough about how helpful they were. I'm grateful.

Jason Southwell and David Millington also made significant contributions to the Factory Pattern chapter. I'm grateful for their help.

I'm quite sure I've forgotten someone who helped me in some significant way. If that is the case, please accept my thanks and apologies for forgetting you. And yes, I'm grateful. :-)

I'd also like to thank Diane Moser for her awesome proof-reading skills.

As always, any errors are totally mine.

Frameworks Used in this Book

This book is about writing code in Delphi. As a result, it uses a number of open source frameworks to facilitate the coding techniques that are discussed herein. I refer to them here at the beginning of the book to enable you to retrieve the code and get them set up before we begin.

All of the frameworks below are available via source control. I recommend that you pull or clone the source code in accordance with the instructions in the source repository. This way you can very easily keep up with the latest changes and fixes. If you have questions about how to setup and use Subversion, Git, or Mercurial, please see Appendix A.

Spring for Delphi Framework

The Delphi Spring Framework is a large collection of libraries, including data structure collections, a dependency injection container, interception, encryption, and other features. In this book we'll be closely examining the interception library.

Homepage: http://www.spring4d.org/[3]

Source Location: https://bitbucket.org/sglienke/spring4d[4]

Repository Type: Git

License: The MIT License[5]

DuckDuckDelphi

DuckDuckDelphi is an open source framework that provides duck-typing to Delphi developers.

Homepage: http://arcana.sivv.com/duckduckdelphi[6]

Source Location: https://code.google.com/p/duckduckdelphi/[7]

Repository Type: Mercurial

License: Apache License V2.0[8]

---

[3]http://www.spring4d.org/
[4]https://bitbucket.org/sglienke/spring4d
[5]http://opensource.org/licenses/mit-license.php
[6]http://arcana.sivv.com/duckduckdelphi
[7]https://code.google.com/p/duckduckdelphi/
[8]http://www.apache.org/licenses/LICENSE-2.0

Six Thoughts Before We Start

As we begin the book, I want to give my thoughts on a few basic, only loosely related topics that I think are useful and of interest. Those topics are:

- Encapsulation
- Coupling
- Cohesion
- Command/Query Separation
- Postel's Law
- Composition Over Inheritance

Thoughts on Encapsulation

Introduction

I remember quite well when the "light bulb went on" when it came to object-oriented programming (OOP). It came while I was reading my favorite technical book of all time, *Borland Pascal 7 Insider* by Paul Cilwa. It was a terrific book, full of excellent writing and exceedingly useful code. It illustrated beautifully the use of objects, including encapsulation, inheritance, and the hardest notion, polymorphism. It was a thrill to finally understand what all the hype was about – and to realize the hype really was worth it.

When someone approaches OOP, I think the first and easiest concept to get is encapsulation. In its most basic form, encapsulation is "information hiding" – the concealment of the internal workings of a class. New developers seem to get that notion pretty quickly. They then move on to inheritance and polymorphism.

Encapsulation looks pretty simple in Delphi:

```
type
  TPerson = class
  private
    FFirstName: string;
    FLastName: string;
  public
    property FirstName: string read FFirstName write FFirstName;
    property LastName: string read FLastName write FLastName;
  end;
```

Easy, right? The internal data is private and protected from prying hands, while it is safely exposed as a property. Couldn't be simpler.

Implementation Hiding

I think that encapsulation is given short shrift as the "easy" part of OOP. I think that it is more important and more nuanced than it is given credit for. Sure, it's about information hiding. That's the basic idea, naturally. But there's more to it. I think that instead of thinking about encapsulation as "information hiding," we should be thinking about it as "implementation hiding."

Consider this class:

```
type
  TCustomers = class
  private
    FList: IList<TCustomer>
  public
    constructor Create; // will create the list.....
    property CustomerList: IList<TCustomer> read FList;
  end;
```

Does this class really hide its information? Is it protected from prying eyes and over-zealous developers?

No, it isn't. Think about this code that could easily be written using this class:

```
MyCustomers.CustomerList.Clear;
```

Is that something that you want the consumer of the class to be able to do? Did you even stop to think that the way the class was designed would allow for such a thing? You may have hiddenFList from your consumers, but you haven't hidden it enough; when you expose it as a property, you've exposed all of it. You haven't hidden the implementation – you've actually exposed it.

True encapsulation would take things a step further. Consider the following code:

```
type
  TCustomers = class
  private
   FList: IList<TCustomer>;
   function GetCustomerList: IEnumerable<TCustomer>;
  public
    constructor Create; // list will be created here
    procedure AddCustomer(aCustomer: TCustomer);
    property Customers: IEnumerable<TCustomer> read GetCustomerList;
  end;
```

There are two important things to note here. First, the list is no longer exposed for change. Instead, it is exposed as an IEnumerable<TCustomer>, giving you full power over the observation of the list, but no power to change the list. Second, there is a single method, AddCustomer, that allows the user of the class to add customers. That's it – they can't do anything else to the list. They can't delete or alter the items in the customer list in any way. They can only read the list via the IEnumerable<T> interface and add customers via the method that you've given them.

This is true encapsulation – you've completely protected the list and given access to it in a safe way. You've limited the ability to change the list merely to adding new customers. Thus, you've protected the internal implementation while still providing the functionality you need. If you want to be able to delete customers, you can add a procedure that does that without losing any of that protection.

Sweet.

A Balance

You need to balance the need for information hiding and implementation protection against the class's usability. You could provide protection for everything by making all your members private, but then of course your class wouldn't be able to do anything. You could make everything public, but then of course you would be neither protecting nor hiding anything. The trick is to find the right balance.

A good rule of thumb is to only make something public if it is needed for the use of the class **and** if it protects the internals of your class. Nothing should be made public that threatens the internal integrity of your class. The balance also comes in when you consider that the public portion of your class should make it obvious what your class does and can do, and what it shouldn't do, as well. A class designer should be very conscious of what is being revealed and take great care to ensure that all internals are properly protected, but properly exposed when necessary.

Never Let a Bad State Happen

Another aspect of encapsulation that gets short shrift is the notion that a class should never allow itself to be put into a bad or non-functional state. Encapsulation dictates that you not only hide your internals, but you protect them from being placed in bad or impossible states.

The first thing this means is that no internal object instance should ever be exposed as nil. If you have an object as an internal member, you should ensure that it is created before it is needed, and that it remains created and valid throughout the time that it is exposed to the end user.

> Note that this position allows for "lazy" initialization of objects, that is, the creation of objects on demand rather than on the initialization of the object. Your internal pointers can be nil, but that fact should never be exposed to the consumer of your object.

Here's an example of what I mean – that is, what not to do:

```
function GetListOfWidgets: TWidgetCollection;
begin
  if Widgets.Count = 0 then
  begin
    Result := nil
  end else
  begin
    Result := Widgets; // Of type TWidgetCollection
  end;
end;
```

This function could return nil. Therefore, any code that consumes GetListOfWidgets had to check for nil every time. This can be tedious. Rather than returning nil, the code should instead return an empty list to indicate that there are no widgets in the collection.

A class should never be allowed to present itself to the consumer as nil. Normally, this means you should create your internal objects in the constructor of the containing class and never free them until the destructor is called. If you have some need to "reset" your class during its lifetime, then have a routine that does that explicitly. Always protect your internal classes so that a consumer can never see a bad state – especially nil.

Dependency Injection

But what about the case of Dependency Injection? In *Coding in Delphi*, I strongly encouraged you to ask for your dependencies rather than create them. If a reference should ever be nil, then you need to be very careful about what you accept from external sources. Consider the following class interface:

```
type
  TWidgetProcessor = class
  private
    FWidgetVerifier: TWidgetVerifier;
  public
    constructor Create(aWidgetVerifier: TWidgetVerifier);
  end;
```

What should the constructor look like? You may be tempted to make it look like the following:

```
constructor TWidgetProcessor.Create(aWidgetVerifier: TWidgetVerifier);
begin
  inherited Create;
  FWidgetVerifier := aWidgetVerifier;
end;
```

That looks great, right? But what happens if the user passes in a nil reference? Well, you'll end up with a nil reference as an internal and that's not good. Instead, you need to protect your internals from ever being nil:

```
constructor TWidgetProcessor.Create(aWidgetVerifier: TWidgetVerifier);
begin
  if aWidgetVerifier = nil then
  begin
    raise ENilParameterException.Create('Cannot pass a nil parameter');
  end;
  inherited Create;
  FWidgetVerifier := aWidgetVerifier;
end;
```

This is called the "Guard Pattern," and the notion is pretty simple: you "guard" against bad data trying to infect your internals. You "Fail Fast" in ensuring – right at the point of entry – that your internals can never be nil. The Spring for Delphi Framework has a class called Guard in the Spring.pas unit that performs this protection for you in one line of code. Here's an example:

```
constructor TWidgetProcessor.Create(aWidgetVerifier: TWidgetVerifier);
begin
  Guard.CheckNotNull(aWidgetVerifier, 'aWidgetVerifier');
  inherited Create;
  FWidgetVerifier := aWidgetVerifier;
end;
```

The Guard class has a number of class procedures that allow you to verify input in any number of ways, ranging from nil checking to making sure strings aren't empty and that any Boolean condition is either True or False. Note that the check in the example is done even before the call to inherited. If the condition is not properly met, the framework will raise an EArgumentException, using the second parameter as part of the error message to tell you which parameter was not valid. The first parameter is obviously the item to be validated.

Whether you choose to use the Guard class or write your own Guard code, it is imperative for proper encapsulation that you use a guard clause to protect your internal classes and other references from ever becoming nil or any other state where they are anything less than usable. Part of the contract you make when you provide a class interface is that the class will always work, and if you allow your class to get itself into an unusable state, then you are breaking the contract you have with the consumer of your code.

Thus, encapsulation becomes a touch more important than mere "information hiding," eh?

Thoughts on Coupling

In *Coding in Delphi* I talked a lot about coupling, but I feel like I assumed that you knew what it meant. I'm guessing most of you do, but I thought I'd talk about it a bit here in more detail.

Coupling is the measure of how dependent your code modules are on each other. Strong coupling is bad and weak coupling is good. Strong coupling means that your modules cannot be easily separated from each other, due to the fact that the internals are mixed and intertwined. When your system is strongly coupled, it is said to be "spaghetti" code, as everything is all mixed up together like a bowl of spaghetti noodles.

Strong coupling often means that a change in one place can have unforeseen effects in unknown other places. It means that your code is harder to understand because complex, intertwined relationships are difficult to understand. Strongly coupled code is difficult to reuse because it is difficult to extract it for use elsewhere due to of all the intertwined dependencies. One should strive to reduce coupling in one's code to as much as possible.

Of course, your code can't be completely decoupled. A collection of completely decoupled modules can't do anything. They need to be coupled in a thin and light manner. I've said before that an interface is like a wisp of smoke – there is something there, but it is really hard to grab onto it. Code that is coupled via interfaces is coupled as thinly as it can possibly be coupled in Delphi.

A real world example of heavy coupling is the Space Shuttle. Now I'm no rocket scientist, but my guess is that the Space Shuttle is made up of hundreds of thousands – if not millions – of unique parts that fit together in one way and one way only. The parts are not generally reusable, and if you need to alter one part – especially if you have to alter the interface of a part – you have a problem because the other parts around it will probably need to be altered as well. This initial alteration could spread a long way throughout the craft and have far-reaching ramifications. The Space Shuttle, then, is a highly coupled system with high cohesion.

What's an example of loose coupling? How about a Space Shuttle built out of Legos. Sure, it won't go anywhere, but it would be easy to change its design as Lego pieces are easily put together and taken apart to make whatever you want. A Lego Space Shuttle would have low coupling.

Most of what I wrote about in my previous book and much of what I'm writing about in this book will be about reducing the coupling of your code.

In summary, uncoupled code will be:

1. Easier to read because it will be simple and not complex.
2. Reusable because it will be connected only by very thin interfaces
3. Easy to change and maintain because changes to the code will be isolated.

Thoughts on Cohesion

Well designed code will have good cohesion, but I really didn't mention this facet of developing clean code in my previous book. I thought it would be a good topic to cover here.

What is cohesion? Wikipedia defines it as the *"degree to which the elements of a module belong together[9]"* High cohesion is considered a good thing. That is, it is a good design to have your classes work well together to form a whole.

An example of good cohesion is an electric drill. It is made of a motor, a power supply, a casing, a trigger, a holder for drill bits, as well as the drill bits themselves. These separate components –- as different as they are individually –- all work together to create something useful.

The same is true for your code: if your classes can be easily combined together to create something useful, then that code is said to be cohesive. There's one catch, though: as we saw in the previous section, you don't want to achieve cohesion at the expense of coupling. A properly designed system has good cohesion and is loosely coupled.

---

[9]http://en.wikipedia.org/wiki/Cohesion_%28computer_science%29

Think about your drill. I bet a well designed drill can be easily taken apart using the proper screwdriver. The motor can be removed from the casing, the electrical system easily fixed or replaced, the drill bit holder removed and repaired, and then the entire drill put back together again. This happens because the drill is both loosely coupled together – each part is replaceable – and has high cohesion among its component parts.

Your code should be the same way: as was said above, it should be loosely but properly coupled. The modules you build should be able to be composed together to form something useful, but in a way that makes the system's decomposition relatively easy. If you realize that a piece of your system is useful for another project, you want to be able to easily reuse that module elsewhere without baggage from the current project. This is what good coupling is about: easily fitting together modules that were not originally intended to do so.

As mentioned above, Legos show high cohesion. They can easily be pieced together to create almost anything you can imagine. Even Duplo blocks have an interface to regular Legos that makes them very cohesive and easy to combine. Legos can be taken apart very easily. They can be put together very easily. There is a reason why they are the one of the most popular toys on the planet. Legos exhibit low coupling and high cohesion – the main reason that they are so popular.

Your code should be like Lego blocks – easy to combine to create useful things.

Thoughts on Command Query Principle

In keeping with our previous discussion on encapsulation, let's look at the notion of separating "commands" and "queries" by using the Command/Query Principle. The notion was first discussed by Bertrand Meyer in his book *Object Oriented Software Construction*[10]. This means that the idea is not new. In its basic form, it means we should separate the things that read data from the system and the things that write data to the system.

The Command/Query Principle states that there should be a clear separation between the updating of information and status in your program and the way that you read information from it. Commands and queries should be separately declared (though you'll find that commands can call queries but not vice-versa). It can be as complex as ensuring that reading and writing take place in completely separate classes, or as simple as ensuring that commands and queries are put in different methods of your classes.

Of course, the first question you'll have is "What do you mean by 'command' and 'query'?" Well, I'll tell you.

Queries

A query is an operation that returns a result without changing the state of the class or the application. In Object Pascal, this is typically a function. As a general rule, queries should not change the state of a class. They should be "idempotent," meaning *"denoting an element of a set that is unchanged in value when multiplied or otherwise operated on by itself."* (I had to look that up, by the way....)

Queries should exhibit two main behaviors: they should return a single value and "asking a question should not change the answer." They should be referentially transparent, which means that they should be perfectly replaceable with their literal result without changing the meaning of the system.

---

[10]http://www.amazon.com/gp/product/0136291554/ref=as_li_tl?ie=UTF8&camp=1789&creative=9325&creativeASIN=0136291554&linkCode=as2&tag=nickhodgeshomepa&linkId=IVMYKYZ22AWZJ2LQ

Your functions shouldn't change the status of the system you are working on, whether that be a class, a framework, or an application. You should be able to run a query, i.e. a function, a hundred times in a row and get the same answer back each time when the input is the same. This makes calling a function at any time possible without repercussions, because it doesn't change the status of the system.

Commands

A command is any operation that has an observable side effect. It is any code that changes something in your class or application. Typically, in Object Pascal a command will be a procedure – that is, code that takes actions without returning a value. Commands can call queries (but queries should never call commands, because commands change the status of the system).

Commands should not in general return values. Thus, the use of var parameters should be discouraged, if not outright banned.

Don't Mix the Two

As a general rule, all your methods and routines should be easily identifiable as either a command or a query. Commands and queries should be separate entities in your code – with the exception that a command can call a query if need be. A query can't call a command, because commands change the system, and that should really not be allowed.

The use of var or out parameters in a procedure will confuse this issue and thus should be discouraged. Following the above rules, you should more easily be able to understand and modify your code.

The Command/Query Principle also encourages you not to violate what I consider to be a bedrock of sound development technique: don't try to make one thing do two things. Here is some code that does exactly that:

```
procedure ProcessWidgets(aCollectionOfWidgets: TWidgetCollection; out aNumberOfProcessedWidgets: integer);
```

This method is a clear violation of CQP as it obviously is trying to be a command and alter the state of the system by processing widgets, but it also tries to be a query by returning, through an out parameter, the number of processed widgets.

Instead, the system should have a simple command to process widgets and a separate query to return the number of widgets that were processed. The procedure is trying to be two things at once, and all kinds of mischief comes from making one thing do two things.

For instance, instead, the code should probably look something like this:

```
procedure ProcessWidgets(aCollectionOfWidgets: TWidgetCollection);
function CurrentProcessedWidgetCount: integer;
```

In this way, you can process widgets all that you want, and any time you want, you can check the state of processed widgets. But you don't do both in one statement, which would be a violation of the admonition to have one thing do one thing.

Following the CQP in the design of your code will help to ensure the proper separation of concerns, resulting in cleaner, easier to read and easier to maintain code.

Thoughts on Postel's Law

Jon Postel wrote an early specification for the Transmission Control Protocol (TCP), one of the core protocols of the Internet protocol suite. You use it every day to surf the web, send emails, etc. One of the guiding principles that he used when writing it was this:

Be conservative in what you do, be liberal in what you accept from others.

This idea is also called the "Robustness Principle", and is sometimes rephrased as *"Be conservative in what you send; be liberal in what you accept."* When applied to TCP, it means that the sender of data should be strict in what is sent, ensuring that it is accurate and precise. It also means that the receiver of data should be forgiving and understanding of data to as large a degree as possible. If you send data, be as clear as possible in what you send. If you can accept sent data, then you should.

Any application programming interface (API) should follow this principle. The same principle should apply to your code. The public interface of your class should be viewed as an API. It should be conservative in what it sends and forgiving in what it receives. When calling another API, your code should send out correctly formatted data, following the rules laid down by the API. It should, however, be willing to receive incorrectly formatted input as long as that input can be understood.

> You shouldn't be so liberal in accepting input that you allow things like SQL injection and buffer overflow exploits. Take care to protect yourself while you are being forgiving in what you accept.

For instance, if passed a string, you might be happy to accept strings with blank spaces on the beginning and end, and use the Trim function to clean things up for the sender. Consider the situation where the input is a name. Clearly, a name should not have spaces at the beginning or end. However, you should accept a string that has such spaces. Why would you reject it? You wouldn't. Nor would you leave it in the form it was sent to you before accepting it.

Another example? Paths. Say you have a function that accepts a path as a parameter. Say,

```
procedure WriteFileToDisk(const aPath: string; const aFilename: string);
```

This procedure should be able to deal with a path that either has or does not have the proper trailing delimiter. You should gladly accept both. Of course, it is up to your internal workings to fix things up properly, but your code should be forgiving and take both "c:\mypath" and "c:\mypath" with equal grace.

Your classes might provide overloads for input methods, accepting both an integer and a string as input, providing a way for your class to be as forgiving as possible. It may be that your class has an ID property of type integer, but the caller of your application holds that ID as a string value. You should, of course, accept the string value as long as you can convert it into a valid value for your application.

On the other hand, when you call another API, your code should be strict and always send data in the correct, expected form. You should trim your string names before they get sent along to the API you are calling. If the system expects integers, you are going to send integers meeting the specification completely.

Another example is the use of nil. Your code should never pass `nil` to a method that you are calling and always provide a valid instance if the API asks for one. Also, as discussed above, your code should accept 'nil', but "fail fast" and immediately raise an exception.

Okay, now let me be clear: I'm not arguing that your code should accept anything. I'm arguing that your code should determine what is acceptable, and if the input sent by the caller can be made acceptable, then you should accept it. It should be as hard as possible to use your API incorrectly.

Thoughts on Composition over Inheritance

Of the three OOP principles, inheritance was probably the second principle that you came to understand after encapsulation. It's a pretty basic idea – you can augment an existing class while still using all the capabilities of the parent class. Easy as pie, right?

Interestingly, inheritance has decidedly fallen out of favor recently, giving way instead to the notion of composition. Inheritance is a powerful feature, but it can get out of control. Let's look at an example to illustrate the point.

Pretend you own a pizza shop. You want to write a system to manage all your pizzas. So you start out with a base class:

```
TPizza = abstract class;
```

Now, of course, that's a nice abstract class, so we have to descend from it. All pizzas have sauce, so we'll create:

```
TTomatoSaucePizza = class(TPizza);
```

And of course, we'll need cheese:

```
TTomatoSauceCheesePizza = class(TTomatoSaucePizza);
```

That's great. But your customers will want more ingredients. Let's start with Pepperoni and Mushrooms. We'll end up with:

```
TTomatoSauceCheesePepperoniPizza = class(TTomatoSauceCheesePizza);
TTomatoSauceCheeseMushroomPizza = class(TTomatoSauceCheesePizza);
```

and of course, your customers may want both, so you'll need:

```
TTomatoSauceCheeseMushroomPepperoniPizza = class(TTomatoSauceCheesePizza);
```

Now lets add in sausage, onions, anchovies and black olives.

Hmmmm. This is going to get complicated really fast, isn't it? Using inheritance, you are going to get a rather deep and wide inheritance model really quickly. Your properties aren't going to cover all the possible situations that happen as more ingredients are added. The overall design quickly becomes unwieldy and inflexible. You'll have a lot of code to write when the boss decides to add pineapple to the pizza, setting aside the fact that pineapple on pizza is an abomination.

Inheritance is cool and everything, but it has its problems.

- It encourages a gaggle of unwieldy subclasses. You can end up with many, many classes that may or may not meet your needs.
- You can never be quite sure what the super-class is going to do. Perhaps it is in a module outside of your control, and is very heavy with many dependencies. Creating it can cause side-effects that you don't want or aren't prepared for.
- Class hierarchies are very hard to change once they've been deployed. You might be stuck with pizzas that no one ever orders, and creating a new, special pizza on the fly will be impossible.
- You can't change a super-class without risking breaking a user's sub-class.

But there is a better way. How about we "compose" a pizza instead:

```
type
  TPizza = class
    Cheese: TCheeseType
    Sauce: TSauceType
    Ingredients: IList<TTopping>;
  end;
```

This is a perfect example of why you should prefer composition over inheritance. The composition version of our pizza is simple. It is more flexible, allowing for multiple cheese types, sauce types, and a practically infinite collection of ingredients. The above example – a very simple one – could easily have private fields, public properties, and a constructor to allow it all to be created in one shot. Okay, let's show that:

```
type
  TPizza = class
  private
    FCheese: TCheeseType
    FSauce: TSauceType
    FToppings: IList<TTopping>;
  public
    constructor Create(aCheese: TCheeseType; aSauce: TSauceType; aIngredients: IList<TIngredient>);
    property Cheese: TCheeseType read FCheese;
    property Sauce: TSauceType read FSauce;
    property Ingredients: IEnumerable<TTopping> read FToppings;
  end;
```

You'd be hard pressed to describe a pizza that this single class can't encompass. If you need to expand the definition of what a pizza is, you can do so easily without affecting existing uses of the TPizza class. You can replace the entire earlier hierarchy with one simple class. Composition allows you to do in one class what might take 2^n classes via inheritance. It also provides a vastly simpler, more testable code-base.

Another way to look at the issue of composition over inheritance is via interfaces (it always comes back to interfaces, doesn't it?). In a coming chapter, we'll discuss SOLID code. As a quick preview, the Interface Segregation principle states that you should keep your interfaces small and simple. If you do that, they can be used to compose classes using those interfaces rather than inheritance, resulting again in more flexibility.

> Note that it is said to *prefer* composition over inheritance. It doesn't say *always* use composition over inheritance. Inheritance has its place – it's just not usually the best choice when designing a class framework.

For example, take the classic example of TVehicle. It's common to create examples of using inheritance to define vehicles, adding wheels and a steering method. Then along comes a boat, and you are screwed. Well, composition of interfaces can allow for this kind of thing.

Consider the following:

```
type
  ISteerable = interface
    procedure TurnLeft;
    procedure TurnRight;
  end;

  IWheel = interface
    procedure Rotate;
  end;

  IMaker = interface
    function GetName: string;
  end;

  IGo = interface
    procedure Accelerate;
  end;

  IStop = interface
    procedure Brake;
  end;

  TCar = class(TInterfacedObject, ISteerable, IMaker, IGo, IStop)
    LeftFrontWheel: IWheel;
    LeftRearWheel: IWheel;
    RightFrontWheel: IWheel;
    RightRearWheel: IWheel;
    procedure TurnLeft;
    procedure TurnRight;
    function GetName: string;
    procedure Accelerate;
    procedure Brake;
  end;
```

```
TBicycle = class(TInterfacedObject, ISteerable, IMaker, IGo, IStop)
  FrontWheel: IWheel;
  RearWheel: IWheel;
  procedure TurnLeft;
  procedure TurnRight;
  function GetName: string;
  procedure Accelerate;
  procedure Brake;
end;

TBoat = class(TInterfacedObject, ISteerable, IMaker, IGo)
  procedure TurnLeft;
  procedure TurnRight;
  function GetName: string;
  procedure Accelerate;
end;
```

Here we have a collection of interfaces that can be put together – composed, if you will – to create any kind of vehicle, even a boat. Note that `TBoat` and `TCar` aren't all that different in their declaration, except that a car has wheels. The various interfaces available are enough to define the functionality of almost any vehicle, and if they aren't, it's pretty simple just to add another one. In the case above, you might think about adding `ILights` and `ITrailerHitch` as interfaces to be used by vehicles that can use them. Both could be added and composed with relative ease and a lack of pain to existing users of the class framework.

Composition thus becomes preferable for a number of reasons:

- Your composed class can be easily added to without repercussion. Perhaps you want to add a new type of cheese to `TPizza` – no problem. Perhaps you decide that you want to add specific kinds of crusts – that can be easily added without fear of breaking existing uses of `TPizza`.
- Composition allows you to delay the creation of components until they are needed, or to never create them at all if they are not needed. Perhaps your TCar is driving in the day, and the lights aren't needed, so they never even need to be created. Instead, the notion of lights could be set up to be either "On" or "Off", and the actual state of any object that manages the lights could be hidden behind those two states.
- You can also design your classes so that components can be dynamically changed if need be. You can't do that with inheritance. Once you've created `TAnchoviesPeppersSausageMozzarrelaThinCrust-Pizza` you are stuck with it. The composed `TPizza` can change its crust type on the fly if need be.

Conclusion

Okay, there you have six thoughts to, well, think about.

- Encapsulation is a bit more complex than you may have thought.
- High cohesion and low coupling are critical to well designed, easily maintained systems.
- Command/Query Principle will have the same effect, making your code more "reasonable".
- Postel's Law will make your API easier to use and your code more concise when using other APIs.

- If you compose your classes instead of using inheritance, you can often create a more flexible design.

All good stuff, eh?

Writing SOLID Code

Introduction

Who doesn't want to write solid code?

Of course, there is solid code and then there is SOLID code. SOLID is an acronym that describes five principles that will help you write solid, clean code.

Just to get it out of the way, the five SOLID principles are:

- Single Responsibility Principle (SRP)
- Open/Closed Principle (OCP)
- Liskov's Substitution Principle (LSP)
- Interface Segregation Principle (ISP)
- Dependency Inversion Principle (DIP)

We'll cover each one in turn, but there they are.

The SOLID principles were first compiled by Robert C. Martin, probably better known as "Uncle Bob". You can read the original articles on Uncle Bob's website at http://butunclebob.com/ArticleS.UncleBob.PrinciplesOfOod[11].

The principles are just that – principles. They are more guidelines than hard and fast rules. They can't be contained in a single framework or code library. They can often be utilized together. For example, applying the Liskov Substitution Principle means you almost can't help writing code that follows the Single Responsibility Principle and the Dependency Inversion Principle.

What SOLID Is

Despite the plethora of OOP based languages, many developers tend to write procedural based code. The classic example is "OnClick" programming that I've railed about so often. All too often we think we are creating a class framework, but we are really just wrapping up our procedural code in classes. The classic example here is a "God Class," where you start out with a single class and keep adding things to it until it can and does do everything. You probably have seen more than one of these as a TForm descendant.

The SOLID principles are designed to ensure that you write true, object-oriented code. They are the true basis of OOP. If you follow them, it will be very difficult to merely write procedural code in objects. They will force you to think about how your objects are designed and how they should be properly written. Their purpose is to help you write better OOP code – code that is properly decomposed and decoupled and thus highly maintainable and testable.

Follow these principles, and you won't be able to help yourself: You'll write better code despite yourself.

---

[11]http://butunclebob.com/ArticleS.UncleBob.PrinciplesOfOod

Now, here's something that is going to happen if you write SOLID code: You are going to have more classes, more code,more modules,and more units than you might be used to. This is okay. For some reason, developers shy away from "lots of classes," preferring fewer classes that do more things. Is there a better definition of "heavily coupled code" than "fewer classes that do more things"? More classes doing one thing each (Single Responsibility Principle) is the path to clean code.

I've said it before and I'll say it again here: There is no end to the mischief that occurs in code when a developer tries to make one thing do more than one thing. So don't be afraid of decomposed, decoupled code even if it results in lots of classes, interfaces, and units.

SOLID code will also answer the problem of many of the Design Smells that plague code.

- Code that is difficult to change because it is tightly coupled and written procedurally is said to be rigid. The SOLID principles will make your code less rigid.
- Code that is easy to break because it is poorly organized with connections that cross all kinds of boundaries is said to be fragile. The SOLID Principles will make your code less fragile.
- Sometimes we write code that is immobile – that is, it is hard to reuse in new places. The SOLID principles will make your code mobile and reusable.
- Viscosity is the measure of your code's ability to make it easy to do the right thing. Following the SOLID principles will make your code more viscous – allowing you to do the right thing when you know you should do it, instead of doing the wrong thing when you know you shouldn't.
- Finally, our code can become over-designed when we give it needless complexity. SOLID code is simple and clean and will help you prevent over-design.

Okay, so let's dive right into it.

Single Responsibility Principle

The Single Responsibility Principle states that a class should do one and only one thing. Uncle Bob says that it means "a class should have only one reason to change." However you look at it, a class should not be doing multiple things. It should be doing one thing. One and only one. Not two, not three – one.

Consider the following class declaration:

```
type
  TBook = class
  private
    FCurrentPage: integer;
    FTitle: string;
    FAuthor: string;
    procedure SetTitle(const Value: string);
    procedure SetAuthor(const Value: string);
  public
    procedure DisplayPage;        // Book Stuff
    function TurnPage: integer;   // Book stuff
    procedure PrintCurrentPage;   // Prints itself
    procedure SaveCurrentPage;    // Saves itself
    property Title: string read FTitle write SetTitle;
    property Author: string read FAuthor write SetAuthor;
  end;
```

This class probably resembles a lot of classes that you may have written or seen. And it all seems reasonable, right? A book does a bunch of things: it should display its pages, turn pages, print things, etc. What's not to like here?

Well, what's not to like is that if you want to change the way the class prints, you have to change the class itself. And maybe someone else is using the class and likes the way that the printing part works. The class is coupled to printing and displaying and saving and who knows what else.

In other words, this class is a pretty gross violation of the Single Responsibility Principle. So what is the solution? How about this:

```
type
  IPrintable = interface
    procedure Print(aString: string);
  end;

  TConsolePrinter = class(TInterfacedObject, IPrintable)
    procedure Print(aString: string);
  end;

  IPageNumberSaver = interface
    procedure Save(aPageNumber: integer);
  end;

type
  TBookManager = class
  private
    FCurrentPage: integer;
    FTitle: string;
    FAuthor: string;
    procedure SetTitle(const Value: string);
    procedure SetAuthor(const Value: string);
  public
    function TurnPage: integer;
    procedure PrintCurrentPage(aPage: IPrintable);
    procedure SavePageNumber(aPageNumberSaver: IPageNumberSaver);
    property Title: string read FTitle write SetTitle;
    property Author: string read FAuthor write SetAuthor;
  end;
```

This TBook doesn't really need to change. We've used dependency inversion (DIP) to remove the functionality of printing and saving. If you don't want to print to the provided console printer, pass in a different implementation of IPrintable. Want to save your page number to an INI file or a database? Pass in the appropriate IPageNumberSaver implementation. TBook knows nothing about the inner workings of those implementations and thus has no reason to change because of them.

TBook does one thing now; it is a book and nothing more. It's not a printer thing or a saver thing. You'd only change it if you want to change the way that it behaves as a book. It turns over the responsibility for printing and saving to external interfaces. No need to change anything if you want to print a different way – just pass in a different IPrintable implementation.

That's what is meant by the Single Responsibility Principle.

Open/Closed Principle

The Open/Closed Principle states that a class should be open for extension but closed to change. That is, a properly defined class, once deployed, shouldn't ever need to be changed (except for bug fixes, of course) and if there is new functionality that needs to be added, it should be added through extension or inheritance.

We are all guilty of violating this one. Shoot, if you have used a case statement in your code, it is very possible that you are violating the Open/Closed Principle. Take a look at this code

```
type

  TItemType = (Normal, TenPercentOff, BOGO, TwentyPercentOff);
  TItem = record
    SKU: string;
    Quantity: integer;
    Price: double;
    ItemType: TItemType;
  end;

  TOrder = class
  private
    FListOfItems: IList<TItem>;
    function GetItems: IEnumerable<TItem>;
  public
    procedure Add(aItem: TItem);
    function TotalAmount: Double;
    property Items: IEnumerable<TItem> read GetItems;
  end;

implementation

{ TOrder }

procedure TOrder.Add(aItem: TItem);
begin
  FListOfItems.Add(aItem);
end;

function TOrder.GetItems: IEnumerable<TItem>;
begin
  Result := FListOfItems;
end;

function TOrder.TotalAmount: Double;
var
  Item: TItem;
  LQuantity: integer;
begin
  for Item in FListOfItems do
  begin
    case Item.ItemType of
      Normal:        begin
                       Result := (Item.Price * Item.Quantity);
                     end;
```

```
    TenPercentOff: begin
                       Result :=(Item.Price * 0.90 * Item.Quantity);
                   end;
      BOGO:        begin
                     LQuantity := Item.Quantity * 2;
                     Result :=  Item.Price * LQuantity;
                   end;

      // More things coming!

    end;
  end;
end;
```

This code is wide open for change. If you want to add a new sale type, you have to dig down into the case statement of the `TotalAmount` function in order to complete that change. The class is most definitely not closed to change.

For instance, if you wanted to add a new `TwentyPercentOff` item, you'd have to add an item to the enumerated type (not that big a deal), but you'd have to add another item to the case statement in the `TotalAmount` function. This isn't the way you want to do things, as altering the class itself makes it easy to introduce bugs, causes you to have to update your test cases, and generally is fraught with peril. Why not design things so that you can deploy the class once, and then extend it easily instead of having to crack it open and change it?

Here's an example of using an interface (ISP) and dependency inversion (DIP) (which we'll look at below) to do the same thing in a way that makes it easy to extend:

```
type
  IItemPricer = interface;

  TItem = record
    ID: string;
    Price: double;
    Quantity: integer;
    Rule: IItemPricer;
    constructor Create(aID: string; aPrice: Double; aQuantity: integer; aRule: IItemPricer);
  end;

  IItemPricer = interface
    function CalculatePrice(aItem: TItem): Double;
  end;

  TNormalPricer = class(TInterfacedObject, IItemPricer)
    function CalculatePrice(aItem: TItem): Double;
  end;

  TTenPercentOffPricer = class(TInterfacedObject, IItemPricer)
    function CalculatePrice(aItem: TItem): Double;
  end;

  TBOGOFreePricer = class(TInterfacedObject, IItemPricer)
    function CalculatePrice(aItem: TItem): Double;
```

```
  end;

  TTwentyPercentOffPricer = class(TInterfacedObject, IItemPricer)
    function CalculatePrice(aItem: TItem): Double;
  end;

  TOrder = class
  private
    FListOfItems: IList<TItem>;
    function GetListOfItems: IEnumerable<TItem>;
  public
    procedure Add(aItem: TItem);
    function TotalAmount: Double;
    property Items: IEnumerable<TItem> read GetListOfItems;
    constructor Create;
  end;
```

(I've shown just the interface declaration here as the implementation should be obvious and straightforward. You can find the implementation on BitBucket if you want to look more closely at how it all works.)

First, we declare the IItemPricer interface which will handle the task of doing special pricing for a given item in our inventory. Then, TItem takes an IItemPricer as a parameter on its constructor. Next, we implement IItemPricer multiple times in separate classes with the various pricing schemes that we want to deploy. Once we have all those implementations of IItemPricer, we can add them to an item in the constructor with ease. We can also create new ones without having to change the TOrder class at all. It's ready to take on any number of items, and those items are ready to take on any pricing rules. Thus, TOrder is closed for change – there's really no reason to alter it – and open for extension – you can easily create new pricing rules and add them to the items list of TOrder.

Sure, we have more classes, but each is super easy to test, extending the system isn't difficult at all, and the base class, TOrder, need not be changed at all even if we want to add a new way to discount items.

So there you have a nice, clean example of being open for extension but closed for change – the Open/Closed Principle.

Liskov's Substitution Principle

Liskov's Substitution Principle is named after Barbara Liskov, the person who identified it. Liskov stated it quite formally:

> "Let q(x) be a property provable about objects x of type T. Then q(y) should be provable for objects y of type S where S is a subtype of T."

Now, it took me a while to decipher that. Actually, I never did quite decipher it without some help. Uncle Bob put it less formally: "Subtypes must be substitutable for their base types." Or as Mark Seemann puts it: "A client should be able to consume any implementation of an interface without changing the correctness of the system." Basically, it means that you should design your system so that either a child class or any implementation of an interface can be substituted for either the base type or that given interface without things being screwed up.

An example will be necessary here, I think. How about the classic `TVehicle` example? That is always prime for problems:

```
TVehicle = class abstract
  procedure Go; virtual; abstract;
  procedure FillWithGas; virtual; abstract
end;
```

Okay, if you have a keen eye, you'll already notice a problem here, but roll with me. `TVehicle` has two abstract methods. Any descendant will have to implement both of those. That's great – here's `TCar`:

```
TCar = class(TVehicle )
  procedure Go; override;
  procedure FillWithGas; override;
end;
```

That works great. The implementations of the methods will be what you'd expect, and a `TCar` can polymorphically be used as a `TVehicle`. All is well.

But of course, what happens when you try to define `TBicycle`:

```
TBicycle = class(TVehicle)
  procedure Go; override;
  procedure FillWithGas; override;
end;
```

The `Go` method looks great:

```
procedure TBicycle.Go;
begin
  WriteLn('Pedal like crazy');
end;
```

But what to do about gas? Hmmm.

```
procedure TBicycle.FillWithGas;
begin
  raise EVehicleException.Create('You silly, you can''t put gas in a bicycle.');
end;
```

Okay, so here's your first clue that you are violating Liskov's Substitution Principle: in order to implement a class, you basically have to raise an exception or otherwise not implement a given method of a descendant class. If your descendant class can't properly implement something it needs to implement, your base class is violating the Liskov Substitution Principle.

What's the right way to do things here? Maybe declare things as follows:

```
type

  TVehicle = class abstract
    procedure Go; virtual; abstract;
  end;

  TGasVehicle = class abstract(TVehicle)
     procedure FillWithGas; virtual; abstract;
  end;

  TCar = class(TGasVehicle )
    procedure Go; override;
    procedure FillWithGas; override;
  end;

  TTruck = class(TGasVehicle)
    procedure Go; override;
    procedure FillWithGas; override;
  end;

  TBicycle = class(TVehicle)
    procedure Go; override;
  end;
```

Here, we've removed the gas requirement from TVehicle and put it in its own class TGasVehicle. That leaves TBicycle clear to only worry about the Go method and not worry about gassing up.

The Liskov's Substitution Principle also works with interfaces. Let's take a look. Here's an interface for a bird:

```
IBird = interface
  procedure Fly;
  procedure Eat;
end;
```

Birds fly and eat, right? Perfect interface. (Hehe.....)

Here's an implementation:

```
TCrow = class(TInterfacedObject, IBird)
  procedure Fly;
  procedure Eat;
end;
```

Now, let's implement TPenguin:

```
TPenguin = class(TInterfacedObject, IBird)
  procedure Fly;
  procedure Eat;
end;
```

Uh oh. What do we do about implementing the Fly method? Penguins are great swimmers but they can't fly at all, so now we are stuck, just like we were before. What to do? Well, how about:

```
IFlyable = interface
  procedure Fly;
end;

IEater = interface
  procedure Eat;
end;

TCrow = class(TInterfacedObject, IFlyable, IEater)
  procedure Fly;
  procedure Eat;
end;

TPenguin = class(TInterfacedObject, IEater)
  procedure Eat;
end;
```

Our first `TPenguin` violated the Liskov Substitution Principle, but when we split up the interfaces, we can apply them as needed and all is well. And here's the fun part – remember when I said that these principles often work together? As we'll see, the above solution used the Interface Segregation Principle to solve the dilemma posed by `IBird` and `TPenguin`.

Here's a list of things that might make you think that you are violating the Liskov's Substitution Principle:

- Your code throws a `NotSupportedException` or something similar when implementing a method.
- If you are doing a lot of typecasting to get a class to be the right class in all cases.
- Extracted interfaces that aren't properly segregated will often result in an Liskov's Substitution Principle violation
- Often times, you might find yourself having to remove features when implementing an interface. This might be an indication that you are violating Liskov's Substitution Principle. One example would be a read-only collection, when you would need to remove things like `Add` and `Insert` to make it all work.

Interface Segregation Principle

The Interface Segregation Principle states that "Clients should not be forced to depend on methods that they do not use." That is, the client should be the one to define what it needs and not be forced to depend on things that it doesn't want to or need to depend on. An interface is defined by the client and not the other way around.

 Do you feel like committing a gross violation of the ISP? Grab one of your classes, copy its public section, and turn that into an interface. I'll almost 100% guarantee that doing that will violate the ISP. Think about it – by doing that, you are having the implementor, and not the client, define what the interface is.

In order to ensure that you follow the ISP, you should favor writing role-based interfaces over header-based interfaces. We saw this in the Liskov's Substitution Principle section previously: Rather than have a single `IBird` with a `Fly` and an `Eat` method, you should instead let the client dictate things – in this case `TCrow` and `TPenguin`, and have two separate interfaces instead – `IFly` and `IEat`.

Don't be afraid of having many small interfaces, even many with just one method. The smaller the interface, the more likely it will be to be used, and the fatter the interface, the less likely it will be to be reused. Reusable code is good, right?

Let's take a look at a more practical, real-world example. Imagine you have decided to ditch all this Delphi programming stuff and take on Netflix by starting a video store. You haven't forgotten Delphi completely, so you decide to build a small application to manage your inventory. As a result, you declare the following interface:

```
type
  IProduct = interface
    procedure SetPrice(aValue: Double);
    function GetPrice: Double;
    procedure SetStock(aValue: integer);
    function GetStock: integer;
    procedure SetAgeLimit(aValue: integer);
    function GetAgeLimit: integer;
    procedure SetRunningTime(aValue: integer);
    function GetRunningTime: integer;

    property Price: Double read GetPrice write SetPrice;
    property Stock: integer read GetStock write SetStock;
    property AgeLimit: integer read GetAgeLimit write SetAgeLimit;
    property RunningTime: integer read GetRunningTime write SetRunningTime;
  end;
```

You then implement that interface for DVD's and Blu-raydiscs. (Here's the DVD declaration....)

```
TDVD = class(TInterfacedObject, IProduct)
private
  FPrice: Double;
  FStock: integer;
  FAgeLimit: integer;
  FRunningTime: integer;

  procedure SetPrice(aValue: Double);
  function GetPrice: Double;
  procedure SetStock(aValue: integer);
  function GetStock: integer;
  procedure SetAgeLimit(aValue: integer);
  function GetAgeLimit: integer;
  procedure SetRunningTime(aValue: integer);
  function GetRunningTime: integer;
public
  property Price: Double read GetPrice write SetPrice;
  property Stock: integer read GetStock write SetStock;
  property AgeLimit: integer read GetAgeLimit write SetAgeLimit;
  property RunningTime: integer read GetRunningTime write SetRunningTime;
end;
```

This works great – you can track sales, what your stock levels are, quickly tell if a 13 year old should be allowed to watch the movie, etc. IProduct works great.

In fact, things are going so well that Netflix is considering suing you, so you decide to sell some T-Shirts that have a defiant comment about them on it. You go to add this to your inventory by implementing TTshirt with IProduct and...... it doesn't go so well. What's the RunningTime for a T-shirt? While defiant, the message isn't crude or anything, so there's no AgeLimit on selling the shirt.

And then it hits you -- the Interface Segregation Principle is being violated! What a fool you've been! You let the implementation -- the DVD's and Blu-rays -- define the interface and not the other way around. So you make the smart move and segregate out your interfaces:

```
IProduct = interface
  procedure SetPrice(aValue: Double);
  function GetPrice: Double;
  procedure SetStock(aValue: integer);
  function GetStock: integer;

  property Price: Double read GetPrice write SetPrice;
  property Stock: integer read GetStock write SetStock;
end;


IVideo = interface(IProduct)
  procedure SetAgeLimit(aValue: integer);
  function GetAgeLimit: integer;
  procedure SetRunningTime(aValue: integer);
  function GetRunningTime: integer;

  property AgeLimit: integer read GetAgeLimit write SetAgeLimit;
  property RunningTime: integer read GetRunningTime write SetRunningTime;
end;
```

Now, you can declare your DVD's like so (Blu-rays will look exactly the same...):

```
TDVD = class(TInterfacedObject, IProduct, IVideo)
  ...
end;
```

and your T-Shirt like:

```
type
  TShirt = class(TInterfacedObject, IProduct)
  private
    FPrice: Double;
    FStock: integer;

    procedure SetPrice(aValue: Double);
    function GetPrice: Double;
    procedure SetStock(aValue: integer);
    function GetStock: integer;
  public
    property Price: Double read GetPrice write SetPrice;
    property Stock: integer read GetStock write SetStock;
  end;
```

Your T-Shirt is not a video, so it shouldn't define nor carry around the baggage of what ends up being the IVideo interface. A T-Shirt can still be a product, but a T-Shirt is not a video. Therefore, they shouldn't be forced to share the same interface. Those two interfaces should be separated – or segregated – from each other. And that is the Interface Segregation Principle.

Dependency Inversion Principle

We've already seen the Dependency Inversion Principle in action when we looked at the Single Responsibility Principle. We saw the printing and saving functionality "inverted" by interfaces so that the class in question stopped printing and saving.

The simplest definition I can think of for DIP is the well-known saying *"Code against abstractions, not implementations."* Another way to put it is *"Always depend on an interface, not an implementation."* A more formal way to say it is *"High level modules should not depend on low-level modules. Both should depend on abstractions. Abstractions should not depend upon details. Details should depend upon abstractions."*

 I should note here that Dependency Inversion is similar to but not exactly the same as Dependency Injection. For an excellent description of this fine distinction, I suggest that you read this blog post by Derick Bailey on the Los Techies blog[12].

In fact, the Dependency Inversion Principle and Liskov Substitution Principle are closely aligned, as well: just as you should always be able to plug a air dryer or a lava lamp or any other electrical appliance into the wall socket of your house, you need to always be able to take one interface implementation and replace it with another implementation of that interface. If your appliances are hardwired into the wall, you can't replace them, just as you can't replace a concrete class with another one without performing surgery on your class (and thus violating the Open/Closed Principle). Therefore, the only thing that your code should know about is the interface. The implementation should be immaterial to your code.

You have probably heard a lot about the relationship between decoupling and writing clean code. But that is what the DIP is all about – having code that is as loosely coupled as possible. You can't have no coupling – your classes would never work together. But as we discussed above, you do want your code as thinly coupled as possible, and in Delphi, that is coupling by interfaces.(I'm not telling you anything you don't already know if you have read *Coding in Delphi*).

Let's look at an example. Here's some code that should be very familiar to you – it depends on concrete instances to do the main work. I see a lot of Delphi code that looks just like this.

---

[12]http://lostechies.com/derickbailey/2011/09/22/dependency-injection-is-not-the-same-as-the-dependency-inversion-principle/

```
unit uCoupled;

interface

type
  TCompressionService = class
  private
    function DoCompression(aByteArray: TArray<Byte>): TArray<Byte>;
  public
    procedure Compress(aSourceFilename: string; aTargetFilename: string);
  end;

implementation

uses
    System.Classes
  , System.SysUtils
  ;

procedure TCompressionService.Compress(aSourceFilename: string; aTargetFilename: string);
var
  LContent, CompressedContent: TArray<Byte>;
  InFS, OutFS: TFileStream;
begin
  // Read content
  InFS := TFileStream.Create(aSourceFilename, fmOpenRead);
  try
    SetLength(LContent, InFS.Size);
    InFS.Read(LContent, InFS.Size);
  finally
    InFS.Free;
  end;

  // Compress
  CompressedContent := DoCompression(LContent);

  // Write compressed content
  OutFS := TFileStream.Create(aTargetFilename, fmCreate);
  try
    OutFS.Write(CompressedContent, Length(CompressedContent));
  finally
    OutFS.Free;
  end;
end;

function TCompressionService.DoCompression(aByteArray: TArray<Byte>): TArray<Byte>;
begin
  // Here's where you'd compress the file..........
  Result := aByteArray;
end;

end.
```

Here is code where the high level module, the TCompressionService, depends on the lower level module, TFileStream. That isn't the way it is supposed to work. Here, we are coupled to TFileStream and have to do radical surgery on the class if we want to change the way our file handling works. And what if someone needs to compress data in memory or a string? We are violating DIP because we aren't depending on an abstraction, and we are having the high level module depend on the lower level module. The Compress method actually creates two hard-coded instances of TFileStream. TFileStream is a detail, and we shouldn't be depending on details; we should be abstracting them away instead.

So let's invert things.

```
unit uDecoupled;

interface

type
  IReader = interface
    function ReadAll: TArray<Byte>;
  end;

  IWriter = interface
    procedure WriteAll(aBytes: TArray<Byte>);
  end;

  TCompressionService = class
  private
    function DoCompression(aByteArray: TArray<Byte>): TArray<Byte>;
  public
    procedure Compress(aReader: IReader; aWriter: IWriter);
  end;

implementation

procedure TCompressionService.Compress(aReader: IReader; aWriter: IWriter);
var
  LContent: TArray<Byte>;
  LCompressedContent: TArray<Byte>;
begin
  // Read Content
  LContent := aReader.ReadAll;
  // Compress
  LCompressedContent := DoCompression(LContent);
  // WriteContent
  aWriter.WriteAll(LCompressedContent);

end;

function TCompressionService.DoCompression(aByteArray: TArray<Byte>): TArray<Byte>;
begin
  // Compression Algorithm would go here, preferrably an abstraction!
  Result := aByteArray;
end;

end.
```

Here we've completely inverted the dependencies. Now, the TCompressionService class is not dependent on the details, but instead is dependent on the two abstractions, IReader and IWriter. No longer is there any hard-coded dependency. Instead, we've put the dependency – or the details if you will – in the low-level modules, abstracted away behind the interfaces.

For completeness, here is but one example of how those details might be implemented. It's critical to note that you can implement `IReader` and `IWriter` in anyway you want – they are details and of no concern to the high-level module `TCompressionService`.

```
unit uFileReaderWriter;

interface

uses
      uDecoupled
    ;

type

  TFileReader = class(TInterfacedObject, IReader)
  private
    FFilename: string;
  public
    constructor Create(aFilename: string);
    function ReadAll: TArray<Byte>;
  end;

  TFileWriter = class(TInterfacedObject, IWriter)
  private
    FFilename: string;
  public
    constructor Create(aFilename: string);
    procedure WriteAll(aBytes: TArray<Byte>);
  end;

implementation

uses
      System.Classes
    , System.SysUtils
    ;

constructor TFileReader.Create(aFilename: string);
begin
  inherited Create;
  FFilename := aFilename;
end;

function TFileReader.ReadAll: TArray<Byte>;
var
  FS: TFileStream;
begin
  FS := TFileStream.Create(FFilename, fmOpenRead);
  try
    SetLength(Result, FS.Size);
    FS.Read(Result, FS.Size);
  finally
```

```
    FS.Free;
  end;
end;

constructor TFileWriter.Create(aFilename: string);
begin
  inherited Create;
  FFilename := aFilename;
end;

procedure TFileWriter.WriteAll(aBytes: TArray<Byte>);
var
  FS: TFileStream;
begin
  FS := TFileStream.Create(FFilename, fmCreate);
  try
    FS.Write(aBytes, Length(aBytes));
  finally
    FS.Free;
  end;
end;

end.
```

Thus, DIP becomes the basis for all decoupling. In the above code, you can change the implementation of `IReader` and `IWriter` without disturbing `TCompressionService` (and thus following the Open/Closed Principle!). You've successfully made all the modules – particularly the details – depend on abstractions (i.e. interfaces). That is the essence of the Dependency Inversion Principle.

Conclusion

Writing SOLID code isn't that tricky. It just requires you to look at your code from a different perspective. Follow the SOLID Principles, and you'll end up with easy to maintain, clean, well-written code. That you end up with more classes and interfaces is a side-effect with no real downsides. Small, discrete classes are easy to test, easy to reuse, and easy to combine into powerful systems. Who doesn't want that?

Patterns

In 1995, a seminal book was released named *Design Patterns: Elements of Reusable Object-Oriented Software* written by four people – Eric Gamma, Richard Helm, Ralph Johnson, and John Vlissides – who came to be known as the "Gang of Four." The book became the "Gang of Four Book," an instant classic because it defined a set of design patterns for writing software. Patterns arise from the notion that there are common problems to be solved in software design and that they can be codified into a set of general patterns that can be recognized and reused.

Sure, the book was written over twenty years ago, but good ideas don't go away, and the patterns in that book are as relevant today as they were then. Uncle Bob Martin defines a Design Pattern as "...a named canonical form for a combination of software structures and procedures that have proven to be useful over the years.[13]" Things found to be useful over the past years tend to stay useful over the future years. In this next section, we'll explore some of these patterns using Delphi code to illustrate them.

Patterns have two main uses. First, they guide your design and development and to lead you down the proper path towards clean good design. Since they have proven to work, you know that you can't go wrong if you follow them.

The other use is to provide a context in which developers can communicate with each other. If you say "I used the Observer pattern to solve the problem," then most developers will (or should) know what you are talking about. They become a *lingua franca* for developers to discuss ideas and design decisions.

 Design patterns are not meant to be recipes to follow step by step; rather, they show the way towards proven solutions to familiar problems. This should not stop you from adapting the code in this book to your particular circumstances, nor from finding a different solution using a given pattern.

I am indebted to the Gang of Four as well as to the authors of *Head First Design Patterns*[14] – Eric Freeman, Elisabeth Freeman, Kathy Sierra, and Bert Bates – for teaching about patterns and leading the way in clear, useful examples.

I can't cover all the patterns in the Gang of Four book – that would be a whole book in itself. I will instead focus on a few of the patterns that I have found useful and interesting in my development. They include:

- Factory
- Adapter
- Observer
- Decorator
- Command

Hopefully these few patterns will give you a taste for learning more.

---

[13] http://blog.cleancoder.com/uncle-bob/2014/06/30/ALittleAboutPatterns.html

[14] http://www.amazon.com/gp/product/0596007124/ref=as_li_tl?ie=UTF8&camp=1789&creative=390957&creativeASIN=0596007124&linkCode=as2&tag=nickhodgeshomepa&linkId=6Z6LCYW3PPWNALT3

Factory Pattern

Introduction

In my previous book[15] and even on my blog[16], I've encouraged you not to create things manually. Instead, I've encouraged you to pass off the responsibility for creating things to some other class whose job is specifically to create things. The reason for this, of course, is that every call to `Create` causes a dependency and a coupling of code. Those things are best avoided.

So in this chapter, we are going to look at the Factory Pattern. First, we'll take an informal look at factories and how they work. Then we'll look at the two main "real" factory patterns from the Gang of Four book, Abstract Factory and Factory Method. There are a lot of ways to do factories – shoot, a Dependency Injection container is really a glorified factory – but we'll try to take a look at the common ways factories are done.

Why do we use the Factory pattern? Well, because we want to write SOLID code. We want to follow the Single Responsibility Principle, and so we don't want our classes taking on the added responsibility of creating things. Instead, we want to create a separate class whose sole responsibility is to create things for us. Also, as we shall see, we want to follow the Open/Closed Principle. In our first example, we'll see a class that is most definitely not closed for modification, and so we want to sequester that problem out to a separate class that makes the class closed for modification.

An Informal Look at Factories

Simple Factory

Let's build some smartphones. Let's do it "wrong" first so we can see the problems with that way, and then we'll move on to take a look at how factories can decouple your code and make things easier to maintain.

First, let's define an enumerated type:

```
TSmartPhoneType = (CheapCrappy, Basic, Deluxe, SuperDuper);
```

This type will define the four different kinds of smartphones we will be assembling at the Nick Phone Assembly plant.

Here's what our smartphones look like:

---

[15]http://www.codingindelphi.com
[16]http://www.nickhodges.com/post/Life-is-Too-Short-To-Call-Create.aspx

```
TBaseSmartPhone = class abstract
  protected
    function GetName: string; virtual; abstract;
  public
    procedure GatherParts; virtual; abstract;
    procedure Assemble; virtual; abstract;
    property Name: string read GetName;
  end;

  TBasicSmartPhone = class(TBaseSmartPhone)
  protected
    function GetName: string; override;
  public
    procedure GatherParts; override;
    procedure Assemble; override;
  end;

  TDeluxeSmartPhone = class(TBaseSmartPhone)
  protected
    function GetName: string; override;
  public
    procedure GatherParts; override;
    procedure Assemble; override;
  end;

  TSuperDuperSmartPhone = class(TBaseSmartPhone)
  protected
    function GetName: string; override;
  public
    procedure GatherParts; override;
    procedure Assemble; override;
  end;

  TCheapCrappySmartPhone = class(TBaseSmartPhone)
  protected
    function GetName: string; override;
  public
    procedure GatherParts; override;
    procedure Assemble; override;
  end;
```

Here are a few things to note about our smartphone classes:

- They all descend from the abstract class TBaseSmartPhone. Remember how I am always saying to code to an abstraction and not an implementation? Well, TBaseSmartPhone is an abstraction. It's declared as an abstract class, and it has three abstract methods. And we are going to code against it instead of the actual concrete phone classes.
- There are four descendants – TBasicSmartPhone, TCheapCrappySmartPhone, TDeluxeSmartPhone, and TSuperDuperSmartPhone, each of which descends from TBaseSmartPhone. (At the Nick Smartphone Company, we know how to segment the market – that is clear.) Each of them overrides the three abstract methods, providing different implementations.
- I'm not showing the implementations because they are simple WriteLn statements that describe what

each method does, identifying each with the name of the phone. You can see the code in the code repository for the book.

Okay, now that we have a set of phones, we can create an assembly plant object that will assemble them:

```
type
  TBadSmartPhoneAssemblyPlant = class
    procedure AssembleSmartPhone(aType: TSmartPhoneType);
  end;

procedure TBadSmartPhoneAssemblyPlant.AssembleSmartPhone(aType: TSmartPhoneType);
var
  SmartPhone: TBaseSmartPhone;
begin
  case aType of
    Basic: begin
             SmartPhone := TBasicSmartPhone.Create;

           end;
    Deluxe: begin
              SmartPhone := TDeluxeSmartPhone.Create;
            end;
    SuperDuper: begin
                  SmartPhone := TSuperDuperSmartPhone.Create;
                end;
  else
    raise ENotImplemented.Create('aType was set to an undefined value');
  end;

  try
    WriteLn(Format('Assemble a %s', [SmartPhone.Name]));
    SmartPhone.GatherParts;
    SmartPhone.Assemble
  finally
    SmartPhone.Free;
  end;
end;
```

Here are some things to note about the above code (and why it's called a "bad" factory):

- It contains a big `case` statement that creates the correct kind of phone based on the parameter passed to the `AssembleSmartPhone` method. If we add more phones, that `case` statement would have to get bigger.
- From there, it uses polymorphism to call the methods `GatherParts` and `Assemble` to metaphorically put the phone together.
- However, there are some problems here. First, as your keen eye has probably noticed, the Assembly Plant object is tightly coupled to the smartphone objects. Second, if we want to add a phone, we have to violate the Open/Closed Principle and change the `TBadSmartPhoneAssemblyPlant` object, specifically by altering the `AssembleSmartPhone` method.

- In addition, the class has more than one reason to change. First, it might change because the assembly plant might need more functionality. Second, it might change because it might need to manufacture a new kind of smart phone, say TSuperCheapSmartPhone. Thus, the class violates the Single Responsibility Principle.

What's the solution for these problems? Well, let's decouple the creation of smartphone objects from the assembly plant by creating some simple smartphone factories. (I know, it's a little ironic to be creating a factory to pass to an assembly plant, but work with me here...)

Here's the declaration of a base class for our smartphone factory:

```
TBaseSmartPhoneFactory = class abstract
public
  function GetSmartPhone: TBaseSmartPhone; virtual; abstract;
end;
```

It's pretty simple, having but one abstract function called GetSmartPhone. And I'm pretty sure you can figure out what is going on here – that method simply will create and return a descendant of TBaseSmartPhone.

Okay, so below is the declaration and implementation of TBasicSmartPhone. I show you only one of the three, because they are all declared basically the same way, and I don't want to repeat myself and waste your time.

```
TBasicSmartPhoneFactory = class(TBaseSmartPhoneFactory)
public
  function GetSmartPhone: TBaseSmartPhone; override;
end;

function TBasicSmartPhoneFactory.GetSmartPhone: TBaseSmartPhone;
begin
  Result := TBasicSmartPhone.Create;
end;
```

There's nothing special going on here. It's just a method that creates the type of phone that the factory is named to create.

Actually, there is something special going on here: by using the factory, we've alleviated the assembly plant of the responsibility of creating things. Thus, we've satisfied the Single Responsibility Principle. As a result, instead of passing an enumerated type to AssembleSmartPhone, we can simply pass a factory:

```
type
  TGoodSmartPhoneAssemblyPlant = class
    procedure AssembleSmartPhone(aFactory: TSmartPhoneFactory);
  end;

procedure TGoodSmartPhoneAssemblyPlant.AssembleSmartPhone(aFactory: TSmartPhoneFactory);
var
  SmartPhone: TBaseSmartPhone;
begin
  SmartPhone := aFactory.GetSmartPhone;
  try
    WriteLn(Format('Assemble a %s', [SmartPhone.Name]));
    SmartPhone.GatherParts;
    SmartPhone.Assemble
  finally
    SmartPhone.Free;
  end;
end;
```

Notice that the case statement is gone, and that we can create any kind of phone that we want with this assembly plant, even phones that haven't been thought of yet. So if our marketing department decides to try to corner the market on cheap, crappy cell phones, we can create:

```
TCheapCrappySmartPhone = class(TBaseSmartPhone)
protected
  function GetName: string; override;
public
  procedure GatherParts; override;
  procedure Assemble; override;
end;
```

along with the factory:

```
TCheapCrappyPhoneFactory = class(TBaseSmartPhoneFactory)
public
  function GetSmartPhone: TBaseSmartPhone; override;
end;

function TCheapCrappyPhoneFactory.GetSmartPhone: TBaseSmartPhone;
begin
  Result := TCheapCrappySmartPhone.Create;
end;
```

And you can pass that to the TGoodSmartPhoneAssemblyPlant without having to change a thing in that class. Thus, we've satisfied the Open/Closed Principle with TGoodSmartPhoneAssemblyPlant – it's open for extension but closed for change. We extend it by enabling the passing of any TBaseSmartPhoneFactory descendant to it. Cool, huh?

Now we can assemble any phone we want:

```
procedure BuildASmartPhone(aFactory: TBaseSmartPhoneFactory);
var
  SmartPhonePlant: TSmartPhoneAssemblyPlant;
begin
  SmartPhonePlant := TSmartPhoneAssemblyPlant.Create;
  try
    SmartPhonePlant.AssemblePhone(aFactory);
  finally
    SmartPhonePlant.Free;
  end;
end;

procedure BuildPhone;
var
  SmartPhoneFactory: TBaseSmartPhoneFactory;
begin
  SmartPhoneFactory := TBasicSmartPhoneFactory.Create;
  try
    BuildASmartPhone(SmartPhoneFactory);
  finally
    SmartPhoneFactory.Free;
  end;
end;
```

Take the Next Step

Hmmm. Those last two methods work great – if you want to create a TBasicSmartPhone. If you want to create a TDeluxePhone, you have to tell the BuildPhone routine to create a TDeluxeSmartPhoneFactory instead of a TBasicSmartPhoneFactory. That's a bit clumsy, no?

Maybe you can see where this is headed – that is, for now, we are going to have to put that big ugly case statement somewhere (we'll get rid of it below, don't worry). So if we have to do that, let's isolate it as much as possible, and make it as easy as possible to add things to it. Okay, let's just go ahead and do that. Basically, let's encapsulate the notion of creating the correct factory like so:

```
type
  TBetterSmartPhoneFactory = class(TBaseSmartPhoneFactory)
  private
    FSmartPhoneType: TSmartPhoneType;
  public
    constructor Create(aPhoneType: TSmartPhoneType);
    function GetSmartPhone: TBaseSmartPhone; override;
  end;

constructor TBetterSmartPhoneFactory.Create(aPhoneType: TSmartPhoneType);
begin
  inherited Create;
  FSmartPhoneType := aPhoneType;
end;

function TBetterSmartPhoneFactory.GetSmartPhone: TBaseSmartPhone;
begin
  case FSmartPhoneType of
```

```
    CheapCrappy: Result := TCheapCrappySmartPhone.Create;
    Basic: Result := TBasicSmartPhone.Create;
    Deluxe: Result := TDeluxeSmartPhone.Create;
    SuperDuper: Result := TSuperDuperSmartPhone.Create;
  end;
end;
```

This factory has a constructor that takes and stores a TSmartPhoneType to define which smartphone should be created. Sure there's still the case statement, but it's been hidden away a bit inside the factory.

We can then modify the helper routine to take such a parameter:

```
procedure BuildPhone(aPhoneType: TSmartPhoneType);
var
  SmartPhoneFactory: TBaseSmartPhoneFactory;
begin
  SmartPhoneFactory := TBetterSmartPhoneFactory.Create(aPhoneType);
  try
    BuildASmartPhone(SmartPhoneFactory);
  finally
    SmartPhoneFactory.Free;
  end;
end;
```

And there you go – you've got a factory that has decoupled the creation of objects from the use of those objects.

Getting Rid of the Case Statement

So far so good. But that dang case statement is still bugging me. How about we design a system without it?

First, we'll use the existing smartphone types, specifically TBaseSmartPhone and its descendants, as well as TSmartPhoneType.

Then, we'll create an anonymous method type that creates a smartphone on demand:

```
TSmartPhoneFunction = reference to function: TBaseSmartPhone;
```

We'll then declare the factory:

```
TSmartPhoneFactory = class
private
  class var FDictionary: IDictionary<TSmartPhoneType, TSmartPhoneFunction>;
public
  class constructor Create;
  class procedure AddPhone(aType: TSmartPhoneType; aFunction: TSmartPhoneFunction);
  class function GetPhone(aType: TSmartPhoneType): TBaseSmartPhone;
end;
```

This factory is kind of interesting. The first thing to note is that everything is class method or variable, including the IDictionary variable. It also has a class constructor. A class constructor is a special constructor used by the compiler. It looks to see if the class is actually used anywhere, and if it is, it adds a call to that constructor in the initialization section of the unit containing the class. (You can read more about class constructors in the Delphi help: http://docwiki.embarcadero.com/RADStudio/XE8/en/Methods[17].)

Okay, so the implementation of the class constructor should be no surprise:

```
class constructor TSmartPhoneFactory.Create;
begin
  FDictionary := TCollections.CreateDictionary<TSmartPhoneType, TSmartPhoneFunction>;
end;
```

It merely creates the internal class variable of type IDictionary from the Spring.Collections unit. The dictionary uses the type of the smartphone as the key, and a function that creates the corresponding smartphone type as the value. It will thus store a way to create a given smartphone based on a variable of type TSmartPhoneType.

The AddPhone method is exactly what you'd think:

```
class procedure TSmartPhoneFactory.AddPhone(aType: TSmartPhoneType; aFunction:    TSmartPhoneFunction);
begin
  FDictionary.AddOrSetValue(aType, aFunction);
end;
```

but the GetPhone method requires a touch of explanation. Here's the implementation:

```
class function TSmartPhoneFactory.GetPhone(aType: TSmartPhoneType): TBaseSmartPhone;
begin
  Result := FDictionary.Items[aType]();
end;
```

There's only one line of code here, but it's a little tricky. First, the code takes the aType parameter and retrieves the anonymous function stored in the dictionary (we'll get to how that happens in a minute). But there's a little "trick" you need to note. See those two little parentheses there? That tells the compiler "Hey, actually execute the procedure and return the result." Thus, the GetPhone class function returns an instance of TBaseSmartPhone based on the type passed to it. Neat, huh?

Okay, how does the dictionary get filled? Well, every time you declare a descendant of TBaseSmartPhone, you call the AddPhone method for it in an initialization somewhere. In our demo app, the initialization for the unit that declares TSmartPhoneFactory looks like this:

---

[17]http://docwiki.embarcadero.com/RADStudio/XE8/en/Methods

```
var
  SPF: TSmartPhoneFunction;

initialization

  SPF := function: TBaseSmartPhone
         begin
           Result := TCheapCrappySmartPhone.Create;
         end;
  TSmartPhoneFactory.AddPhone(CheapCrappy, SPF);

  SPF := function: TBaseSmartPhone
         begin
           Result := TBasicSmartPhone.Create;
         end;
  TSmartPhoneFactory.AddPhone(Basic, SPF);

  SPF := function: TBaseSmartPhone
         begin
           Result := TDeluxeSmartPhone.Create;
         end;
  TSmartPhoneFactory.AddPhone(Deluxe, SPF);

  SPF := function: TBaseSmartPhone
         begin
           Result := TSuperDuperSmartPhone.Create;
         end;
  TSmartPhoneFactory.AddPhone(SuperDuper, SPF);
```

Thus, in this way, all the smartphone types are registered and available for use at runtime.

Now that we have everything registered and ready to go, we can actually use the factory to create types on demand:

```
procedure DoIt;
var
  SmartPhone: TBaseSmartPhone;
  SmartPhoneType: TSmartPhoneType;
begin
  for SmartPhoneType := Low(TSmartPhoneType) to High(TSmartPhoneType) do
  begin
    SmartPhone := TSmartPhoneFactory.GetPhone(SmartPhoneType);
    WriteLn('About to assemble ', SmartPhone.Name);
    SmartPhone.GatherParts;
    SmartPhone.Assemble;
    WriteLn;
  end;
end;
```

and we get an output that looks like this:

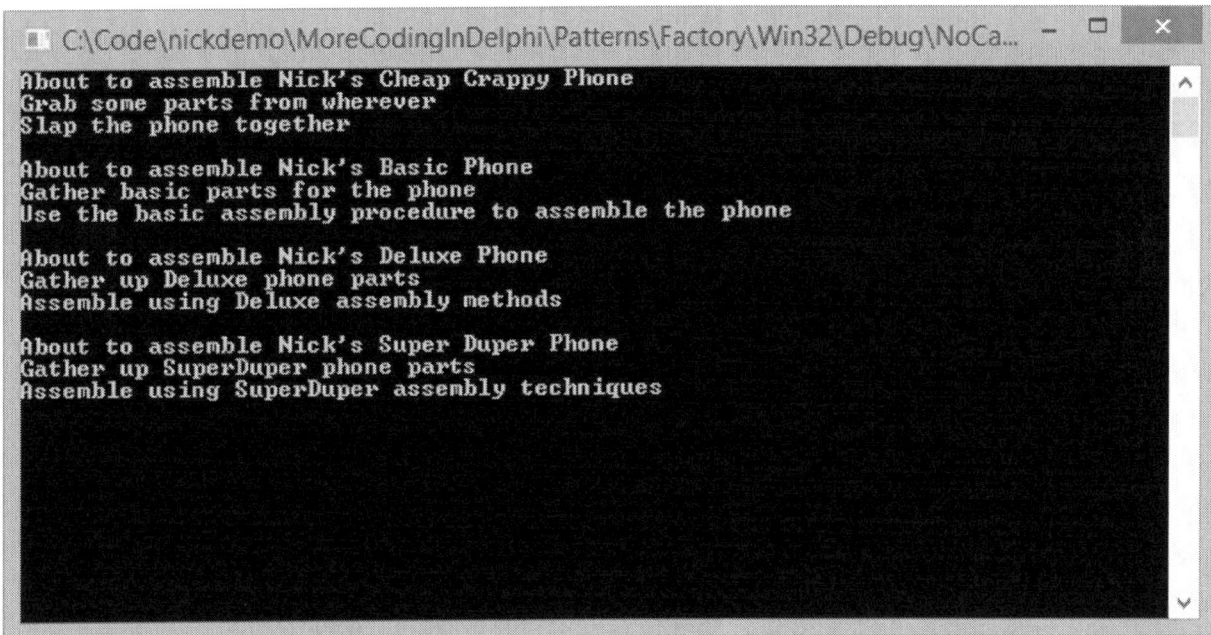

This method is obviously better than an ugly `case` statement. You can add functionality by putting all the new functionality in a separate unit, without having to touch any existing code. It even allows you to dynamically extend the functionality by registering things from an external library. It is generally more flexible, more easily maintained, and easier to extend.

Some General Thoughts on Factories

Factories abstract the notion of creation

Sometimes creation of objects is complicated, and you don't want your main class coupled to the things that are required to create a class. This is where factories can come in to do the creation without the coupling. They can encapsulate and abstract away the notion of object creation.

Factories can return interfaces

As we'll see below, factories can return interfaces, something that a constructor cannot do. This enables you to create a factory that can return various, unrelated classes as long as they implement the required interface. Thus, a class using a factory doesn't have to care at all about how an interface gets implemented, as long as the interface is implemented.

Raising an exception in a factory doesn't have side effects

When you raise an exception in a constructor, there are various ramifications that happen. For instance, an exception in a constructor results in the destructor being called. Raising an exception in a factory has no such side effects. You may want to have finer control over things when creating objects, and a factory can give you that.

Factories can return null objects

Well, a factory can actually return nil itself, but we never want to do that, right? What a factory can do is to return an object that follows the Null Object Pattern.

Factories can have generic type parameters

You cannot parameterize a constructor. You can parameterize a factory. Thus, you can take advantage of the power of generics with factories –– something a constructor cannot do.

Factories can create complex types

Factories can encapsulate the creation of complex types, enabling you to keep the construction of complex objects isolated. This can relieve a class's constructor of the burden of having many dependencies and having to coordinate the construction of these complex types.

A More Formal Look at Factories

So far, we've just looked at the general notion of factories, and we haven't really followed the "strict" definitions put out by the Gang of Four. They define two different factory patterns: Abstract Factory and Factory Method. Below, we'll take a look at these more formal pattern definitions.

Factory Method

The Gang of Four defines the Factory Method pattern as follows:

> Define an interface for creating an object, but let subclasses decide which class to instantiate. Factory Method lets a class defer instantiation to subclasses.

What does that really mean? Well, let's take a look at a simple example.

Delphi has a cool feature not found in many other languages – the class reference. In fact, a class reference itself can act as a class factory, and when embedded into a class, can be a good demonstration of the Factory Method pattern.

The Factory Method pattern occurs when you – surprise! – use a method on a class as a factory for creating a class. Usually, the Factory Method will take some form of an abstraction, allowing the class user to determine via polymorphism which exact class will be created.

For example, here's a class reference that we'll use as a simple factory:

```
TSmartPhoneFactory = class of TBaseSmartPhone;
```

then, we can create a class that will have a class method to create instances of our smartphones:

```
TSmartPhoneAssemblyPlant = class
  class function MakeUnAssembledSmartPhone(aSmartPhoneFactory: TSmartPhoneFactory): TBaseSmartPhone;
  class function MakeAssembledSmartPhone(aSmartPhoneFactory: TSmartPhoneFactory): TBaseSmartPhone;
end;
```

Note that there are two ways to create the `TBaseSmartPhone` – assembled or unassembled. This is a main reason to use a factory – when you want to vary the construction of the class, and the varying of the construction makes things a bit more complicated. Here we can produce a fully assembled phone, or a phone ready to be assembled. The two factory methods allow us easily and cleanly to choose by encapsulating the two assembly types.

Here's some code that shows how you can use the factory to create any type of smartphone that you want by merely passing in a class reference to the proper factory method:

```
procedure DoItAgain;
var
  SmartPhone: TBaseSmartPhone;
begin
  SmartPhone := TSmartPhoneAssemblyPlant.MakeUnAssembledSmartPhone(TDeluxeSmartPhone);
  SmartPhone.GatherParts;
  SmartPhone.Assemble;
  WriteLn;
  SmartPhone := TSmartPhoneAssemblyPlant.MakeAssembledSmartPhone(TCheapCrappySmartPhone);
  // Phone is already assembled.
end;
```

Abstract Factory

Sometimes you want to have a factory that defines a given interface for the creation of an object, but you don't want to specify the implementation of that interface until you decide at runtime.

The Gang of Four defines the Abstract Factory Pattern as follows:

> Provide an interface for creating families of related or dependent objects without specifying their concrete classes.

Of course, an example will do the trick. Let's imagine the notion of electrical devices that run on batteries. Here we'll use interfaces as our abstractions:

```
IBattery = interface
['{AE55BF10-3945-43BC-886D-AC8556334D55}']
  function GetType: string;
end;

IElectricalDevice = interface
['{14655F2F-8B5A-4A45-BC7F-459FEB99F8B6}']
  function GetName: string;
  procedure UseBattery(aBattery: IBattery);
end;

IElectricalDeviceFactory = interface
['{EFB88733-99B0-4E3C-B626-19D6C6CDA111}']
  function CreateBattery: IBattery;
  function CreateElectricalDevice: IElectricalDevice;
end;
```

`IBattery` represents – yes – a battery, and `IElectricalDevice` represents any device that needs a battery.

However, there are lots of different kinds of devices and lots of different kinds of batteries. Let's declare a few of them:

```
TLitiumIonBattery = class(TInterfacedObject, IBattery)
  function GetType: string;
end;

TCellPhone = class(TInterfacedObject, IElectricalDevice)
  function GetName: string;
  procedure UseBattery(aBattery: IBattery);
end;

TAABatteries = class(TInterfacedObject, IBattery)
  function GetType: string;
end;

TToyRaceCar = class(TInterfacedObject, IElectricalDevice)
  function GetName: string;
  procedure UseBattery(aBattery: IBattery);
end;
```

We've declared two types of batteries and two types of electrical devices that use different kinds of batteries.

So, what might be a good way to create all the right things in all the right places and at the right times in a way that is decoupled and flexible? We could create an Abstract Factory:

```
// Abstract Factory
IElectricalDeviceFactory = interface
['{EFB88733-99B0-4E3C-B626-19D6C6CDA111}']
  function CreateBattery: IBattery;
  function CreateElectricalDevice: IElectricalDevice;
end;
```

Yep, that's a factory, and since it is an interface, it is abstract, containing two functions that create a battery and an electrical device for use. By using it, you can implement any battery type and any electrical device that you want.

Now that we have an abstract factory, we can create a "client" class that uses it, and we can do that even before we write any concrete factories. That's the power and flexibility of factories. Watch:

```
// Client class
TElectrical = class
private
  FBattery: IBattery;
  FElectricalDevice: IElectricalDevice;
public
  constructor Create(aElectricalDeviceFactory: IElectricalDeviceFactory);
  procedure TurnOnDevice;
end;

constructor TElectrical.Create(aElectricalDeviceFactory: IElectricalDeviceFactory);
begin
  inherited Create;
  FBattery := aElectricalDeviceFactory.CreateBattery;
  FElectricalDevice := aElectricalDeviceFactory.CreateElectricalDevice;
end;

procedure TElectrical.TurnOnDevice;
begin
  FElectricalDevice.UseBattery(FBattery);
end;
```

TElectrical creates any electrical device for which you have a factory and then lets you power it up. It does all that without actually calling a constructor on anything. It defers to the factory for the creation of the batteries and the actual device.

What is needed now are some concrete factory implementations:

```
// Concrete Factories
TCellPhoneFactory = class(TInterfacedObject, IElectricalDeviceFactory)
    function CreateBattery: IBattery;
  function CreateElectricalDevice: IElectricalDevice;
end;

TToyRaceCarFactory = class(TInterfacedObject, IElectricalDeviceFactory)
  function CreateBattery: IBattery;
  function CreateElectricalDevice: IElectricalDevice;
end;

function TCellPhoneFactory.CreateElectricalDevice: IElectricalDevice;
begin
  Result := TCellPhone.Create;
end;

function TCellPhoneFactory.CreateBattery: IBattery;
begin
  Result := TLitiumIonBattery.Create;
end;

function TToyRaceCarFactory.CreateElectricalDevice: IElectricalDevice;
begin
  Result := TToyRaceCar.Create;
end;

function TToyRaceCarFactory.CreateBattery: IBattery;
begin
  Result := TAABatteries.Create;
end;
```

As you can see, each of the factories decides what electrical device will be created and what type of battery that device needs. You could create many more of these similar factories, and pass them to TElectrical without changing anything in the existing code. TElectrical can create any electrical device, even ones that haven't been invented yet. Expanding the universe of electrical devices involves nothing more than creating new classes. That's what an abstract factory lets you do.

Here's the procedure to make it all work:

```
procedure DoIt;
var
  CellPhoneFactory: IElectricalDeviceFactory;
  ToyCarFactory    : IElectricalDeviceFactory;
  Electrical: TElectrical;
begin
  CellPhoneFactory := TCellPhoneFactory.Create;
  Electrical := TElectrical.Create(CellPhoneFactory);
  try
    Electrical.TurnOnDevice;
  finally
    Electrical.Free;
  end;

  ToyCarFactory := TToyRaceCarFactory.Create;
```

```
  Electrical := TElectrical.Create(ToyCarFactory);
  try
    Electrical.TurnOnDevice;
  finally
    Electrical.Free;
  end;
end;
```

Conclusion

We've pretty thoroughly decoupled creation of objects from the classes that use them, eh? (And let's all say it together: "Loose coupling is good! Tight coupling is bad!") We've created factories, which are classes that take over the responsibility of creating objects so your main classes don't have that responsibility anymore. Our general classes no longer depend on concrete classes, but instead can rely on abstractions. And relying on abstractions makes for clean, easy to maintain code. Yay!

Observer Pattern

Introduction

The next pattern we'll look at is the Observer Pattern. You should use it when you have one object that needs to notify any number of other objects when events occur. The Observer Pattern creates a one-to-many relationship between an event-generating object and the objects that need to be notified about that event.

The Observer Pattern is a good way to separate your concerns. First, you have a concern of data production. Data production is useless unless it can be used or displayed in someway. However, there may be any number of ways that you want that data saved, displayed, or otherwise distributed. So the "Subject" – the thing being observed – keeps track of all the "Observers" that want the data. The observers should be separated from the subject via interfaces.

A good way of thinking about the Observer Pattern is to think of magazine subscriptions. You might subscribe to a news magazine that is delivered to you weekly. That magazine is the "Subject" and you are the "Observer." You read (observe) the magazine each week as it is delivered. You can stop subscribing at any time. But you aren't the only subscriber – other people, dentist's offices, businesses, etc., all might subscribe or stop subscribing at any time. The magazine producer doesn't know much if anything about where its magazines are going beyond the address, and you don't know much about what it takes to create the magazine – you just know it shows up each week.

The Observer Pattern is like this – observers can subscribe to the subject, and the subject can notify the subscribers of "news."

Baseball Data

Let's take a sports example – a baseball game. Baseball games traditionally keep track of the runs in each half of each inning as well as the score, the hits, and the errors for each team. These statistics are updated as the game goes on and are displayed and transmitted all over in real time - to websites, to the scoreboard at the game, to sports TV shows, etc.

The idea here is that the baseball game is the Subject – it is the object being observed and doing the notifying. The different displays for the game statistics are the observers – they wait for news of what happens during the baseball game and update themselves based on the notifications that they receive from the game. Another way to look at it is that the baseball game is a publisher of information, and the displays are subscribers.

The formal definition from the Gang of Four book for the Observer Pattern states: "The Observer Pattern defines a one-to-many dependency between objects so that when one object changes state, all of its dependents are notified and updated automatically."

When it comes time to implement this, however, the temptation is to simply embed the displays inside of a method of the baseball game itself. You might create classes for each view, instantiate them in the baseball game's constructor, and then simply update the views in a method called GameChanged.

Of course, if you do this you are breaking some of the base design rules. First, you'd be coding against an implementation instead of against an interface. Second, you've made it really hard to add a new data display should that become necessary. Displays are hard-coded into the baseball game and can't be added or removed at runtime. (Note that this way of doing things would violate the Open/Closed principle because the baseball game class would have to be changed to add a display.) If we do want to add more displays, we'd need to modify the baseball game itself. Or, put more succinctly, the baseball game and its displays are tightly coupled to each other. And if you know one thing about me, I despise tight coupling. You should too.

In any event, there is a better way – the Observer Pattern. As noted above, the Observer Pattern is made up of a Subject that is monitored by Observers. We'll implement a very simple version of the observer pattern. The first thing we will do of course, is declare two interfaces:

```
type
  IObserver = interface
  ['{69B40B25-B2C8-4F11-B442-39B7DC26FE80}']
    procedure Update(aGameInfo: TGameInfo);
  end;

  ISubject = interface
  ['{A9240295-B0C2-441D-BD43-932AF735832A}']
    procedure RegisterObserver(aObserver: IObserver);
    procedure RemoveObserver(aObserver: IObserver);
    procedure NotifyObservers;
  end;
```

The first interface is IObserver, which the observing classes will implement. In it they'll be updated with all the baseball statistics that the baseball game has for us. The second is ISubject, which will be implemented by the baseball game. It defines three methods, two for handling the connecting and disconnecting of IObservers, and the third for doing the actual notification to the observers.

But first, we'll need to declare a few data structures that we'll use to track the game.

```
type
  TInningHalf = (Top, Bottom);
  TTeam = (Home, Away);

  TInning = record
    Top: integer;   // will hold score for that half inning
    Bottom: integer;
    constructor Create(aTop, aBottom: integer);
  end;

  TRuns = record
    Home: integer;
    Away: integer;
    constructor Create(aHome, aAway: integer);
  end;

  THits = record
    Home: integer;
    Away: integer;
    constructor Create(aHome, aAway: integer);
```

```
  end;

  TErrors = record
    Home: integer;
    Away: integer;
    constructor Create(aHome, aAway: integer);
  end;

  TInningNumber = 1..9; // There are normally nine innings in a baseball game

  TGameInfo = record
    Innings: array[TInningNumber] of TInning;
    Runs: TRuns;
    Hits: THits;
    Errors: TErrors;
    procedure SetInning(aInningNumber: integer; aInningHalf: TInningHalf; aValue: integer);
  end;
```

The basic data for a baseball game includes the score for each half inning as well as the total runs, hits, and errors that occur during the game. These are aggregated into a record called TGameInfo for easier access.

Next, we'll look at the Subject – the thing being observed. Note that it implements ISubject, and thus it contains code for tracking any number of observers in an internal list.

```
type
  TBaseballGame = class(TInterfacedObject, ISubject)
  private
    FHomeTeam: string;
    FAwayTeam: string;
    FGameInfo: TGameInfo;
    FObserverList: TList<IObserver>;
    procedure NotifyObservers;
  public
    constructor Create(aHomeTeam: string; aAwayTeam: string);
    destructor Destroy; override;
    procedure RegisterObserver(aObserver: IObserver);
    procedure RemoveObserver(aObserver: IObserver);
    procedure SetInning(aInningNumber: TInningNumber; aInning: TInning);
    procedure SetRuns(aRuns: TRuns);
    procedure SetHits(aHits: THits);
    procedure SetErrors(aErrors: TErrors);
    procedure GameChanged;
    property GameInfo: TGameInfo read FGameInfo write FGameInfo;
    property HomeTeam: string read FHomeTeam;
    property AwayTeam: string read FAwayTeam;
  end;
```

The plumbing for managing the TBaseballGame implementation is what you'd expect. The interesting part, of course, is the implementation of ISubject: internally, it uses a TList<IObserver> to manage all the observers that get registered. The RegisterObserver and RemoveObserver methods simply insert and remove, respectively, instances of classes that implement the IObserver interface.

The real action occurs in the NotifyObservers method. We'll get to that in a second. First, though, let's take a look at the observers; they are going to implement different ways to display the baseball score. Since all the displays are very similar, this is a good time to use good old-fashioned inheritance to declare a base class that implements the needed functionality, and then have descendant classes that do the work of providing the specified displays. Here, then, is the interface for TBaseballGameDisplay:

```
TBaseballGameDisplay = class(TInterfacedObject, IObserver, IDisplay)
private
  FSubject: TBaseballGame;
public
  constructor Create(aBaseballGame: TBaseballGame);
  procedure Update(aGameInfo: TGameInfo); virtual;
  procedure Display; virtual; abstract;
end;
```

The IDisplay interface that it implements is here:

```
IDisplay = interface
['{1517E56B-DDB3-4E04-AF1A-C70CF16293B2}']
  procedure Display;
end;
```

TBaseballGameDisplay has an internal field to keep track of the baseball game that it is observing. Its descendants can do as they please with the data it contains. The class also implements the IDisplay interface so that it can report out what it has to say. The Update method will allow the Subject -- in this case the baseball game -- to update all of the displays that are observing the game. Update is a virtual method, by the way, so that descendants can do different things with the incoming information.

In addition, here are the constructor and destructor for TBaseballGameDisplay:

```
constructor TBaseballGameDisplay.Create(aBaseballGame: TBaseballGame);
begin
  inherited Create;
            if aBaseballGame = nil  then
  begin
    raise Exception.Create('You cannot pass a nil baseball game');
  end;

  FSubject := aBaseballGame;
  FSubject.RegisterObserver(Self);
end;

destructor TBaseballGameDisplay.Destroy;
begin
  FSubject.RemoveObserver(Self);
  inherited;
end;
```

Note that it takes a TBaseballGame as a parameter, and registers itself with that TBaseballGame via a call to RegisterObserver.

Okay, so let's look under the hood. The baseball game can accept and remove IObserver implementations at runtime. It implements the NotifyObservers method as part of the ISubject interface. It gets called whenever the baseball game information changes. It is implemented as follows:

```
procedure TBaseballGame.NotifyObservers;
var
  Observer: IObserver;
begin
  for Observer in FObserverList do
  begin
    Observer.Update(GameInfo);
  end;
end;
```

This is pretty simple – it merely enumerates over each item in the observer list and calls the `Update` method on each display, passing along the new `GameInfo` data. The base class stores the information, and its descendants process it.

The real "work" gets done when the baseball updates the inning data and calls `NotifyObservers`:

```
procedure TBaseballGame.SetInning(aInningNumber: TInningNumber; aInning: TInning);
begin
  FGameInfo.Innings[aInningNumber].Top := aInning.Top;
  FGameInfo.Innings[aInningNumber].Bottom := aInning.Bottom;
  GameChanged;  // simply calls NotifyObservers
end;
```

What about the displays? Well, I define two and hint at a third. The first one prints out a traditional baseball line score:

```
TFullGameDisplay = class(TBaseballGameDisplay)
strict private
  procedure Display; override;
end;

procedure TFullGameDisplay.Display;
var
  i: Integer;
begin
  WriteLn('1 2 3 4 5 6 7 8 9  R H E');
  WriteLn('------------------------');
  for i := Low(TInningNumber) to High(TInningNumber) do
  begin
    Write(FSubject.GameInfo.Innings[i].Top, ' ');
  end;
  WriteLn(' ', FSubject.GameInfo.Runs.Away, ' ', FSubject.GameInfo.Hits.Away, ' ',
        FSubject.GameInfo.Errors.Away);

  for i := Low(TInningNumber) to High(TInningNumber) do
  begin
    Write(FSubject.GameInfo.Innings[i].Bottom, ' ');
  end;
  WriteLn(' ', FSubject.GameInfo.Runs.Home, ' ', FSubject.GameInfo.Hits.Home, ' ',
        FSubject.GameInfo.Errors.Home);

end;
```

The next display simply prints out the score of the game:

```
{ TGameScore }

procedure TGameScore.Display;
begin
  WriteLn;
  WriteLn(FSubject.AwayTeam, ': ', FSubject.GameInfo.Runs.Away);
  WriteLn(FSubject.HomeTeam, ': ', FSubject.GameInfo.Runs.Home);
  WriteLn;
end;
```

The third one, THTMLOutput, would, if I were really ambitious, provide an HTML output of the baseball data. But I'm not that ambitious, and provide it here merely as an illustration of what could be done with the baseball data.

```
THTMLOutput = class(TBaseballGameDisplay)
strict private
  procedure Display; override;
end;

procedure THTMLOutput.Display;
begin
  Writeln('An HTML output here is beyond the scope of the demo, but you can imagine it, right?');
end;
```

So all of this comes together in a method to create a baseball game and add observers:

```
procedure DoBaseballGame;
var
  BaseballGame: TBaseballGame;
  // Displays
  FullDisplay: IDisplay;
  ScoreDisplay: IDisplay;
  HTMLDisplay: IDisplay;
begin
  BaseballGame := TBaseballGame.Create('Bisons', 'Gazelles');
  try
    FullDisplay := TFullGameDisplay.Create(BaseballGame);
    ScoreDisplay := TGameScore.Create(BaseballGame);
    HTMLDisplay := THTMLOutput.Create(BaseballGame);

    BaseballGame.SetRuns(TRuns.Create(1, 0));
    BaseballGame.SetHits(THits.Create(2, 0));
    BaseballGame.SetInning(1, TInning.Create(0, 1));
    ReadLn;

    BaseballGame.SetRuns(TRuns.Create(1, 4));
    BaseballGame.SetHits(THits.Create(2, 5));
    BaseballGame.SetErrors(TErrors.Create(0, 1));
    BaseballGame.SetInning(4, TInning.Create(4, 0));
    ReadLn;

    ReadLn;
  finally
```

```
    BaseballGame.Free;
  end;
end;
```

Here are some interesting things to note:

- This code doesn't write anything to the console. All of that is done by the display objects that get registered as observers. Each observer is registered, and the code pretty much forgets about them. To the baseball game, they are merely IObserver interfaces, and the only thing you can do to an IObserver is call its Update method. From the baseball game's perspective, there's nothing else to it.
- The screen is updated each time the inning information is updated. Note that this is obviously demo code, and if I updated after every change, the data would be scrolling by pretty quickly. So for illustrative purposes, I simply update the game when the inning information changes.
- TBaseballGame doesn't know anything about game displays – it only knows about IObservers. This means that you could have observers doing other things such as streaming the results over the network. You could simply store the game data, or do anything else with it that you like. For instance, you could create a TStoreBaseballGame class that implements the IObserver interface and uses a database. The baseball game itself neither knows nor cares. IObservers are under no obligation to do anything specific with the data passed to them.
- We can change the observers anytime we want without altering the Subject. We can add new ones and remove existing ones as well. Basically, observers and subjects are very loosely coupled, and either can be changed, altered, updated, and added to without having to worry about the other.

That should be a quick rundown on how the observer pattern works. Note that our IObserver interface is very specific to baseball data. You can create your own interface for your specific implementation of the observer. The pattern remains the same no matter how the IObserver interface is designed. This is obviously a good place for generics to enter the picture, and in fact, the Delphi Spring framework implements a generic IObservable<T> interface and implementing class. Let's take a look at that, creating our baseball game using it.

Generic Observer with Spring4D

Building an application with the Spring4D's IObservable<T> is pretty simple. First, we'll create a new TBaseballGame. This one is a touch simpler:

```
type
  TBaseballGame = class(TObservable<IDisplay>)
  private
    FGameInfo: TGameInfo;
  protected
    procedure DoNotify(const observer: IDisplay); override;
  public
    procedure SetInning(aInningNumber: TInningNumber; aInning: TInning);
    procedure SetRuns(aRuns: TRuns);
    procedure SetHits(aHits: THits);
    procedure SetErrors(aErrors: TErrors);
    property GameInfo: TGameInfo read FGameInfo;
  end;
```

TBaseballGame descends from TObservable<IDisplay>. That class has an abstract method DoNotify that needs to be overridden. TBaseballGame does so and thus provides a way to notify the class's Observers that something has changed.

```
procedure TBaseballGame.DoNotify(const observer: IDisplay);
begin
  observer.Update(Self.GameInfo);
end;
```

We'll let our observers know that an update has happened in the game in the SetInning method:

```
procedure TBaseballGame.SetInning(aInningNumber: TInningNumber; aInning: TInning);
begin
  FGameInfo.Innings[aInningNumber].Top := aInning.Top;
  FGameInfo.Innings[aInningNumber].Bottom := aInning.Bottom;
  Notify;
end;
```

This baseball game class looks a lot like the baseball game from the previous example, except it doesn't have any of the ISubject methods. Instead, it descends from TObservable<T>, which looks like this:

```
IObservable<T> = interface
  procedure Attach(const observer: T);
  procedure Detach(const observer: T);
  procedure Notify;
end;

TObservable<T> = class(TInterfacedObject, IObservable<T>)
private
  fLock: TMREWSync;
  fObservers: IList<T>;
protected
  procedure DoNotify(const observer: T); virtual; abstract;
  property Observers: IList<T> read fObservers;
public
  constructor Create;
  destructor Destroy; override;
```

```
  procedure Attach(const observer: T);
  procedure Detach(const observer: T);
  procedure Notify;
end;
```

You should see the similarities in IObservable<T> and TObservable<T> and the first demo application. They both track observers (listeners) and they both have Subjects (TObservable).

We'll just declare a single observer, TConsoleDisplay, which implements IDisplay, an interface that we'll pass as the parameterized type (as seen above in the declaration of TBaseballGame). TConsoleDisplay is basically declared the same way as in the first example.

```
type

  IDisplay = interface
  ['{E118BD99-37BD-461C-AF69-770FD8E18702}']
    procedure Update(aGameInfo: TGameInfo);
  end;

  TConsoleDisplay = class(TInterfacedObject, IDisplay)
    procedure Update(aGameInfo: TGameInfo);
  end;
```

The main body of the application is basically the same as the previous example:

```
var
  BaseballGame: TBaseballGame;

begin
  BaseballGame := TBaseballGame.Create;
  BaseballGame.Attach(TConsoleDisplay.Create);


  BaseballGame.SetRuns(TRuns.Create(1, 0));
  BaseballGame.SetHits(THits.Create(2, 0));
  BaseballGame.SetInning(1, TInning.Create(0, 1));
  ReadLn;

  BaseballGame.SetRuns(TRuns.Create(1, 4));
  BaseballGame.SetHits(THits.Create(2, 5));
  BaseballGame.SetErrors(TErrors.Create(0, 1));
  BaseballGame.SetInning(4, TInning.Create(4, 0));
  ReadLn;

end.
```

Here are a couple of things to note:

- Because it takes advantage of the generic infrastructure provided by the Spring for Delphi framework, the amount of code you have to write to enable the Observer pattern goes way down.

- `TBaseballGame` is the subject. It takes in listeners, and then notifies them when the score changes.
- `TBaseballGame` is structured basically like our first demo. The data for runs, hits, and errors can be updated at any time, and when it is, it simply calls its `Notify` method. `Notify` iterates over all the observers and calls their `DoNotify` method.

Conclusion

So in summation, the Observer pattern ensures that publishing classes (subjects) can communicate updates to their subscribing (observer) classes with very loose and flexible coupling. Observers can be updated and removed at runtime. Adding observers requires no change to subjects and observers can be created and added at anytime. Subjects don't know much at all about what the observers are up to. It's all very easy and elegant and loosely coupled – just like you want it.

The Adapter Pattern

Introduction

Many of you have traveled, I'm sure, and many of you have no doubt traveled to a country where the standard power outlet is different from the one in your home country. Here in the US, our power outlets consist of two parallel slots and a hole below them. One of the slots is "hot" with electricity, and the hole provides the ground.

Countries in Europe have a different power outlet. When I go there, I have to bring a power adapter – a device that has the US output on one side and the European input on the other. I plug the adapter into the European outlet, and then plug my device – usually my computer – into the adapter. My computer's power adapter can perform the job of converting a range of voltages – usually 110V or 220V – into something that the computer can consume. Depending on where I am in the world, my computer is using up to two adapters to power itself.

A typical power adapter

Sometimes in our code we need an adapter. Sometimes two things we want to work together don't quite fit and we need to write a class that makes them fit. It's the job of the "adapter" to make one interface match up with a s second one. This is called the Adapter Pattern. The purpose of the Adapter Pattern is to allow us to wrap up something to make it look and work like something it is not. Often those two things will be similar already, but they need not be. Just like our power adapter, the Adapter Pattern will allow us to take a `TSquarePeg` and fit it into a `TRoundHole`.

The Adapter Pattern's definition is "*A pattern that converts one interface into another interface expected by a different class. The Adapter Pattern allows two disparate systems work together by providing a common interface to objects that otherwise would be incompatible.*"

You'd use the Adapter Pattern when you need to use an existing class and its interface doesn't match the interface that you need to use. An adapter will change an existing class into something expected by the consuming class.

A Simple Example

Let's start with a simple but illustrative example. Let's try to find a way to get a house cat to look like a cougar. First, we'll define a house cat:

```
type
  IHouseCat = interface
  ['{4A5537CF-60D7-4617-95F9-9E4DC3660FB4}']
    procedure Hunt;
    procedure Meow;
  end;

  THouseCat = class(TInterfacedObject, IHouseCat)
    procedure Hunt;
    procedure Meow;
  end;

  procedure THouseCat.Hunt;
  begin
    WriteLn('Catch a mouse');
  end;

  procedure THouseCat.Meow;
  begin
    WriteLn('Meow!');
  end;
```

Then we'll define a cougar:

```
type
  ICougar  = interface
  ['{DD635959-ED9E-4A55-B17A-ABCE7B49204F}']
    procedure Hunt;
    procedure Growl;
  end;

  TCougar = class(TInterfacedObject, ICougar)
    procedure Hunt;
    procedure Growl;
  end;

procedure TCougar.Growl;
begin
```

```
    WriteLn('GROWL!');
end;


procedure TCougar.Hunt;
begin
  WriteLn('Run down a mule deer');
end;
```

The two have similar but not identical interfaces. You can imagine a situation where you might need to use a house cat as a cougar. Okay, maybe not really, but lets do it anyway. We'll create an adapter class to make a house cat look like a cougar.

```
THouseCatAdapter = class(TInterfacedObject, ICougar)
private
  FHouseCat: IHouseCat;
public
  constructor Create(aHouseCat: IHouseCat);
  procedure Hunt;
  procedure Growl;
end;


constructor THouseCatAdapter.Create(aHouseCat: IHouseCat);
begin
  inherited Create;
  FHouseCat := aHouseCat;
end;


procedure THouseCatAdapter.Growl;
var
  i: Integer;
begin
  // Try to be a cougar by meowing a bunch of times to simulate a growl
  for i := 1 to 5 do
  begin
    FHouseCat.Meow;
  end;
end;


procedure THouseCatAdapter.Hunt;
begin
  WriteLn('Catch a really big mouse and pretend it is a deer.');
end;
```

Okay, so what is happening here?

- First, note that THouseCatAdapter implements the ICougar interface, meaning that it will do the things that a cougar does, using a house cat as the thing being adapted.
- Next, the THouseCatAdapter has a constructor that takes an IHouseCat as a parameter. It stores that internally, and uses it to "pretend" that it is a Cougar. This is really the trick of the adapter – it takes the adaptee as a parameter and uses it to be the thing being adapted.
- Next, the Hunt method has the cat catch a big mouse and pretend that it is a deer. This is the adaption part where the house cat again acts like a cougar.

- Finally, the house cat meows five times in an effort to imitate a cougar's large growl.

Basically, the THouseCatAdapter class is an ICougar that uses an IHouseCat to do the cougar role. In other words, it takes a house cat and adapts it into a cougar.

In order to demonstrate the adapter in action, let's create a method that takes a cougar and does cougar-y things:

```
procedure DoCougarStuff(aCougar: ICougar);
begin
  aCougar.Hunt;
  aCougar.Growl;
end;
```

Obviously, we can pass a cougar into DoCougarStuff:

```
Cougar := TCougar.Create;
DoCougarStuff(Cougar);
```

And that has the expected output, with the cougar things getting done.

Here's the fun part. You can create a house cat, pass it to the adapter, and have that house cat behave like a cougar. Watch:

```
HouseCat := THouseCat.Create;
HouseCat.Meow;
HouseCat.Hunt;

HouseCatAdapter := THouseCatAdapter.Create(HouseCat);
DoCougarStuff(HouseCatAdapter);
```

Call that code, and you get the following output:

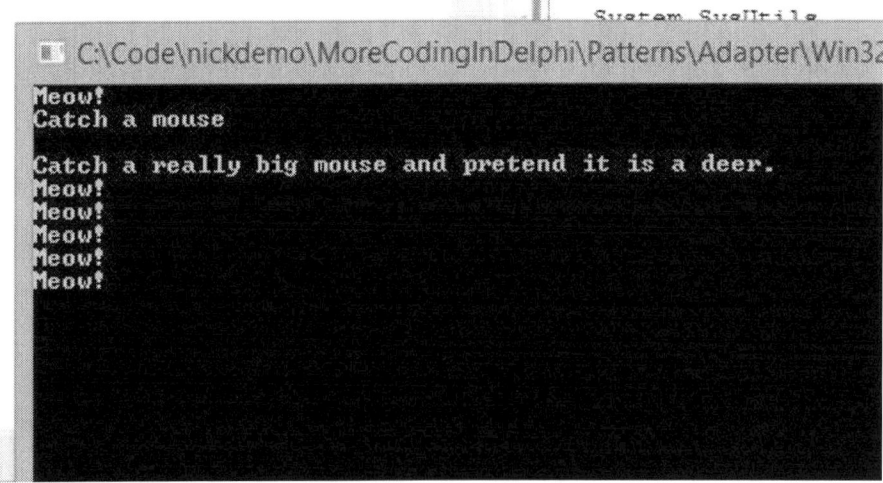

Thus a cat can become a cougar. I know my four cats at home would like that.

A More Practical Example

Here's a more practical example. Imagine that you are working for a company, and you acquire a small startup. You get charged with integrating their Customer Management System with your current one. You look at the problem, and it doesn't seem too difficult, but one of the main differences is in how the new system handles Customer birthdays and Names. Your system simply has a 'Name' property, but the new system has `FirstName` and `LastName`. Your system stores the customer's date of birth in this structure:

```
TDateOfBirth = record
  Month: integer;
  Day: integer;
  Year: integer;
end;
```

while the new system uses a good old `TDate`. What to do?

Well, first, let's design interfaces for the two systems:

```
IOldCustomer = interface
['{14C3F1DB-0901-4AB7-8F6E-346C4BBA2E43}']
  function GetName: string;
  procedure SetName(aName: string);
  function GetDateOfBirth: TDateOfBirth;
  procedure SetDateOfBirth(aDateOfBirth: TDateOfBirth);

  property Name: string read GetName write SetName;
  property DateOfBirth: TDateOfBirth read GetDateOfBirth write SetDateOfBirth;
end;

INewCustomer = interface
['{BDACD6A1-C181-4A06-978F-6CAB72CD229B}']
  function GetFirstName: string;
  procedure SetFirstName(aFirstName: string);
  function GetLastName: string;
  procedure SetLastName(aLastName: string);
  function GetDateOfBirth: TDate;
  procedure SetDateOfBirth(aDOB: TDate);

  property FirstName: string read GetFirstName write SetFirstName;
  property LastName: string read GetLastName write SetLastName;
  property DateOfBirth: TDate read GetDateOfBirth write SetDateOfBirth;
end;
```

Then let's create implementations for both interfaces:

```
TOldCustomer = class(TInterfacedObject, IOldCustomer)
strict private
  FName: string;
  FDOB: TDateOfBirth;
  function GetName: string;
  procedure SetName(aName: string);
  function GetDateOfBirth: TDateOfBirth;
  procedure SetDateOfBirth(aDateOfBirth: TDateOfBirth);
public
  constructor Create(aName: string; aYear, aMonth, aDay: integer);
  property Name: string read GetName write SetName;
  property DateOfBirth: TDateOfBirth read GetDateOfBirth write SetDateOfBirth;
end;

TNewCustomer = class(TInterfacedObject, INewCustomer)
strict private
  FFirstName: string;
  FLastName: string;
  FDOB: TDate;
  function GetFirstName: string;
  procedure SetFirstName(aFirstName: string);
  function GetLastName: string;
  procedure SetLastName(aLastName: string);
  function GetDateOfBirth: TDate;
  procedure SetDateOfBirth(aDOB: TDate);
public
  property FirstName: string read GetFirstName write SetFirstName;
  property LastName: string read GetLastName write SetLastName;
  property DateOfBirth: TDate read GetDateOfBirth write SetDateOfBirth;
end;
```

The implementations for both are what you'd expect, so I won't show them here. What is important is that we have two classes that are similar, but don't quite fit. They are both pegs, but one is round and one is square. What to do? The Adapter Pattern to the rescue!

Here's a customer adapter:

```
TCustomerAdapter = class(TInterfacedObject, INewCustomer)
strict private
  FFirstName: string;
  FLastName: string;
  FDOB: TDate;
  function GetFirstName: string;
  procedure SetFirstName(aFirstName: string);
  function GetLastName: string;
  procedure SetLastName(aLastName: string);
  function GetDateOfBirth: TDate;
  procedure SetDateOfBirth(aDOB: TDate);
  function ParseFirstName(aName: string): string;
  function ParseLastName(aName: string): string;
public
  constructor Create(aOldCustomer: IOldCustomer);
  property FirstName: string read GetFirstName write SetFirstName;
  property LastName: string read GetLastName write SetLastName;
```

```
  property DateOfBirth: TDate read GetDateOfBirth write SetDateOfBirth;
end;
```

Here the real work gets done in the constructor:

```
constructor TCustomerAdapter.Create(aOldCustomer: IOldCustomer);
begin
  inherited Create;
  FFirstName := ParseFirstName(aOldCustomer.Name);
  FLastName := ParseLastName(aOldCustomer.Name);
  FDOB := EncodeDate(aOldCustomer.DateOfBirth.Year, aOldCustomer.DateOfBirth.Month,
                     aOldCustomer.DateOfBirth.Day);
end;
```

`ParseFirstName` and `ParseLastName` are just simple methods that parse the first and last names out so that we can convert an "old" name to a "new" name.

More importantly, though, is to note that the constructor for `TCustomerAdapter` takes an `IOldCustomer` interface as a parameter. In this way, if you have an old customer – one from the original system – and you need to use it in the new system, you can simply call:

```
var
  OldCustomer: IOldCustomer;
  NewCustomerAdapter: INewCustomer;
...
OldCustomer := TOldCustomer.Create('Marvin Martian', 1945, 12, 25);
NewCustomerAdapter := TCustomerAdapter.Create(OldCustomer);
OutputNewCustomer(NewCustomerAdapter);
```

`OutputNewCustomer` is declared as follows:

```
procedure OutputNewCustomer(aCustomer: INewCustomer);
begin
  WriteLn('First Name: ', aCustomer.FirstName);
  WriteLn('Last Name: ', aCustomer.LastName);
  WriteLn('DOB: ', DateToStr(aCustomer.DateOfBirth));
end;
```

Notice that it takes an `INewCustomer` as a parameter, and that it gladly accepts the `NewCustomerAdapter` variable as an input knowing that that variable will behave exactly like a customer in the new system.

> It should come as no surprise that all these connections are made with interfaces. Interfaces, as discussed in *Coding in Delphi*, make your code very flexible, and the Adapter Pattern is just another example of that. You can even use it to add interfaces to classes that don't have them without changing the original code.

Conclusion

And that is the Adapter Pattern in a nutshell: Create an adapter that takes the "old" thing as a parameter in the constructor, and have it behave as the "new" thing in its implementation. We use the adapter pattern when the old interface and the new interface are incompatible, but need to work together.

Decorator Pattern

One of the themes of the book is to make your code as flexible as possible at runtime and to design your code to prefer runtime flexibility over compile-time flexibility. Any time you determine something at compile-time, you lock that feature into your code. It can't be changed at runtime.

Inheritance is a pillar of OOP, but it is a compile-time construct. As we saw back in the *Six Things* chapter, inheritance is powerful, but inflexible at run time. You have the classes you have, and they can't be altered or changed once you set them in the stone that is compiled code. If you are trying to come up with differing combinations to define each inherited class, you can end up having a huge number of descendant classes, which can become difficult to manage and maintain. Changes to one of the features means any number of descendants might need to change as well. We talked about how you should prefer composition over inheritance.

The decorator pattern is a way of circumventing these limitations and providing the power of inheritance, while at the same time providing runtime flexibility. It can be a different way of adding new behaviors at runtime from what we saw in the Six Things chapter. It actually uses some simple inheritance to "wrap up" a given class and provide additional functionality without having to change the original class.

Here is the formal definition from Wikipedia: *The Decorator Pattern attaches additional responsibilities to an object dynamically. Decorators provide a flexible alternative to subclassing for extending functionality.*

It's actually pretty straight-forward. Here's what you do:

First, you start with the notion of a class that needs to be decorated. It becomes the "base" class. We'll use the example of a pizza. We'll create just two, one with Parmesan cheese and one with Mozzarella cheese. (We'll assume all pizzas have tomato sauce on them.) Each will be decorated with various toppings such as sausage, pepperoni, black olives, and onions.

Then you create a single descendant that will be the base decorator class. That class will take as a property an instance of the original base class. The base decorator should have a constructor that takes the original base class as a parameter.

Next, you create concrete instances of decorators that override the necessary methods and properties of the base decorator class.

From there you can start with the base class, and then chain together as many decorators as you want.

Okay, let's take a look at that in code. Here is the base class, TPizza:

```
type
  TPizza = class
  private
    FDescription: string;
  protected
    function GetDescription: string;  virtual;
    procedure SetDescription(const Value: string);
  public
    function Cost: Currency; virtual; abstract;
    property Description: string read GetDescription write SetDescription;
  end;
```

The base class is abstract. It has two properties – well, one actually – with Cost being a virtual abstract function.

TPizza is the base class for the beginning of the wrapping process. We create descendants that will form the base class described above. These classes override the Cost method, providing their own prices. They will be the starting point for decorating. In our case, we'll create specific base pizza types that can be wrapped:

```
TParmesanCheesePizza = class(TPizza)
  constructor Create;
  function Cost: Currency; override;
end;

TMozarellaCheesePizza = class(TPizza)
  constructor Create;
  function Cost: Currency; override;
end;
```

The interesting part comes in the base decorator class:

```
TPizzaDecorator = class(TPizza)
private
  FPizza: TPizza;
public
  constructor Create(aPizza: TPizza);
  destructor Destroy; override;
end;
```

TPizzaDecorator does three things. One, it descends from TPizza. Two, it gets another instance of TPizza from its constructor in order to "wrap" itself around the starting base class. And three, the destructor ensures that the internally stored instance gets freed properly when that time comes.

Since TPizzaDecorator is itself a TPizza, you can continue wrapping the previous result in a new one, decorating the decorator as it were. In addition, it will have the exact same interface as the base pizza class, so it can act like a pizza because, well, it is one.

As for classes that do the decorating, they will descend from TPizzaDecorator:

```
TPepperoni = class(TPizzaDecorator)
protected
    function GetDescription: string; override;
public
  function Cost: Currency; override;
end;

TSausage = class(TPizzaDecorator)
protected
  function GetDescription: string; override;
public
  function Cost: Currency; override;
end;

TBlackOlives = class(TPizzaDecorator)
protected
  function GetDescription: string; override;
public
  function Cost: Currency; override;
end;

TOnions = class(TPizzaDecorator)
protected
  function GetDescription: string; override;
public
  function Cost: Currency; override;
end;
```

Each of these classes does two things.

First, they override the getter for the `Description` property. They do it in an interesting way. Since they are decorating the base Pizza, they assume that they are "additive", that is that they will be adding on to the base description. The `TPepperoni.GetDescription` method looks like this:

```
function TPepperoni.GetDescription: string;
begin
  Result := FPizza.GetDescription + ', Pepperoni';
end;
```

This method grabs the description from the class that it is wrapping and adds on a comma and its own description.

Second, the `Cost` method is overridden to add the cost to the price of the class that it is decorating.

```
function TPepperoni.Cost: Currency;
begin
  Result := FPizza.Cost + 1.20;
end;
```

So, now we have a bunch of types of pizza – the base classes –and a bunch of toppings to wrap around those classes and themselves. Let's put it all together:

First, we'll create a routine to write out the pizza type to the console:

```
procedure OutputPizza(aPizza: TPizza);
begin
  WriteLn('A ', aPizza.Description, ' costs ', '$', Format('%2f', [aPizza.Cost]));
  WriteLn;
end;
```

Then, we'll create a Mozarella pizza and wrap it with Sausage and Pepperoni:

```
Pizza := TMozarellaCheesePizza.Create;
try
  Pizza := TPepperoni.Create(Pizza);
  Pizza := TSausage.Create(Pizza);
  OutputPizza(Pizza);
finally
  Pizza.Free;
end;
```

This will build the description and calculate the correct price, and result in:

```
■ C:\Code\nickdemo\MoreCodingInDelphi\Patterns\Decorator\Win32\Debug\D
A Mozarella Cheese Pizza, Pepperoni, Sausage costs $9.14
```

Another way that you can create a pizza is by simply nesting each decorator in the constructor of the previous one. This method actually provides a coding representation of how each decorator wraps up the previous one:

```
Pizza := TBlackOlives.Create(TPepperoni.Create(TPepperoni.Create(TParmesanCheesePizza.Create)));
try
  OutputPizza(Pizza);
finally
  Pizza.Free;
end;
```

You should note that the use of the Decorator pattern above (and the one we'll look at below) illustrates the Open/Closed Principle – TPizza remains closed, yet we've used the decorator pattern to make it open for extension. TPizza doesn't even know it's being decorated. It also helps to preserve the Single Responsibility Principle by ensuring that TPizza remains just a Pizza and doesn't do anything more than that.

Decorator and Interfaces

The previous example used pure inheritance to illustrate one way to implement the Decorator Pattern. But you know me and you know that I am obsessed with programming to an interface (you should be, too, by the way…). So how about implementing the Decorator Pattern with interfaces instead of just the inheritance of classes? I thought you'd like that idea.

Something to Decorate

First, we'll declare a simple interface that we can later decorate with other functionality. We'll start with a simple order processor interface:

```
IOrderProcessor = interface
['{193966C6-BD40-487F-8A2F-E36BC707CA7D}']
  procedure ProcessOrder(aOrder: TOrder);
end;
```

Then, a just as simple implementation:

```
TOrderProcessor = class(TInterfacedObject, IOrderProcessor)
  procedure ProcessOrder(aOrder: TOrder);
end;

procedure TOrderProcessor.ProcessOrder(aOrder: TOrder);
begin
  WriteLn('Processed order for Order #', aOrder.ID);
end;
```

Here's the declaration for TOrder. It's very basic and actually only incidental to what we are doing:

```
type

  TOrder = class
  private
    FID: integer;
  public
    constructor Create(aID: integer);
    property ID: integer read FID;
  end;

constructor TOrder.Create(aID: integer);
begin
  inherited Create;
  FID := aID;
end;
```

Now we have a basic class that we can decorate using interfaces.

Okay, now we want to decorate IOrderProcessor – or more accurately, decorate its implementation. We'll start out with declaring a new class that also implements IOrderProcessor:

```
TOrderProcessorDecorator = class abstract(TInterfacedObject, IOrderProcessor)
private
  FInnerOrderProcessor: IOrderProcessor;
public
  constructor Create(aOrderProcessor: IOrderProcessor);
  procedure ProcessOrder(aOrder: TOrder); virtual; abstract;
end;
```

The constructor is implemented as follows:

```
constructor TOrderProcessorDecorator.Create(aOrderProcessor: IOrderProcessor);
begin
  inherited Create;
  FInnerOrderProcessor := aOrderProcessor;
end;
```

The `TOrderProcessorDecorator` class will be the base class for all decoration of `IOrderProcessor`. It is also an abstract class with the `ProcessOrder` method requiring implementation in descendant classes. `ProcessOrder` also happens to be the only method on the `IOrderProcessor` interface. Coincidence? I think not. Its purpose is to be a "gateway" of sorts for inserting other interfaces into implementations of `IOrderProcessor` and enhance – "decorate" if you will – the functionality of the interface.

Notice that the constructor stores what is called `FInnerProcessor`. That will be our original `IOrderProcessor` that will be decorated. We'll see it used in a second.

Let's wrap some functionality around `IOrderProcessor` – how about some logging. We'd naturally want to log everything that happens with the order process, and so we'll descend from `TOrderProcessorDecorator`, inserting a new interface into it, and wrapping the `IOrderProcessor` functionality with the new logging interface.

Here is that interface with a simple implementation:

```
ILogger = interface
['{955784CD-D867-4B41-A8F2-3D31B4593F39}']
  procedure Log(const aString: string);
end;

TLogger = class(TInterfacedObject, ILogger)
  procedure Log(const aString: string);
end;

procedure TLogger.Log(const aString: string);
begin
  WriteLn(aString);
end;
```

Here we are logging to the console, but of course, your logging implementation could be anything you want it to be. Since we are coding to an interface, it really doesn't matter how the logging gets implemented.

So, now we declare `TLoggingOrderProcessor` as follows:

```
TLoggingOrderProcessor = class(TOrderProcessorDecorator)
private
  FLogger: ILogger;
public
  constructor Create(aOrderProcessor: IOrderProcessor; aLogger: ILogger);
  procedure ProcessOrder(aOrder: TOrder); override;
end;

constructor TLoggingOrderProcessor.Create(aOrderProcessor: IOrderProcessor; aLogger: ILogger);
begin
  inherited Create(aOrderProcessor);
  FLogger := aLogger;
end;

procedure TLoggingOrderProcessor.ProcessOrder(aOrder: TOrder);
begin
  FLogger.Log('Logging: About to process Order #' + aOrder.ID.ToString);
  FInnerOrderProcessor.ProcessOrder(aOrder);
  FLogger.Log('Logging: Finished processing Order #' + aOrder.ID.ToString);
end;
```

Here are a few things to notice about this code:

- The constructor takes two parameters. The first is the IOrderProcessor that we are going to decorate. The second parameter is an instance of an implementation of ILogger, which represents the new functionality we are going to wrap around the first parameter. It stores the new functionality, FLogger, for later use.
- If you recall from my previous book, this is Dependency Injection in action – specifically Constructor Injection. See? That stuff really does come in useful.
- The class overrides the abstract ProcessOrder method, and wraps – decorates – the call to FInnerOrderProcessor.ProcessOrder with the logging code.
- The decorating functionality is provided by the FLogging field which is, of course, an interface. It was injected in the constructor, and we use it in the ProcessOrder method to decorate the inner functionality of the original order processing class.

Of course, it wouldn't be any fun to stop there. We need to show how now, we can wrap this wrapped class in more functionality. How about we add some authorization to the mix? Often, you'll want to protect a particular method with a password, giving authorization to only particular people to execute a given chunk of code.

We'll declare an interface and a simple implementation:

```
type

  IAuthentication = interface
  ['{10793CD1-B1C4-4A59-9C5B-A48B64B4AC2A}']
    function Authenticate(const aPassword: string): Boolean;
  end;


  TAuthentication = class(TInterfacedObject, IAuthentication)
  private
    function Authenticate(const aPassword: string): Boolean;
  end;

function TAuthentication.Authenticate(const aPassword: string): Boolean;
var
  S: string;
begin
  Write('Enter the Password: ');
  ReadLn(S);
  Result := S = aPassword;
end;
```

This is a really simple implementation that merely asks for a password and returns True if it matches what was passed in. I wouldn't protect my bank account with this, but it illustrates the point, eh?

Then, let's declare the following code that once again wraps IOrderProcessor with a new interface and applies the authentication functionality to it.

```
TAuthenticationOrderProcessor = class(TOrderProcessorDecorator)
private
  FAuthentication: IAuthentication;
public
  constructor Create(aOrderProcessor: IOrderProcessor; aAuthentication: IAuthentication);
  procedure ProcessOrder(aOrder: TOrder); override;
end;

constructor TAuthenticationOrderProcessor.Create(aOrderProcessor: IOrderProcessor; aAuthentication: IAuthentic\
ation);
begin
  inherited Create(aOrderProcessor);
  FAuthentication := aAuthentication;
end;

procedure TAuthenticationOrderProcessor.ProcessOrder(aOrder: TOrder);
begin
  if FAuthentication.Authenticate('password') then
  begin
    FInnerOrderProcessor.ProcessOrder(aOrder);
  end else
  begin
    WriteLn('You failed authentication!');
  end;
end;
```

Again, here are some things to notice in this code:

- The constructor once again takes two parameters, the original `IOrderProcessor` and an interface to the new functionality – in this case, `IAuthentication`.
- The `ProcessOrder` method makes a call to the `IAuthentication.Authenticate` method, passing in a really secure password. If the function returns `True`, then the inner order processor is allowed to do its thing. If not, you get a nasty message.
- Now, note that this class, as well as the previous class, both implement (via inheritance) the `IOrder-Processor` interface. Therefore, it will be possible as we'll see below, to wrap any of these classes around any other ones.

Okay, so let's exercise this stuff. Here is a simple procedure that we'll call in our console application that shows how all of this works:

```
procedure DoIt;
var
  OrderProcessor: IOrderProcessor;
  Order: TOrder;
begin
  Order := TOrder.Create(42);
  try
    OrderProcessor := TOrderProcessor.Create;
    OrderProcessor := TLoggingOrderProcessor.Create(OrderProcessor, TLogger.Create);
    OrderProcessor.ProcessOrder(Order);

    WriteLn;

    OrderProcessor := TAuthenticationOrderProcessor.Create(OrderProcessor, TAuthentication.Create);
    OrderProcessor.ProcessOrder(Order);

  finally
    Order.Free;
  end;
end;
```

First, we create an order to be processed. Then, we create the base class, `TOrderProcessor`. Once we do that, we create a `TLoggingOrderProcessor`, passing to it our existing instance of `TOrderProcessor` as well as an instance of the `ILogger` interface. Then we call the `ProcessOrder` method. Our output will show the logging (see below).

After that, we pass the wrapped-by-logging version of `OrderProcessor` to the authentication implementation of `IOrderProcessor`, thus "double wrapping" the original order processor. Then, when we call the `ProcessOrder` event, we'll first get authentication and then the logging functionality, as well as the original processing of the order.

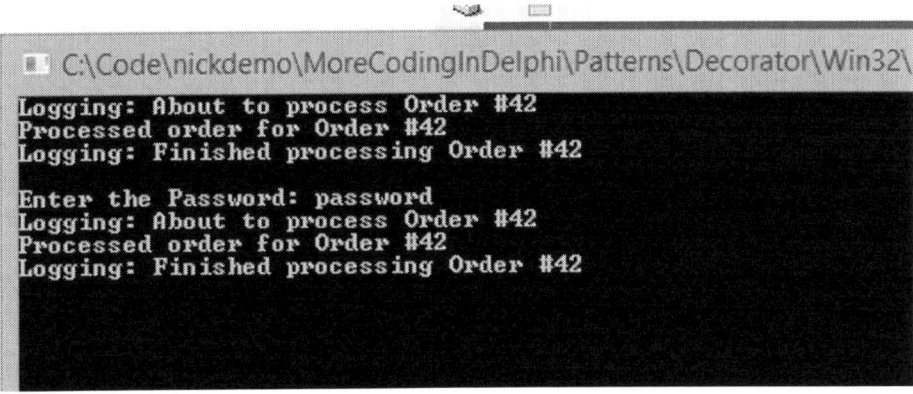

Pretty cool, eh?

Once again, interfaces allow for a powerful yet clean way to implement the separation of concerns. And once again, we've supported the Single Responsibility Principle and the Open/Closed Principle. One could even say that the Liskov Substitution Principle came into action here, as well, since we can pass any implementation of logging and authentication to the decorators.

> Folks who are a little more advanced might notice that this example of the Decorator pattern is actually doing a simple form of Aspect Oriented Programming, which we'll be covering more in a future chapter. We'll actually be doing much the same thing in the early part of that chapter that we are doing here.

Summary

So, to summarize:

- The whole thing starts with a base class or an interface that will be decorated. We then can add functionality to that base class or interface without having to change it. Notice this follows the Open/Closed Principle.
- When using simple inheritance, the decorator classes both descend from and maintain a reference to that base class. This means that they will have the same interface, yet the reference will allow composition instead of inheritance. Remember how we talked about that back at the beginning of the book?
- When using interfaces, we can easily pass an interface into a decorator class to enhance the functionality of the initial interface.
- One or more decorators can be wrapped around the base class and each other to produce a single entity. One or more interfaces can be chained together to add multiple decorators to a starting interface.
- You can dynamically decorate objects at anytime, enabling you to create any combination of decorators without having to create a descendant class for each.
- Decorators allow you to extend behavior of existing classes without needing to modify existing code. In our inheritance example, adding a new pizza ingredient is as easy as creating a simple new class overriding TPizzaDecorator. In the interface example, all we need to do is declare a new interface and pass it into the constructor of the Decorator class.

- The basic idea is to simplify and add flexibility to your code instead of a complex inheritance model. In addition, it makes it easier to build a single instance at runtime of complicated combinations of features or items that you may have never thought of before.

Command Pattern

Introduction

In the first chapter I talked about the importance of Encapsulation. Hopefully, you ended up wanting to encapsulate everything that you can. In this chapter, we'll take a look at encapsulating method invocation. We'll learn how to encapsulate the execution of code so that the objects running it don't even have to know anything about how or what it does. We can easily choose different code to run depending on the situation. Your objects will just make a call to a simple method, and the invocation will be taken care of by an external object. You can queue up commands and save them to undo actions. And along the way, we'll even use our Dependency Injection skills to further separate our concerns between objects and the functionality that they provide.

 If you have used the TAction components in the VCL, you are using the Command Pattern. Actions provide an abstraction of the notion of a VCL event, and allow you to separate the invocation of a command from the command itself.

The formal definition of the Command Pattern from the "Gang of Four" is:

> *Encapsulate a request as an object, thereby letting you parameterize clients with different requests, queue or log requests, and support undoable operations.*

A Simple Example: An Auto Key Fob

Most new cars these days don't just come with a set of keys – they come with a key fob that allows you to remotely lock and unlock the car. Most also have an "emergency button" that sets the car horn blaring away. Some even allow you to remotely start your car. In any event, this is a good example of an object that executes commands that can be encapsulated.

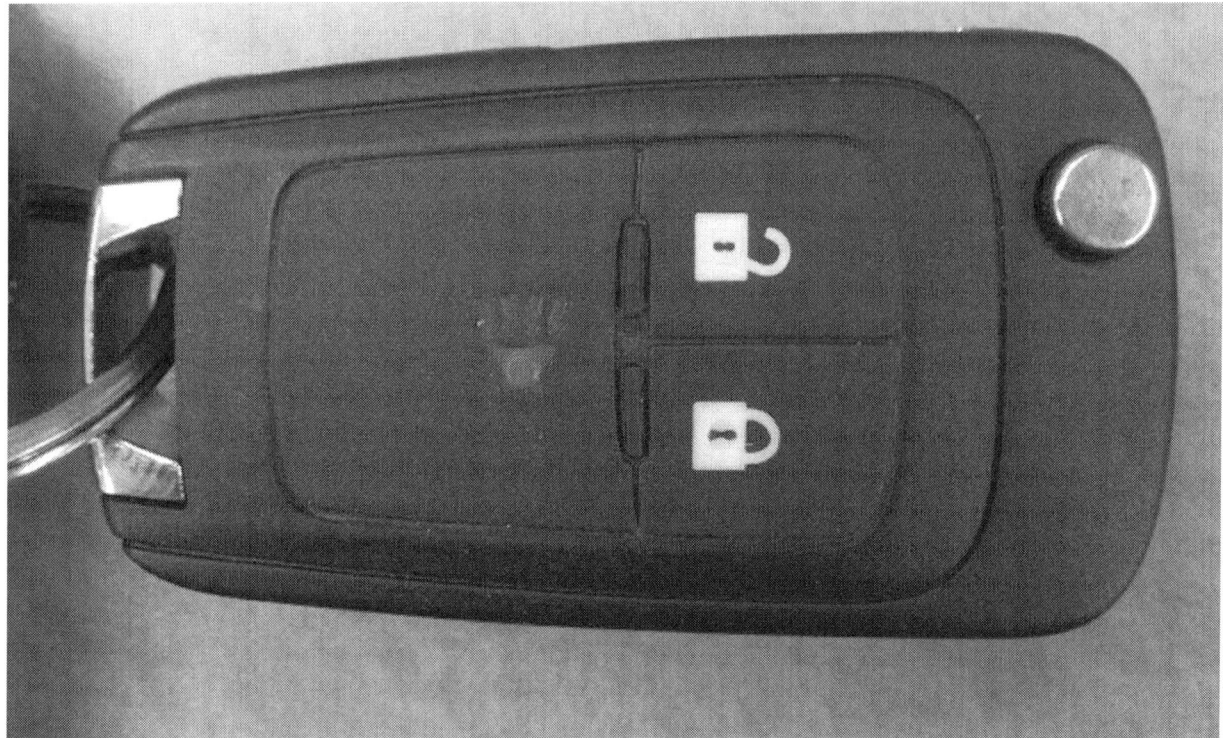

The key fob from my 2014 Chevy Spark

First, lets define a simple interface:

```
type

  ISimpleCommand = interface
  ['{364D931B-CBE5-44AF-BA40-935DC28B497F}']
    procedure Execute;
  end;
```

ISimpleCommand defines, well, a simple command. It has a single method, Execute, that we'll use to invoke some desired functionality. Can't get much simpler than that.

The real power of ISimpleCommand comes in implementing commands that can be executed. Most of these key fobs work locally with a small transmitter. Let's implement some commands that can be executed using a local radio to do the work of the key fob:

```
TLocalCarLocker = class(TInterfacedObject, ISimpleCommand)
  procedure Execute;
end;

TLocalCarUnlocker = class(TInterfacedObject, ISimpleCommand)
  procedure Execute;
end;

TLocalEmergencyHorn = class(TInterfacedObject, ISimpleCommand)
  procedure Execute;
end;

procedure TLocalEmergencyHorn.Execute;
begin
  WriteLn('HONK, HONK, HONK, HONK!!!');
end;

procedure TLocalCarUnlocker.Execute;
begin
  WriteLn('The car is now unlocked');
end;

procedure TLocalCarLocker.Execute;
begin
  WriteLn('The car is now locked');
end;
```

Notice that these classes are specific to the functionality of a key fob. They follow the Single Responsibility Principle by doing one thing and one thing only. They all do their work in the Execute method of ISimpleCommand. But the most important thing is that they are easily injected into a class called TAutoKeyFob.

```
type
  TAutoKeyFob = class
  private
    FLockButton: ISimpleCommand;
    FUnLockButton: ISimpleCommand;
    FEmergencyButton: ISimpleCommand;
  public
    constructor Create(aLocker: ISimpleCommand; aUnlocker: ISimpleCommand; aEmergencyHorn: ISimpleCommand);
    procedure PressLockButton;
    procedure PressUnlockButton;
    procedure PressEmergencyButton;
  end;

constructor TAutoKeyFob.Create(aLocker: ISimpleCommand; aUnlocker: ISimpleCommand;
                               aEmergencyHorn: ISimpleCommand);
begin
  inherited Create;
  FLockButton := aLocker;
  FUnlockButton := aUnlocker;
  FEmergencyButton := aEmergencyHorn;
end;

procedure TAutoKeyFob.PressEmergencyButton;
```

```
begin
  FEmergencyButton.Execute;
end;

procedure TAutoKeyFob.PressLockButton;
begin
  FLockButton.Execute;
end;

procedure TAutoKeyFob.PressUnlockButton;
begin
  FUnLockButton.Execute;
end;
```

Here are a few things to note about the above class:

- It uses Dependency Injection – specifically constructor injection – to get its dependencies. That's always a good thing.
- Its dependencies are all of type ISimpleCommand.
- The fob has three buttons, and thus three methods that "press" each of the three buttons.
- Bottom line: This class couldn't be much simpler, yet it still gets the job done.

You can then create a TAutoKeyFob and execute its commands as follows:

```
var
  AutoKeyFob: TAutoKeyFob;
begin
  AutoKeyFob := TAutoKeyFob.Create(TLocalCarLocker.Create,
                                   TLocalCarUnlocker.Create,
                                   TLocalEmergencyHorn.Create);
  try
    AutoKeyFob.PressLockButton;
    AutoKeyFob.PressUnlockButton;
    AutoKeyFob.PressEmergencyButton;
  finally
    AutoKeyFob.Free;
  end;
```

and you get the following output:

So what is the deal here? Why provide this level of indirection, when you could just as easily add the functionality right into the methods of TAutoKeyFob? Well, I'll tell you and then show you. First, the indirection allows for the functionality itself to be properly encapsulated in separate classes. Second, and more importantly, it makes it very easy to replace, update, or otherwise change the functionality of the class without having to open it up. Thus, not only does the command pattern enforce the Single Responsibility Principle, it demonstrates the Open/Closed Principle.

How so? By allowing you to completely change what happens when the buttons get pushed without changing or touching the code in TAutoKeyFob. Watch: First, we declare a new kind of functionality. My car has an application built into it that allows me to remotely control it with an app on my phone via a satellite. We can create a set of commands that use that satellite to control the car instead of the local transmitter.

```
TSatelliteCarLocker = class(TInterfacedObject, ISimpleCommand)
  procedure Execute;
end;

TSatelliteCarUnlocker = class(TInterfacedObject, ISimpleCommand)
  procedure Execute;
end;

TSatelliteEmergencyHorn = class(TInterfacedObject, ISimpleCommand)
  procedure Execute;
end;

procedure TSatelliteCarLocker.Execute;
begin
  WriteLn('The care is locked via satellite');
end;

procedure TSatelliteCarUnlocker.Execute;
begin
  WriteLn('The care is unlocked via satellite');
end;

procedure TSatelliteEmergencyHorn.Execute;
begin
  WriteLn('The car goes "HONK" via satellite');
end;
```

Here, the functionality is again encapsulated in simple, clean classes. And we can easily assign that functionality to the key fob:

```
AutoKeyFob := TAutoKeyFob.Create(TSatelliteCarLocker.Create,
                                 TSatelliteCarUnlocker.Create,
                                 TSatelliteEmergencyHorn.Create);
try
  AutoKeyFob.PressLockButton;
  AutoKeyFob.PressUnlockButton;
  AutoKeyFob.PressEmergencyButton;
finally
  AutoKeyFob.Free;
end;
```

And now, without changing the fob, we have one that communicates with the car via satellite. Note that we could even mix and match the functionality by, say, having the doors locked and unlocked via a satellite and having the emergency function executed via a local radio.

The key message here is that the Command pattern decouples the functionality from the thing using it. The fob has no idea what will happen when its buttons are pushed. It just knows that the work will get done when Execute is called. In theory, we could easily have one of the buttons turn on the car lights or start the car up. We could even write code to change the functionality at runtime if we needed to. Shoot, we could program the fob to run a toaster. That is the power and flexibility we get when we use the Command Pattern.

Undoing Commands

The Command Pattern also makes providing undo functionality possible. To do so, your command should know how to undo itself, and your application should maintain a stack of commands that have been executed, allowing you to call that undo functionality in reverse order.

To make this happen, our command interface adds another method called – not surprisingly – Undo:

```
type
  IPointCommand = interface
  ['{5D792581-9D05-4A52-BE44-4EB0CB0D3B3B}']
    procedure Execute;
    procedure Undo;
  end;
```

Now, the interface will be able to represent a class that can Execute its command, and then Undo that command when asked to do so.

In order to demonstrate this, I'm going to use a VCL application that draws and "un-draws" little red dots. Here are the steps to get going:

1. Create a new VCL application.
2. Drop a TPanel, clear its Caption property, and then set its Align property to alTop.
3. Drop a TPaintBox on the main area of the form and set its Align property to alClient.
4. Place two TButtons on the TPanel, giving one the Caption of "Undo", and the other "Clear".
5. Place a TLabel on the Panel.
6. Align them all up and make them look pretty. You should get something that looks like this:

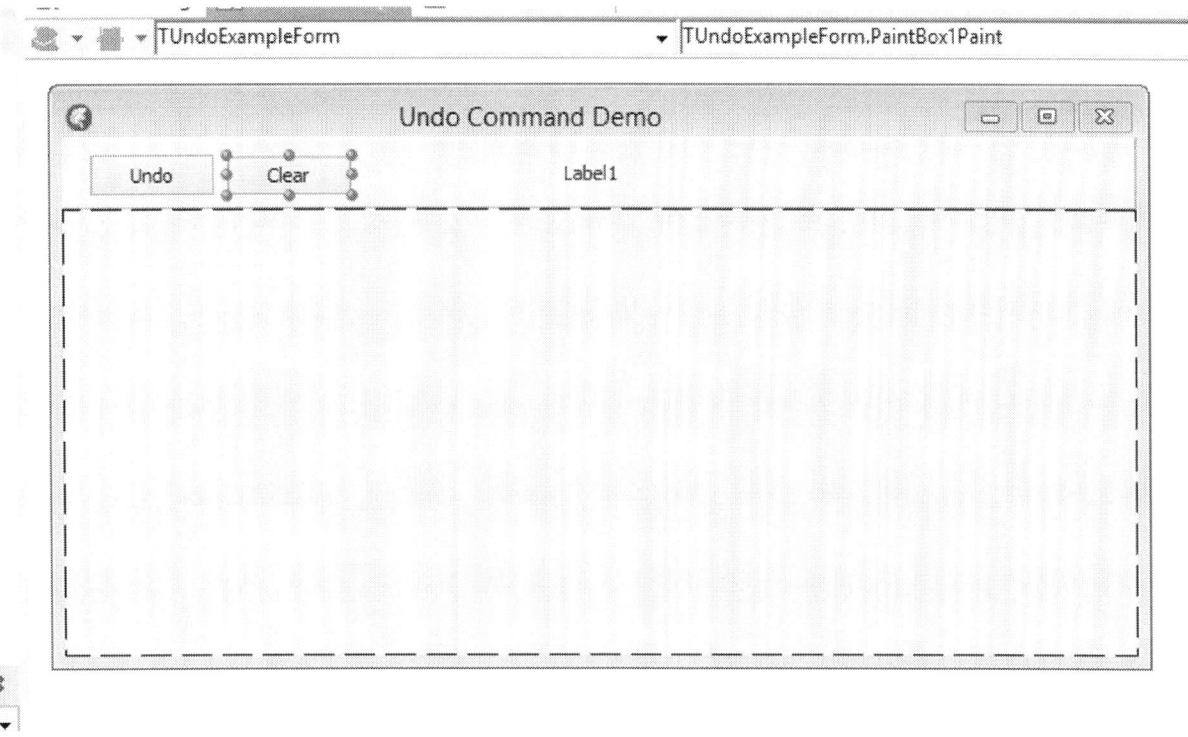

Next, create a separate unit and name it uPointCommand.pas. First, we'll add the above IPointCommand interface to this unit. Then, we'll add an implementation of IPointCommand:

```
type
  IPointCommand = interface
  ['{5D792581-9D05-4A52-BE44-4EB0CB0D3B3B}']
    procedure Execute;
    procedure Undo;
  end;

  TPointPlacerCommand = class(TInterfacedObject, IPointCommand)
  private
    FCanvas: TCanvas;
    FPoint: TPoint;
  public
    constructor Create(aCanvas: TCanvas; aPoint: TPoint);
    procedure Execute;
    procedure Undo;
  end;

const
  CircleDiameter = 15;

constructor TPointPlacerCommand.Create(aCanvas: TCanvas; aPoint: TPoint);
begin
  inherited Create;
  FCanvas := aCanvas;
  FPoint := aPoint;
end;
```

```
procedure TPointPlacerCommand.Execute;
var
  FOriginalColor: TColor;
begin
  FOriginalColor := FCanvas.Brush.Color;
  try
    FCanvas.Brush.Color := clRed;
    FCanvas.Pen.Color := clRed;
    FCanvas.Ellipse(FPoint.X, FPoint.Y, FPoint.X + CircleDiameter, FPoint.Y + CircleDiameter);
  finally
    FCanvas.Brush.Color := FOriginalColor;
    FCanvas.Pen.Color := FOriginalColor;
  end;
end;

procedure TPointPlacerCommand.Undo;
begin
  FCanvas.Ellipse(FPoint.X, FPoint.Y, FPoint.X + CircleDiameter, FPoint.Y + CircleDiameter);
end;
```

Notice that the command does all the work of painting on the canvas that is passed to it. The constructor takes a TCanvas and a TPoint. Those are stored away so that the command can remember them. In the Execute command, it draws a small red dot on the Canvas. The Undo command simply paints over the same spot with the original color of the canvas.

Now, let's go back to the main form. First, we'll need a way to collect and manage all the dots we plan on placing on the TPaintBox via a mouse click. We'll also want to be able to remember them in reverse order, so that we can undo them in the reverse order that they were laid down. And what else but a stack will do the job? We'll dig into our bag of tricks, otherwise known as Spring for Delphi, and use its IStack implementation. Thus, we'll declare this variable as private:

```
FDots: IStack<IPointCommand>;
```

and we'll initialize it in the OnCreate event of the form:

```
procedure TUndoExampleForm.FormCreate(Sender: TObject);
begin
  FDots := TCollections.CreateStack<IPointCommand>;
end;
```

Next up we'll create an IPointCommand every time the OnMouseUp event occurs:

```
procedure TUndoExampleForm.PaintBox1MouseUp(Sender: TObject; Button:
                                            TMouseButton; Shift:
                                            TShiftState; X, Y: Integer);
var
  LCommand: IPointCommand;
begin
  LCommand := TPointPlacerCommand.Create(PaintBox1.Canvas, TPoint.Create(X, Y));
  LCommand.Execute;
  FDots.Push(LCommand);
  UpdateLabel;
end;
```

Here, we create a new command, call the `Execute` method that paints a dot on the `TPaintBox`, and then push it onto the stack for later use during the Undo process. `UpdateLabel` is a simple method that updates the `TLabel` that outputs the total number of dots on the screen.

```
procedure TUndoExampleForm.UpdateInfo;
begin
  Label1.Caption := 'Number of Dots: ' + FDots.Count.ToString();
end;
```

Now for the "why we are here" part: the actual undoing of the dots. Remember that the commands are saved in the stack, and that they remember where they are located. So undoing things is pretty easy. We provide an `OnClick` event handler for the Undo button:

```
procedure TUndoExampleForm.btnUndoClick(Sender: TObject);
begin
  if FDots.Count > 0 then
  begin
    FDots.Pop.Undo;
  end;
  UpdateLabel;
end;
```

First we check to see if there are any dots, and if so, we just `Pop` the top one – that is, the last dot we put down – off the stack. We then call the `Undo` method for the command so that the last dot we drew is covered up by the original color of the canvas.

The Clear button does the same thing for all of the dots:

```
procedure TUndoExampleForm.btnClearClick(Sender: TObject);
begin
  if FDots.Count > 0  then
  begin
    repeat
      FDots.Pop.Undo;
    until FDots.Count = 0;
  end;
  UpdateLabel;
end;
```

One final thing – any good Window needs to be able to paint itself on demand, and so we provide an `OnPaint` handler for the paintbox which simply calls the `Execute` method of each Dot.

```
procedure TUndoExampleForm.PaintBox1Paint(Sender: TObject);
var
  LDot: IPointCommand;
begin
  for LDot in FDots do
  begin
    LDot.Execute;
  end;
end;
```

And that is about it. Run the application, and you should see a red dot wherever you click the mouse on the paintbox. Hit the "Undo" button, and they will be "undone" in reverse order. Hitting the "Clear" button will make them all go away. If you want to see the undoing at work, click a whole bunch on the same basic spot, and then undo them. You should see portions of the dots that are painted over when the dots on top of them are removed.

The form really only knows about `IPointCommand` – we would probably use a Factory or a Dependency Injection container to actually create an instance of `TPointPlacerCommand` for us so the form could be ignorant of any implementation. The `IPointCommand` interface gives us the `Execute` method, which paints a dot, and the `Undo` method that knows how to un-paint a dot. Thus, we basically have separated the calling of commands from the execution of the actual code while providing undo capabilities. Pretty slick. Again – separation of concerns makes for clean, maintainable code.

A Simple Queue of Commands

Part of the definition of the Command Pattern states that you can queue up commands and execute them as needed or desired. In this section, we'll look at a simple application of that notion by enqueuing commands using a timer, and then dequeuing them when you press a button. In this way, you can collect up commands for later execution. You can define the command however you like and have it do its thing in the Execute method. It's just another example of being able to "store up" functionality for execution at a later time.

QueueCommand

First we'll define a simple command interface:

```
type
  IQueueCommand = interface
  ['{380B35B6-3157-4835-BDC7-6BD7746F1147}']
    procedure Execute(aMemo: TMemo);
  end;
```

The Execute method takes a TMemo because the command will simply report out to a Memo about its existence. We'll implement this interface as follows:

```
TQueueCommand = class(TInterfacedObject, IQueueCommand)
private
  FID: integer;
public
  constructor Create(aID: integer);
  procedure Execute(aMemo: TMemo);
  property ID: integer read FID;
end;
```

Here are the constructor and the Execute method implementations:

```
constructor TQueueCommand.Create(aID: integer);
begin
  inherited Create;
  FID := aID;
end;

procedure TQueueCommand.Execute(aMemo: TMemo);
begin
  aMemo.Lines.Add('Command #' + ID.ToString());
end;
```

The constructor just stores the ID for the command. The Execute method merely takes the passed-in memo and writes out the command number. It is very simple and illustrative. Again, your command interface will be simple, but the command's implementation can do whatever you need it to do.

Let's create a new VCL application that looks like this:

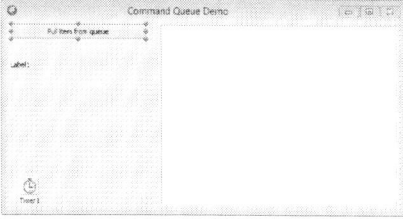

The timer will be used to add up to ten commands in the queue, and the button will pull them out and execute them.

We'll be using the Spring.Collections unit, so add that to your interface section uses clause. Next, add these two variables to the private section of your form:

```
Counter: integer;
CommandQueue: IQueue<IQueueCommand>;
```

Double click on the form, and add the following code to the `OnCreate` event for the form:

```
procedure TForm49.FormCreate(Sender: TObject);
begin
  Counter := 1;
  CommandQueue := TCollections.CreateQueue<IQueueCommand>;
end;
```

Here, we just set things up to run the application. Double click on the timer, and add the following code to its `OnTimer` event:

```
procedure TForm49.Timer1Timer(Sender: TObject);
var
  LCommand: IQueueCommand;
begin
  if CommandQueue.Count <= 10 then
  begin
    LCommand := TQueueCommand.Create(Counter);
    Inc(Counter);
    CommandQueue.Enqueue(LCommand);
    Label1.Caption := CommandQueue.Count.ToString();
  end;
end;
```

First, we only allow ten items in the queue. If there are less than ten we create a new command, assign it to the interface, increment the counter, add the command to the queue, and then update the label with the number of items in the queue. The timer will start when the application does and places commands in the queue.

Then, double click on the button and add the following code to its `OnClick` event handler:

```
procedure TForm49.Button1Click(Sender: TObject);
var
  LCommand: IQueueCommand;
begin
  if CommandQueue.Count > 0  then
  begin
    LCommand := CommandQueue.Dequeue;
    LCommand.Execute(Memo1);
    Label1.Caption := CommandQueue.Count.ToString();
  end;
end;
```

If there is anything in the queue then we `Dequeue` the leading item (Queues are First In, First Out data structures) and call its `Execute` method. Finally, we update the label with the number of items in the queue since it has changed.

Now, you should be able to run the application and watch commands being added to the queue. You can press the button and remove items from the queue, and you'll see them declare themselves in the memo.

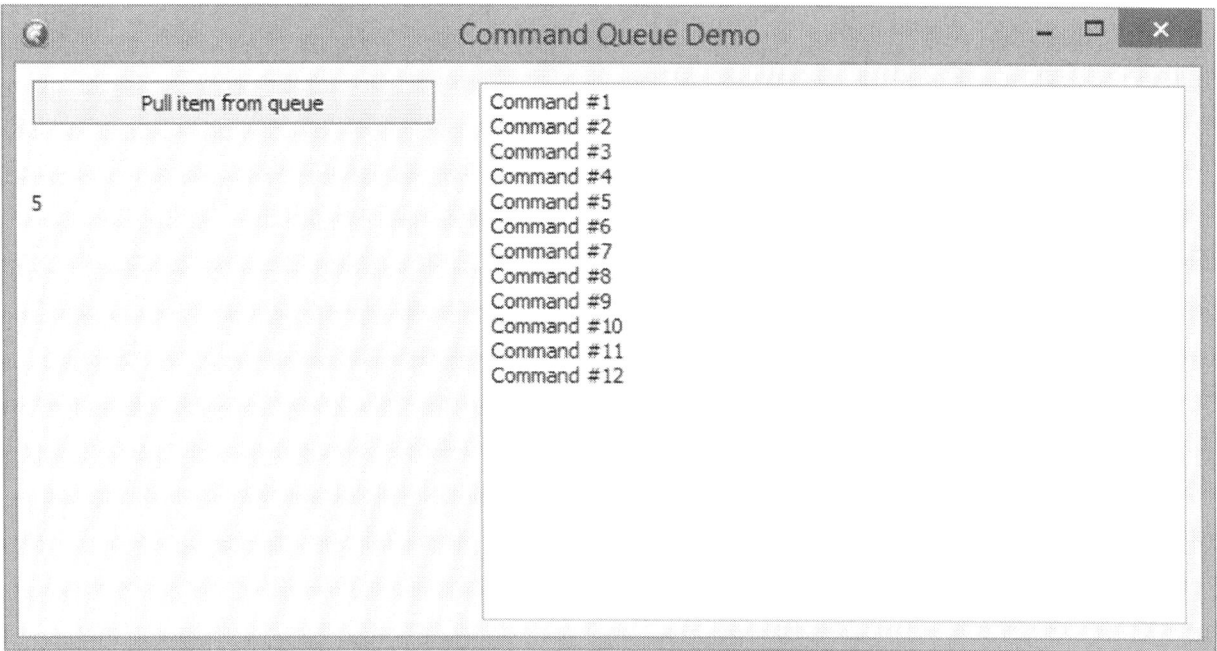

It's a pretty simple application, but it illustrates an important part of the Command Pattern – the ability to queue up the execution of code. One could imagine keeping a queue of external requests or requests that come in over a TCP/IP connection or some other communication mode. You could even create separate threads for each command. The pattern allows for flexible execution of specific actions. You might need to limit how many requests are processed at any given time because of resource limitations. (Imagine having print requests come in and only having two printers.)

You might also use the Command Pattern to create a transactional system, storing up commands, and then ensuring that either they all run or none of them do.

Summary

We've seen a number of different ways that the command pattern can separate the concerns in your code while still enabling powerful functionality. We decoupled the actions of a car key fob from what the buttons do. You could do the same with your applications. In fact, if you use TActions in your applications, you are doing that very thing.

We saw how we can utilize the pattern to add an Undo feature to our application. We were able to erase dots on our form using a stack of commands that knew how to un-draw themselves.

And finally, we saw how we can store up commands for later execution using a queue to manage the incoming requests and execute them on demand.

The Command Pattern is just another example of how we can decouple our code. In this case, we can decouple the code for a given action from the mechanism that executes that code. This is yet another example of how writing clean code that separates our concerns can make for maintainable, extensible code. In addition to reducing coupling, the Command Pattern can also be a great way of managing mutability, not just for implementing Undo as we have done here, but perhaps by extending it so that you can roll back to any prior state of the underlying objects.

Operator Overloading

Operator Overloading is kind of hard to describe. I must confess that the Wikipedia entry[18] made no sense at all to me. So instead of the Wikipedia entry, you can use this chapter to figure out operator overloading.

First, what are operators? Operators are the symbols used by a programming language to perform many standard functions. For instance, we use the '+' symbol to indicate addition.

We could simply define

```
function Add(A, B: integer): integer;
```

to do addition. However, that isn't nearly as convenient as simply typing:

```
A + B
```

Thus, operators provide a simpler way to express many common functions.

Of course, the list of operators is pretty long. It includes all the common mathematical symbols

```
+, - ,* , /, =, <, >, etc
```

as well as logical operators like and and or, and bitwise operators like shl and shr, etc. In addition, in Delphi you can overload the Inc, Dec, Trunc, and Round operators.

Operator Overloading is the addition of functionality to operators for different data types. A familiar example is the Delphi compiler, which overloads the '+' symbol for strings allowing you to do things like:

```
SomeString := 'Why did the dog lay in the shade?  ' + 'Because it didn''t want to be a hot dog';
```

So operator overloading is the ability to add functionality to operators by applying them to new data types.

Delphi allows you to do operator overloading of record data types. You can define a record, and then overload any of a long list of operators to apply new functionality to those new record types. (The complete list of operators that can be overloaded can be found in the Delphi documentation[19]).

> Because they support Automatic Reference Counting (ARC), newer versions of the mobile compiler allow for class overloading. However, as mentioned in the Preface, we are going to stick with the Windows compiler here, and thus focus on operator overloading with records.

---

[18]http://en.wikipedia.org/wiki/Operator_overloading

[19]http://docwiki.embarcadero.com/RADStudio/XE7/en/Operator_Overloading_%28Delphi%29

An Example: `TFraction`

An example should make things clearer. Computers deal in integers and floating point numbers, but there may be an occasion for you to need to use good old fashioned fractions. So how about we create a `TFraction` type, overloading the general mathematical operators that allow us to add, subtract, multiply, divide and compare fractions? Sounds good, right?

Okay, so let's start out with a simple definition of `TFraction`:

```
type
  TFraction = record
  strict private
    FNumerator: Integer;
    FDenominator: Integer;
    class function GCD(a, b: Integer): Integer; static;
    function Reduced: TFraction;
  public
    class function CreateFrom(aNumerator: Integer; aDenominator: Integer): TFraction; static;

    property Numerator: Integer read FNumerator;
    property Denominator: Integer read FDenominator;
  end;
```

It's a simple record with `Numerator` and `Denominator` properties. It also has a constructor of sorts called `CreateFrom` that allows you to initialize a `TFraction`. That function is probably a little more complicated that you might think:

```
class function TFraction.CreateFrom(aNumerator, aDenominator: Integer): TFraction;
begin
  if aDenominator = 0 then
  begin
    raise EZeroDivide.CreateFmt('Invalid fraction %d/%d, numerator cannot be zero', [aNumerator, aDenominator]\
);
  end;
  if (aDenominator < 0) then
  begin
    Result.FNumerator := -aNumerator;
    Result.FDenominator := -aDenominator;
  end else
  begin
    Result.FNumerator := aNumerator;
    Result.FDenominator := aDenominator;
  end;
  Assert(Result.Denominator > 0); // needed for comparisons
end;
```

First, since we are dealing only with rational numbers, you can't have a `Denominator` that is zero, so an exception is raised if you try to create a fraction with a zero on the bottom. Next, in order to allow for better code when doing the comparison operators a little later, if the denominator is negative, we move the sign to the numerator.

Now we can create a fraction like so:

```
var
  OneThird: TFraction;
begin
  OneThird := TFraction.CreateFrom(1, 3);
end;
```

But what good is that? Wouldn't it be better if we could do math on these fractions? Well, we could do it this way:

```
function AddFractions(a, b: TFraction): TFraction;
```

but that would be clumsy and no fun. It would be much better to be able to do:

```
var
  A, B, C: TFraction;
begin
  A := TFraction.Create(1, 2);
  B := TFraction.Create(1, 3);
  C := A + B;
end;
```

Well, lets make that happen. In order to do that, we need to add some `class operator` methods to the `TFraction` record. We want to be able to add fractions together, so in order to do addition, we'll need this method:

```
class operator Add(const Left, Right: TFraction): TFraction;
```

The `class operator` declaration is a special class method that indicates that an operator is to be overloaded. In this case, we are overloading addition, as indicated by the method name `Add`. The compiler recognizes `Add` as a special method name and uses it to override the '+' operator. A `class operator` must be followed by a specific operator name as defined in the documentation link above. For instance, if you declare

```
class operator FooBar(const AValue: TFraction): TFraction;
```

you'll get an error like this one:

```
[dcc32 Error] uFractions.pas(36): E2393 Invalid operator declaration
```

In other words, you need to have a correct, valid operator name for the `class operator` declaration to compile. Here we have `Add`, but in a minute we'll add more, like `Subtract` and `Negative`.

However, there are no restrictions on parameters and return value types. You can provide overloads and converters for any Delphi type if it is appropriate for your overload.

So, how do you add two fractions?

```
class operator TFraction.Add(const Left, Right: TFraction): TFraction;
begin
  Result := CreateFrom(Left.Numerator * Right.Denominator + Left.Denominator * Right.Numerator, Left.Denominat\
or * Right.Denominator).Reduced;
end;
```

This code creates a new instance of TFraction, and performs the formula for adding two fractions together. And finally, it calls Reduced to reduce the resulting fraction to have the least common denominator. Reduced is declared as follows:

```
function TFraction.Reduced: TFraction;
var
  LGCD: Integer;
begin
  LGCD := GCD(Numerator, Denominator);
  Result := CreateFrom(Numerator div LGCD, Denominator div LGCD);
end;
```

and GCD is declared as:

```
class function TFraction.GCD(a, b: Integer): Integer;
var
  rem: Integer;
begin
  rem := a mod b;
  if rem = 0 then
    Result := b;
  else
    Result := GCD(b, rem)
end;
```

I'm no mathematician, but I understand that the GCD function is a recursive implementation of the Euclidean Greatest Common Denominator algorithm. Impressive, eh?

In any event, the code ensures that all results are properly reduced, and you'll see the call to Reduced on the end of any method that returns a TFraction.

Okay, so that's the implementation for adding two fractions together. The code for adding a fraction to an integer is very similar, as an integer is just a fraction with a denominator of 1, so I won't show it here. (You can check it out on the BitBucket[20] repository for the book's code).

How about subtraction? Well, before we look at subtraction, we need to look at another operator:

```
class operator Negative(const AValue: TFraction): TFraction;
```

This is the overload for the minus sign in front of a fraction, which of course makes it negative. It's implemented as follows:

---

[20]https://bitbucket.org/NickHodges/nickdemocode/src/11f331ec18dc0f2f4f6ade17153bff0b31ab13cf/MoreCodingInDelphi/?at=default

```
class operator TFraction.Negative(const AValue: TFraction): TFraction;
begin
  Result := CreateFrom(-aValue.Numerator, AValue.Denominator);
end;
```

It's implementation is pretty obvious – it just creates a negative version of the TFraction passed to it by making the numerator negative. I showed it to you first before looking at the Subtraction method, because the Subtraction method uses it. Here's the implementation for subtracting one fraction from another:

```
class operator TFraction.Subtract(const Left, Right: TFraction): TFraction;
begin
  Result := Left + (-Right);
end;
```

Note that the class operators can build on one another. The subtraction uses the Add operator and the Negative operator together to create Subtraction, resulting in easier code to read and maintain.

The Multiply and Divide methods are implemented exactly like you would think, so I won't cover them here.

The next set of operators that we'll look at are the comparison operators, that is, =, <>, >, <, <=, and >=. Again, they'll build on each other, so we'll start with Equal and NotEqual.

```
class operator TFraction.Equal(const Left, Right: TFraction): Boolean;
begin
  Result := Left.Numerator * Right.Denominator = Right.Numerator * Left.Denominator;
end;

class operator TFraction.NotEqual(const Left, Right: TFraction): Boolean;
begin
  Result := not (Left = Right);
end;
```

Note that the Equal method uses the classic algorithm you learned in fourth grade to determine if two fractions are equal, but the NotEqual method simply takes advantage of the Equal operator by using not to get the proper result.

Naturally following from that is the greater than/less than operators, including the equals. And guess what, they build on each other as well:

```
class operator TFraction.LessThan(const Left, Right: TFraction): Boolean;
begin
  Result := Left.Numerator * Right.Denominator < Right.Numerator * Left.Denominator;
end;

class operator TFraction.GreaterThan(const Left, Right: TFraction): Boolean;
begin
  Result := Left.Numerator * Right.Denominator > Right.Numerator * Left.Denominator;
end;

class operator TFraction.LessThanOrEqual(const Left, Right: TFraction): Boolean;
begin
  Result := (Left < Right) or (Left = Right);
end;

class operator TFraction.GreaterThanOrEqual(const Left, Right: TFraction): Boolean;
begin
  Result := (Left = Right) or (Left > Right);
end;
```

Again, the code is quite simple and pretty much what you'd expect. Note that GreatThanOrEqual and LessThanOrEqual both use existing functionality to do their work.

Assignments

So now we have a TFraction that can perform basic math and do comparisons. But what if you want to assign a TFraction to another type, say, a Double, or if you want to assign an integer to a TFraction?

Well, you can do that by using a call to class operator Implicit. Implicit is the operator that allows you to write code that assigns one type to another. For TFraction, we'll declare two of them:

```
class operator Implicit(const aValue: Integer): TFraction;
class operator Implicit(const aValue: TFraction): Double;
```

One will allow an integer to be turned into a TFraction and the other will convert a TFraction into a double. The implementations are simple:

```
class operator TFraction.Implicit(const AValue: Integer): TFraction;
begin
  Result := TFraction.CreateFrom(aValue, 1);
end;

class operator TFraction.Implicit(const aValue: TFraction): Double;
begin
  Result := aValue.Numerator/aValue.Denominator;
end;
```

Delphi's strong typing prevents me from wanting to allow TFraction to be assignable to a string, but I have provided a ToString method that turns the fraction into something readable:

```
function TFraction.ToString: string;
begin
  Result := Format('%d/%d', [Numerator, Denominator]);
end;
```

In addition, I've used the `class operator Explicit` method to allow hard casting of a `TFraction` to a `string`. This operator allows code like the following:

```
SomeString := string(TFraction.CreateFrom(1, 3));
```

Implicit vs. Explicit

Implicit casting is what happens when, for example, you pass a string to a function taking a `Variant`, or if you directly assign an `integer` to a `Double`. In our example, we can use implicit conversion to add a `TFraction` to an integer. This keeps us from having to implement multiple `Add` operators:

```
// Don't need these because of implicit conversions
class operator Add(const Left: TFraction; const Right: Integer): TFraction;
class operator Add(const Left: Integer; const Right: TFraction): TFraction;
```

So, we can implicitly `Add` a `TFraction` to an `integer`. How about adding a `TFraction` and a `double` to result in a double? Well, we have the following:

```
class operator Implicit(const aValue: TFraction): Double;
```

so you'd think that this test would pass:

```
procedure TFractionTests.TestAddDouble;
var
  a: TFraction;
  b: Double;
begin
  a := TFraction.CreateFrom(1, 3);
  b := a + 0.5;
  Assert.AreEqual(b, 5/6);
end;
```

but in fact it won't even compile, giving the error:

```
[dcc32 Error] uFractionsTests.pas(111): E2015 Operator not applicable to this operand type
```

This is due to the limitations in the Delphi compiler. It doesn't "see" that by converting the `TFraction` to a `Double` via the implicit cast it can actually do the addition.

In order to have the above test compile and pass, you can implement directly the `Add` operator for a `TFraction` and a `TDouble` like so:

```
class operator TFraction.Add(const Left: TFraction; const Right: double): double;
var
  LDouble: Double;
begin
  LDouble := Left;
  Result := LDouble + Right;
end;
```

and then our test will pass.

Note that I don't have an implicit converter for changing a TFraction into an integer. Why not? Well, because such a conversion would be "lossy". That is, you'd lose information by doing so. Think about it – how do you convert 3/4 into an integer? You really can't, and thus the functionality is not provided.

I've made that decision for the user. But if I wanted to allow the user to choose to make such a lossy conversion, I could provide an Explicit conversion method that would allow the user to do a "hard" cast of a TFraction to an integer. Hard casts are the responsibility of the developer, and so an Explicit conversion could be provided if desired, realizing that it passes responsibility for the loss of data to the user. Such a conversion might truncate or round the fraction to an integer.

Using TFraction

Okay, so let's exercise this a bit. Here are some things that you can do with TFraction. First, let's add some fractions:

```
var
  A, B, C, D: TFraction;
  S: string;
  Dub: Double;
begin
  A := TFraction.CreateFrom(2, 6);
  B := TFraction.CreateFrom(4, 18);
  C := A + B;
  S := C.ToString;
  WriteLn(S);
end;
```

This outputs 5/9. Note that the fraction has been Reduced from 10/18.

How about the Negative and Explicit methods? Do they allow you to turn a fraction negative, and hard cast a fraction to a string? Sure they do.

```
C := TFraction.CreateFrom(7, 12);
D := -C;
S := string(D);
WriteLn(S);
```

will result in -7/12.

How about inequality?

```
A := TFraction.CreateFrom(1, 2);
B := TFraction.CreateFrom(2, 5);
if A <> B then
begin
  WriteLn('Not Equal');
end else
begin
  WriteLn('Inequality check failed');
end;
```

Yep, that outputs `Not Equal` as expected.

How about `GreaterThan`:

```
A := TFraction.CreateFrom(1, 3);
B := TFraction.CreateFrom(1, 100);
if A > B then
begin
  WriteLn('Greater Than');
end else
begin
  WriteLn('Greater than check failed');
end;
```

Yep, that works. In fact, it all works, and I won't repeat demos for all of the possible method calls here. You can look in the BitBucket[21] repository for test code. The bottom line is that we now have the ability to do pretty much whatever we want and need with `TFraction`.

> The demo code that is part of this chapter includes a complete set of unit tests that show `TFraction` works as it is designed to work.

Conclusion

So there we have it – a new record `TFraction` that can be used with all the major mathematical operators. You have to admit, that the code is not complicated at all.

> Delphi ships with a more complicated example of operator overloading that deals with complex numbers. That can be found on your hard drive, most likely at:
> C:\Users\Public\Documents\Embarcadero\Studio\16.0\Samples\Object Pascal\RTL\ComplexNumbers
> That demo is written by the great Hallvard Vassbotn, and is very complete.

It is, however, a powerful technique that can result in much cleaner code. Nobody wants to see

```
Sum := ThisFraction.Add(ThatFraction);
```

when you could write

---

[21] https://bitbucket.org/NickHodges/nickdemocode/src/11f331ec18dc0f2f4f6ade17153bff0b31ab13cf/MoreCodingInDelphi/?at=default

```
Sum := ThisFraction + ThatFraction;
```

Seems pretty obvious, right?

Operator Overloading doesn't fit every situation – not every `record` is going to require or need it, but it can be a very useful technique for those data types that can be "operated" on. Generally, only records that can be used with mathematical expressions should have their mathematical operators overloaded. Don't go crazy – you can easily produce some very confusing code by overloading records that shouldn't be overloaded.

Multi-Threading and Parallelism

Introduction

Don't you wish you had a dollar for every time someone asked "Is <some library/framework/class> thread-safe?" It's never that easy, is it?

Writing multi-threaded and parallel code is hard – really hard. It's very easy to get it wrong and difficult to get it right. It is incredibly powerful and useful when used correctly and a debugging nightmare when not. It's fraught with peril. It's scary. The wise developer approaches it with fear and trepidation. Even the most seasoned, experienced developers will tread with a very light step when dealing with multi-threaded and parallel programming. Just because your processor has a ton of cores doesn't mean that you can run off willy-nilly and write multi-threaded code with impunity. And just because Delphi XE7 introduces the System.Threading.pas unit doesn't mean that all your performance problems will all go away by using it.

Shoot, just writing these chapters is hard.

Do I have you sufficiently nervous? Good. You should be.

About These Three Chapters

As I said, writing these chapters has been hard. My approach is designed to suit an experienced developer who may have dabbled in writing simple multi-threaded code and yet needs a good introduction and a solid foundation to the many issues deriving from the use of multi-threading and parallelism. I assume that you have only a passing familiarity with the basics of using TThread. This is not going to be a treatise on thread scheduling and the depths of the Windows threading system.

The first chapter will cover TThread and its usage. Then the next two chapters will focus on the System.Threading.pas unit introduced in Delphi XE7. My goal is to introduce you to the power that is available in multi-threaded and parallel programming, warn you about the dangers and pitfalls inherent in that power, and leave you with the ability to write parallel code that will improve the performance of your applications. Multi-threaded and parallel programming is challenging, but there is help out there in the form of RTL support. Tread carefully, but know that these libraries are there to take away much – but not all – of the complexity of multi-threaded development.

What is a Thread?

A thread is a single execution context used by the operating system to schedule the execution of code on the CPU. All code is executed in a thread. Every application has a main thread. From the main thread, an application can "spawn" new threads to perform specific tasks across the multiple cores in your machine. A thread runs within the context of a specific CPU core, though the operating system can move threads from one core to another within your CPU. If your computer has multiple CPU cores – and what machine these days doesn't? – you can use additional threads to spread the work of your application across those multiple cores. An application that is tied to one CPU, because it doesn't take advantage of parallelism, isn't using the resources of a computer as efficiently as it could be.

In these power-conscious days, using the CPU and all of its cores at maximum usage for a short period of time can be better for power management than using a fraction of the CPU for a longer time. Thus, parallelism can actually help with battery life, particularly on hand-held devices.

Thus, parallel programming can make your applications run more efficiently. Parallelism allows you to split your application into smaller chunks and use all those cores you've got in your CPU. The Operating System – in our case, Windows – is responsible for scheduling all the threads and doling them out to various cores of your multi-core processor. That's what parallel programming is – running multiple tasks at the same time, on separate cores of a multi-processor system.

Think of each core as the lane of a highway: each can handle a stream of cars. A four lane highway, say, can therefore handle four streams of cars simultaneously. More cars can get to a destination faster in four lanes than in two or one. Likewise, a system with four CPU cores can handle four threads at a time. If you have four, eight or sixteen cores available, it can pay dividends in performance to utilize them all.

Your application can be broken up into "lanes," but doing that level of coordination and decomposition is often beyond the ability of most developers. You almost certainly need some assistance in splitting your application's functionality into discrete chunks. This is where things like TThread and the Parallel Programming Library (PPL) come in – they can aid in that decomposition into separate threads. They provide "buckets," if you will, where you can place your code and allow the operating system to take control to distribute the work among multiple cores.

Continuing with the highway metaphor, sometimes a given lane will be jammed. This may result from a thread simply waiting on another thread, or as a result of a long process. The other lanes, however, may be open for business, and a well-designed program will take advantage of that, letting you "change lanes" to get on your way. For instance, you may have a text editor that waits for user input, but have a spell-checker running in the background that checks spelling as the user types.

Think Differently

The only way to make your code multi-threaded is by thinking about it in a completely new way.

You need to think about the proper decomposition of your code, that is, how the code is broken down into separate, discrete tasks that can be made parallel. If code is going to run in "lanes," you need to be able to break the code into chunks that can fit inside that lane comfortably and properly.

Then you need to think about how your tasks will coordinate with all the other tasks that need to be executed. Often, multiple tasks must be coordinated and allowed to work together.

In addition, you need to keep in mind which thread is executing a given block of code. This is especially important when you use Queue or Synchronize or otherwise call methods from multiple threads. Keeping context in mind is always critical to good multi-threaded code.

Finally, you need to think about how to handle data that will be shared by those tasks. Frequently tasks will share, or even compete for, common resources, and you need to think about how those common resources will be shared. This is one of the main challenges of parallel programming – how to ensure that you don't actually make things worse.

Fortunately, Delphi provides classes and libraries that abstract much of this for you. If you ever worked with the TThread class, you will be happy to know that the Parallel Programming Library (PPL) goes up one level of abstraction from that, making things even easier. This, however, does not mean that it's an easy going: there are still lots of pitfalls to watch out for.

I remember the days when people were calling for a "thread-safe VCL." Thank goodness we appear to be past that now. People somehow wanted the VCL to magically become "thread-safe" so that they could create threads without having to worry about corrupting their user interface. But if you stop to think about it, the term "thread-safe VCL" is meaningless. Well, not meaningless -- more of a case of "be careful what you wish for." Given how a modern GUI works, a thread safe VCL would be slower than a tired sloth on cough medicine. It would have to be filled from top to bottom with locks, drastically degrading performance. Asking for a thread-safe VCL is asking for the wrong thing. What you should be asking for is a way to write parallel code – and that is why the PPL exists.

Why Should I Care About Multi-threaded and Parallel Programming?

Good question. It should be pretty easy to answer. Moore's Law[22] marches on. Historically, Moore's Law meant more transistors on a single CPU chip. It recently took a bit of a detour. The ability to add transistors to an individual CPU core became more difficult, and so instead of putting the transistors into one CPU, chip makers started putting multiple CPU cores into a single CPU chip.

What has happened to make Moore's Law still relevant is that CPUs have become multi-cored – the transistor count still increases, but they increase by adding more cores. That is, a given CPU chip actually has multiple CPUs in it. I don't know the clock speed of the CPU in this computer I am writing on, but I do know that it has four real cores, and eight virtual ones. In addition, the cache on chips is growing, as is the memory attached to them. Shoot, even my phone has a multi-core CPU in it.

Multi-threaded and parallel programming aims at taking advantage of these multiple cores. If you have multiple cores but tie your application to only a single core, you aren't fully utilizing the speed and power of your machine. The days of fixing performance by using better hardware are now sadly gone. Your application needs to use all the cores within your CPU.

All of this boils down to two things that multi-threaded and parallel programming will get you: better speed and better responsiveness. Obviously, if you separate a task into multiple execution paths, it is going to run faster. In addition, if you split the task into parallel threads, your application can remain responsive while doing complicated and intense calculations because the main thread – where the user interface runs – has its own, separate lane. Almost all of the demo applications we'll look at can be moved and sized while intense calculating is going on in them.

That's why you should care about multi-threaded and parallel programming.

---

[22]http://en.wikipedia.org/wiki/Moore%27s_law

A Long Task

In order to illustrate the use of the Multi-threading and the PPL, we need a method that takes up some serious CPUtime. Most demos I see use the good old Sleep command, but I don't want to do that. I want my demos to do something at least semi-real. Instead, let's use a very inefficient algorithm for calculating prime numbers, and then check for the "primeness" of a fixed group of numbers. Calculating the total number of primes between 2 and 100,000 should take some serious CPU time – just what we are looking for. This task will do well for taking up the CPU time we need to illustrate parallel programming.

Here's the code we'll use:

```pascal
// An incredibly inefficient way to calculate primes
function SlowIsPrime(aInteger: integer): Boolean;
var
  i: integer;
begin
  Assert(aInteger > 0);
  // Remember, 1 is not prime
  if aInteger = 1 then
  begin
    Result := False;
    Exit;
  end;
  Result := True;
  for i := 2 to aInteger - 1 do
  begin
    if aInteger mod i = 0 then
    begin
      Result := False;
      Exit;
    end;
  end;
end;

function PrimesBelow(aInteger: integer): integer;
var
  i: integer;
begin
  Result := 0;
  for i := 1 to aInteger do
  begin
    if SlowIsPrime(i) then
    begin
      Result := Result + 1;
    end;
  end;
end;
```

Thus, you can call something like the PrimesBelow(200000) function, which will take the CPU time we need to illustrate a time-consuming process. On my machine, the following code:

```
Stopwatch := TStopwatch.StartNew;
Total := PrimesBelow(200000);
ElapsedSeconds := StopWatch.Elapsed.TotalSeconds;
WriteLn('There are ', Total, ' primes under 100,000');
WriteLn('It took ', ElapsedSeconds, ' seconds to calculate that') ;
ReadLn;
```

reports taking about six seconds to run, which ought to serve our purposes very well. We can adjust this to create `PrimesBelow(50000)` and `PrimesBelow(100000)` as needed or desired.

We are also going to use simple VCL apps to run our code, because part of using threads involves producing responsive applications during CPU-intensive processes. Part of what I'll ask you to do when you run the code we'll be looking at is to try to move the application using the title bar. Without multi-threading, a CPU-intensive application is usually not responsive to simple requests like moving the main window. However, that's not good, and we'll see how you can use threads and parallelism to both speed up your applications while at the same time keeping them responsive. Nice, eh?

Okay, with all that scary talk out of the way, let's get started.

Multi-threading with TThread

Introduction

When Delphi 1 was introduced – way back in 1995 – it was a 16-bit tool that ran on Windows 3.1. Those were the days, eh? Anyway, Windows 3.1 didn't do multi-threading; it did something called "cooperative multitasking." This meant that the OS would manage the "passing of the baton" around to different processes, simulating a multi-threaded system. Problems could and would easily occur when an application refused to give up the baton. It was sub-optimal to say the least.

Delphi 2 came out about a year after Delphi 1, and it was a 32-bit system running on Windows 95. Windows 95 allowed for true multi-threading, and thus Delphi 2 supported threading via a class called TThread.

Delphi 2's TThread was fairly straight forward, and since then, TThread has been enhanced and expanded, taking advantage of things like anonymous methods.

This chapter will cover the basics of TThread. We won't delve into the low-level Win32/64 API calls that TThread encapsulates. Instead we'll stick to the functionality that Delphi provides.

Descending from TThread

TVerySimpleThread

Okay, let's start with a very, very simple demo that illustrates the basics of how to create a thread class and how a thread goes about its business. The first thing we want to do is to create a descendant of TThread. Here's one:

```
unit uVerySimpleThread;

interface

uses
    System.Classes
  , VCL.StdCtrls
  , System.SysUtils
  ;

type
  TVerySimpleThread = class(TThread)
  private
    FMemo: TMemo;
    FConcatenatedString: string;
  protected
    procedure Execute; override;
  public
    constructor Create(aMemo: TMemo; String1, String2: string);
```

```
  end;

implementation

constructor TVerySimpleThread.Create(aMemo: TMemo; String1, String2: string);
begin
  if aMemo = nil then
  begin
    raise Exception.Create('You must pass a valid Memo');
  end;

  inherited Create(False);
  FreeOnTerminate := True;
  FMemo := aMemo;
  FConcatenatedString := String1 + ' ' + String2;
end;

procedure TVerySimpleThread.Execute;
begin
  Synchronize(procedure
              begin
                FMemo.Lines.Add('The concatenated string is: ' + FConcatenatedString);
              end);
end;

end.
```

TVerySimpleThread is – surprise! – a very simple thread that does nothing more than take two strings, concatenate them, and write the result out to a TMemo. Here are some things to note:

- TVerySimpleThread descends from TThread. TThread is a wrapper around the notion of a thread. I say "notion" because TThread is cross-platform abstraction of a thread.
- Any creator of a TThread descendant has the obligation to override the abstract Execute method, which TVerySimpleThread does. The Execute method is where a thread does its work. Nothing a thread does happens outside of Execute. A thread will do nothing until its Execute method is called. The Execute method is always called by the new thread after it is created by the operating system as part of the TThread encapsulation. You should never call Execute yourself.
- The constructor does some interesting things. First, it checks to make sure you aren't passing a nil memo. Then, it calls the inherited constructor, passing False. TThread has a single constructor that takes a Boolean parameter called CreateSuspended. This parameter determines if the thread should start right away, or wait to be manually started. In this case, we pass False, meaning that the thread will be not be suspended when it is created. What does this mean? It means that the Execute method will be called when the thread is done being created. And remember, nothing in a thread happens until Execute is called. *The next line of constructor code sets FreeOnTerminate to True. This states that the thread will be freed automatically when it is done doing what it has to do – that is, when the Execute method is finished. When the Execute method ends, the thread is terminated. That is, its Terminated property is set to True. Once that happens, the thread will destroy itself. Now when you do this, you need to be careful that the Execute method will definitely finish and not hang or run past the end of the application yourself, as you won't have any control over the thread once it is set. The thread might still be running when the application terminates, so use it with care.

- The constructor takes a `TMemo` as a parameter and stores it for later use after making sure that it isn't `nil`.
- In the `Execute` method, we write a simple message out to the memo we stored.

Pretty simple, as I said. But wait, there's something interesting happening in the `Execute` method, eh?. There's a call to `Synchronize` in there with an anonymous method wrapping up the call to the memo. What's that all about?

The VCL isn't "thread-safe". That means that you can't rely on the VCL to do the right thing in a multi-threaded environment. The VCL involves painting and drawing and monitoring UI inputs and all kinds of things that can't function properly when multiple threads are involved. Thus, any actions in the VCL that a thread takes need to be "synchronized" with the main thread. That's what the `Synchronize` call is doing here. Basically it says "Hey, I have some VCL code that needs to run here. Let's stop everything, let the VCL code run in the main thread, then get back to business". Thus, anytime you want to run VCL code in a thread, you need to use `Synchronize`. (Or `Queue`, which we'll look at in a bit.)

Using TVerySimpleThread

Okay, so we've created a very simple thread – now how do we use it?

I've created a simple VCL application that looks like this:

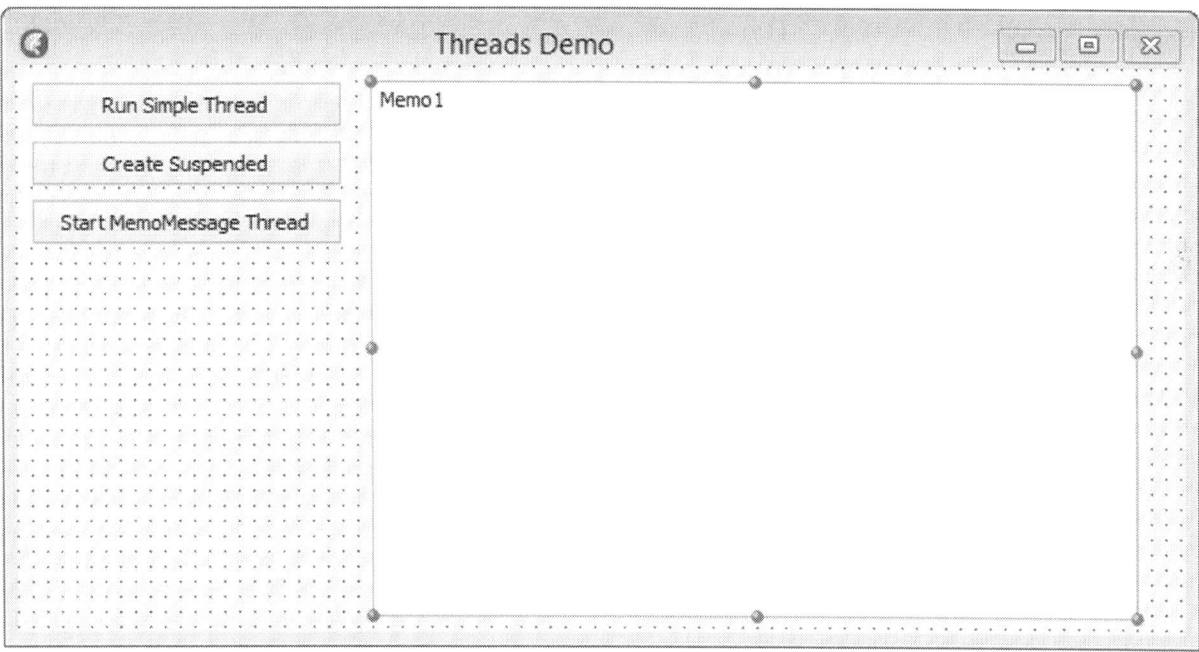

Double-click the first button and add this code:

```
procedure TThreadsDemoForm.Button1Click(Sender: TObject);
begin
  TVerySimpleThread.Create(Memo1);
  Memo1.Lines.Add('This comes from the main thread');
end;
```

When you run the app and press the button, you should see the following:

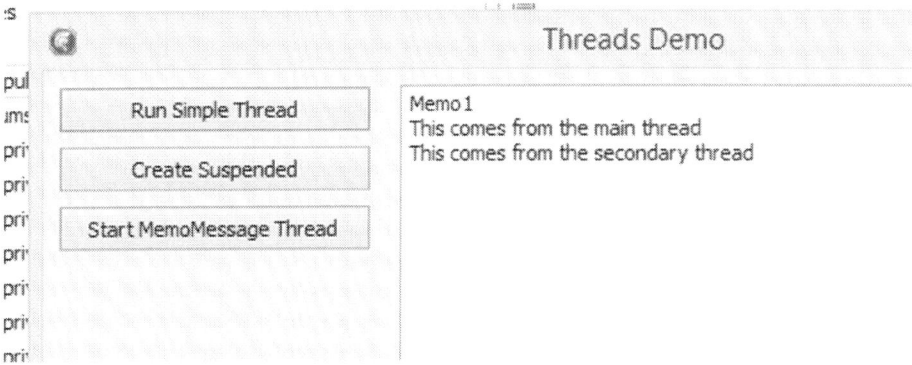

Now, that's interesting. The first line of code executes second, and the second line first. Hmmm. Why? Well, because threads run independently and possibly at the same time on different CPU cores. When synchronizing access to a shared resource (the memo in this case), which thread gets access first is unpredictable. As we'll see in the coming chapters on Parallelism, threads can often run in varying and unpredictable ways.

The other interesting thing is that when we called the thread, we simply called the constructor, leaving the reference unassigned to any variable. We can do that because the thread is created unsuspended and with FreeOnTerminate set to True. This means that the thread will start when called and free itself when it is done. I like to call this a "Fire and Forget" thread – one that you can create and set on its way and not worry about again.

Creating a Suspended Thread

But we don't always want our threads to be "Fire and Forget". How about we create a similar one that is created suspended:

```
unit uMemoMessageThread;

interface

uses
    System.Classes
  , VCL.StdCtrls
  ;

type
  TMemoMessageThread = class(TThread)
  private
    FMemo: TMemo;
    FMemoMessage: string;
```

```
  protected
    procedure Execute; override;
  public
    constructor Create(aMemo: TMemo);
    property MemoMessage: string read FMemoMessage write FMemoMessage;
  end;


implementation

uses
      uSlowCode
    ;


{ TMemoMessageThread }

constructor TMemoMessageThread.Create(aMemo: TMemo);
begin
  inherited Create(True);
  FreeOnTerminate := True;
  FMemo := aMemo;
end;

procedure TMemoMessageThread.Execute;
begin
  // Do Something busy
  PrimesBelow(150000);
  Synchronize(procedure
              begin
                FMemo.Lines.Add(FMemoMessage);
              end);
end;

end.
```

TMemoMessageThread is a little different than TVerySimpleThread. First, it is created suspended, meaning it just sits there, waiting for someone or something to call the Execute method. It still sets FreeOnTerminate to True, and keeps a reference to the memo passed to it.

> When you create a TThread descendant, you will almost certainly be passing in dependencies to the constructor. This is, of course, a classic case of Dependency Injection via Constructor Injection. Very often a thread will utilize external data, and the best way to get that information to the thread is via the constructor.

The Execute implementation is a little different as well. It contains a call to PrimesBelow that will take up some CPU time, a thing that threads are often asked to do. And, since the thread is created suspended, we'll need to call Start to get it rolling. Double click on the third button and add this code:

```
procedure TThreadsDemoForm.Button3Click(Sender: TObject);
begin
  MemoMessageThread.Start;
  MemoMessageThread := nil;
end;
```

Okay, so let's use this thread. Double click on the second button on the form and enter the following in its OnClick handler:

```
procedure TThreadsDemoForm.Button2Click(Sender: TObject);
begin
  MemoMessageThread := TMemoMessageThread.Create(Memo1);
  MemoMessageThread.MemoMessage := 'Hello from the TMemoMessageThread thread';
end;
```

Notice that this time we've maintained a reference to the thread after its creation so that we can fire it up later (the reference is a field of the form). Notice, too, that we nil the thread after we call Start. Since FreeOnTerminate is True, the thread may be destroyed immediately. The reason is, of course, scheduling, and that the main thread may end its time slice immediately after starting the thread, but before it actually returns. Then, depending on the system load and CPU, the thread may run and do its job before the main thread is scheduled to resume execution. And since we are using Synchronize, this could be immediately after the OnClick runs. Without Synchronize, it could be destroyed by the time Start returns. Thus, if we were to try to use the reference in another place – to set Terminate, for instance – we could be doing so on a destroyed object. Better to try to do so on a nil'ed object rather than on a dangling pointer.

Next, press the third button (make sure to press the second one first!), and the thread will start. It will calculate a bunch of prime numbers in about five seconds or so, but because it is doing so on a separate thread, the application will remain responsive during those five seconds. After you press the start button, grab the window by the title bar and move it around. You can do it, and if you do it long enough, the message will appear in the memo box while you do. Thus, you've seen your first use of a thread to create a more responsive application.

Thread Termination

I mentioned above that setting the Terminated property to True signals that the thread should be destroyed. Let's take a look at that. Here's a thread that does nothing but increment and display an integer:

```
unit uTerminatedDemoThread;

interface

uses
    System.Classes
  , VCL.StdCtrls
  ;

type
  TCountUntilTerminatedThread = class(TThread)
  private
```

```pascal
    FLabel: TLabel;
    i: integer;
  protected
    procedure Execute; override;
  public
    constructor Create(aLabel: TLabel);
  end;

implementation

uses
      System.SysUtils
    , WinAPI.Windows
    ;

{ TCountUntilTerminatedThread }

constructor TCountUntilTerminatedThread.Create(aLabel: TLabel);
begin
  inherited Create(True);
  FLabel := aLabel;
end;

procedure TCountUntilTerminatedThread.Execute;
begin
  inherited;
  while not Terminated do
  begin
    Synchronize(procedure
                begin
                  FLabel.Caption := i.ToString;
                end);
    Sleep(1000);
    TInterlocked.Increment(i);
  end;
end;

end.
```

This thread has a few more things in it than previous examples. The constructor is straight-forward. But the Execute method is more interesting.

First, it starts with a while clause that waits for the thread's Terminated property to be True. In other words, the thread will run until it is requested to be terminated. Then, it outputs via Synchronize the value of a field variable.

 Actually, what it does is set the thread internal FTerminated field to True. Once that happens, the thread will notice that Terminated is set and will finish up what it is doing, call the OnTerminate event (which we'll discuss below) and destroy itself. Notice that the thread doesn't necessarily get destroyed immediately upon Terminate being called because it may still have code to execute.

Then it uses TInterlocked.Increment to safely increment the variable i. TInterlocked is in the System.SyncObjs unit and is a sealed class that implements a number of common actions that can be done on variables that can be accessed by different threads. We'll discuss more about thread synchronization below.

The interesting thing here is how we end up destroying this thread. Create a form that looks something like this:

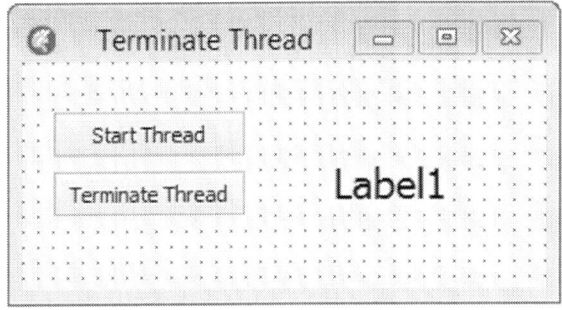

Add a private field to maintain a reference to the created thread:

```
FThread: TCountUntilTerminatedThread;
```

Double click on the first button and add this event handler:

```
procedure TForm49.Button1Click(Sender: TObject);
begin
    FThread := TCountUntilTerminatedThread.Create(Label1);
    FThread.FreeOnTerminate := True;
    FThread.OnTerminate := HandleTermination;
    FThread.Start;
end;
```

The interesting part here is that third line of code after the begin. TThread has an event called OnTerminate. It occurs when you'd expect it to – when the thread terminates. The event is fired in the main thread via Synchronize. Let's add a method to the form that can be assigned to the event (as we've done above). The implementation is simple:

```
procedure TForm49.HandleTermination(Sender: TObject);
begin
   Label1.Caption := 'Ended at ' + FThread.i.ToString;
end;
```

Then, let's actually terminate the thread in the OnClick handler for the second button:

```
procedure TForm49.Button2Click(Sender: TObject);
begin
   FThread.Terminate;
end;
```

Now, run the app and press the "Start Thread" button. The label will start counting up, and will continue to do so until it reaches MaxInt unless you press the second button which merely calls FThread.Terminate. Doing so will, well, terminate the thread.

Here's what the application looks like after the thread is terminated:

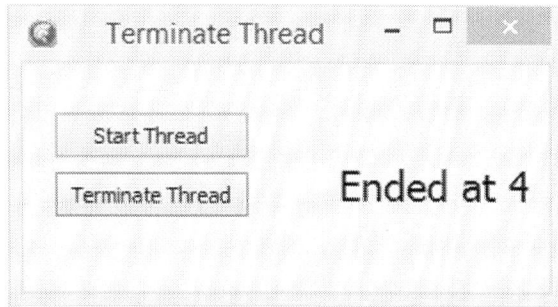

The OnTerminated event is also a good place for you to pass information from the thread to the VCL. Notice that the application knew the final value of the integer when the OnTerminated event was called. We used the FThread field, but we could have just as well used the Sender parameter, which in the case of the OnTerminate event is the thread being terminated.

Handling Exceptions in Threads

What happens if an exception gets raised in the middle of thread execution? Well, let's find out.

The first thing to know is that if an exception is raised during the execution of a thread, the thread is immediately terminated. Since an unhandled exception on a secondary thread would immediately kill your application and make it immediately disappear, TThread is kind enough to grab the exception and handle it for you. It takes the exception and wraps it up into the TThread.FatalException property.

Thus, you can give your thread an OnTerminated event handler and deal with the exception however you like. If you don't, the exception will just be "eaten". If you do, you can deal with the exception as desired.

Here's a thread that does a little work and then raises an exception:

```
unit uExceptionInThread;

interface

uses
    System.Classes
  , VCL.StdCtrls
  , uSlowCode
  , System.SysUtils
  ;

type
  TExceptionThread = class(TThread)
  private
    FMemo: TMemo;
  public
    constructor Create(aMemo: TMemo);
    procedure Execute; override;
  end;
```

```
implementation

{ TExceptionThread }

constructor TExceptionThread.Create(aMemo: TMemo);
begin
  inherited Create(True);
  FreeOnTerminate := True;
  FMemo := aMemo;
end;

procedure TExceptionThread.Execute;
begin
  PrimesBelow(50000);
  raise Exception.Create('This exception was raised on purpose');
end;

end.
```

We'll use our classic button/memo form again, and create the thread as follows:

```
procedure TForm52.Button1Click(Sender: TObject);
begin
  FThread := TExceptionThread.Create(Memo1);
  FThread.OnTerminate := HandleException;
  FThread.Start;
end;
```

The HandleException method will look like this:

```
procedure TForm52.HandleException(Sender: TObject);
var
  LThread: TExceptionThread;
begin
  if Sender is TExceptionThread then
  begin
    LThread := TExceptionThread(Sender);
  end else
  begin
    Memo1.Lines.Add('Sender is not a TExceptionThread');
    Exit;
  end;

  if LThread.FatalException <> nil then
  begin
    if LThread.FatalException is Exception then
    begin
      // Cast to Exception needed because FatalException is a TObject
      Memo1.Lines.Add(Exception(LThread.FatalException).Message)
    end;
  end;
end;
```

The HandleException method first ensures that the Sender parameter is an Exception, and if it is, it casts it to a local variable. It then makes sure that the exception isn't nil, and if it isn't, it reports out the exception's message in the memo. Pretty simple, but it shows how you can capture and deal with exceptions in your threads.

TThread Class Methods

So far we've looked at creating TThread descendants as the way to get code to run in a separate thread. But what if you just have a small chunk of code that you want to run in a thread and don't want to go to the trouble of creating a whole new thread class to run it?

TThread provides three class methods that let you execute code in the context of a thread, without having to actually create a thread descendant.

The first class method we'll look at is TThread.CreateAnonymousThread. This method will take the anonymous method that you pass to it, create a separate thread, execute the anonymous method, and then clean everything up for you. It's a straight-forward, easy way to execute some code in a separate thread.

Let's create another VCL form that looks like this:

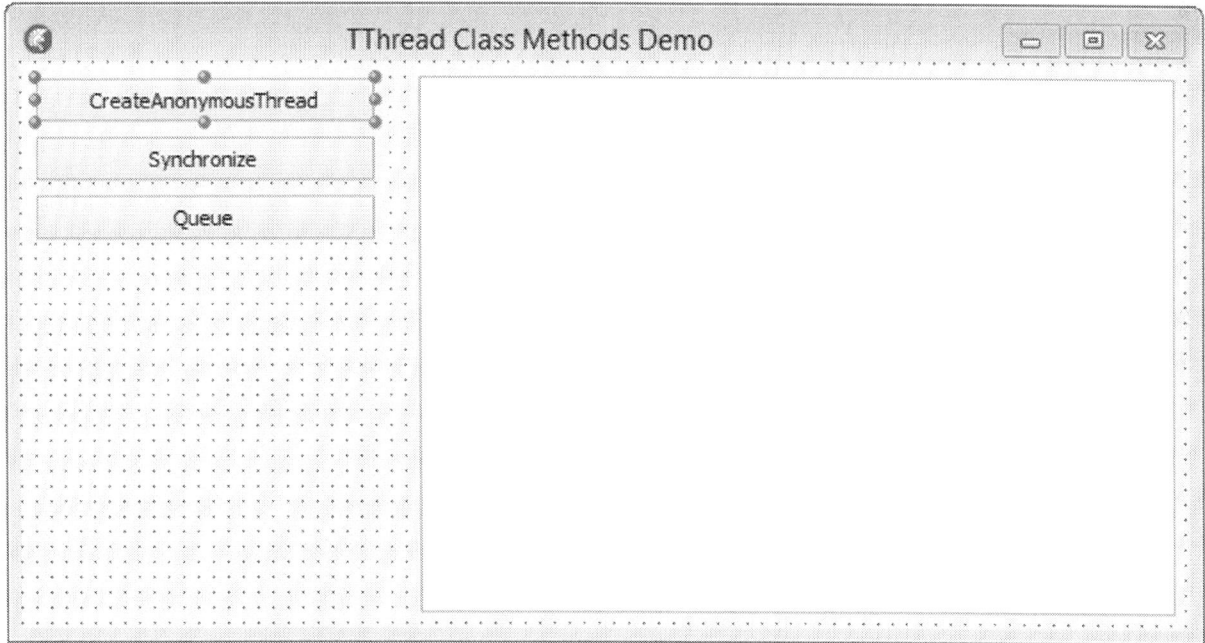

Double click on the first button, and add the following code:

```
procedure TForm50.Button1Click(Sender: TObject);
var
  LTotal: integer;
begin
  TThread.CreateAnonymousThread(procedure
                                begin
                                  LTotal := PrimesBelow(150000);
                                  TThread.Synchronize(TThread.CurrentThread,
                                  procedure
                                  begin
                                    Memo1.Lines.Add('Total: ' + LTotal.ToString);
                                    Memo1.Lines.Add('All Done from an Anonymous thread');
                                  end);
                                end).Start;

end;
```

The first thing you'll notice is that `CreateAnonymousThread` takes an anonymous method as its only parameter. Then, it calculates how many prime numbers there are below 150,000. Then it uses the second class method we've seen – `Synchronize` – to write out the information to the memo. Notice that the prime calculations are happening outside of the `Synchronize` call. (We'll discuss the `Synchronize` call below.)

If you run this app, the prime number calculations will take some time. You should note, though, that the form remains responsive because the code is running in the context of a separate thread. You can move the form around as the calculations are being done.

Queue and Synchronize

The two other class methods that are available – and commonly used, I should add – are `Queue` and `Synchronize`. Both are usually used to coordinate events in the context of another thread, as we saw above. During the coming chapters on the Parallel Programming Library, you'll see them used all the time. Generally, they are used to coordinate the processing of background threading code with the main thread. For instance, consider this code from the `OnClick` of the second button on our form:

```
procedure TForm50.Button2Click(Sender: TObject);
var
  LTotal: integer;
begin
  TThread.Synchronize(TThread.CurrentThread, procedure
                                             begin
                                               LTotal := PrimesBelow(150000);
                                               Memo1.Lines.Add('Total: ' + LTotal.ToString);
                                               Memo1.Lines.Add('All done from the Synchronize class procedure'\
);
                                             end);
end;
```

The `Synchronize` call takes two parameters. One is the thread whose context will run the code, and then an anonymous method to run the code itself. In this case, there isn't a lot of point in doing what we are doing here, because the anonymous method ends up being run on the current – in this case main – thread. If you run the application and then press the second button, you'll notice that the code runs, but the application itself is not responsive because the code is running in the context of the main thread. The same happens when we use Queue instead of Synchronize.

```
procedure TForm50.Button3Click(Sender: TObject);
var
  LTotal: integer;
begin
TThread.Queue(TThread.CurrentThread, procedure
                                      begin
                                        LTotal := PrimesBelow(150000);
                                        Memo1.Lines.Add('Total: ' + LTotal.ToString);
                                        Memo1.Lines.Add('All Done from the Queue class procedure');
                                      end);
end;
```

Queue vs Synchronize

We've seen the similar uses of Queue and Synchronize, and by now you are no doubt asking, "When should I use one or the other?" The quick answer is that you should almost always use Queue.

The longer answer is that you should avoid Synchronize because it always suspends the operation of the current thread to run the code in its anonymous method. If there are two or more active Synchronize calls, they will all block the main thread and be called in a serialized fashion. This doesn't sound like something you'd necessarily want to have happen, especially the blocking part.

Instead, it is better to queue the requests up and do them one at a time. Thus, the call to Queue is generally preferable. Queue submits a request to the main thread and returns immediately. When the main thread is out of work/idle, it will check for any pending requests and execute the associated anonymous method.

Synchronize does the same but waits until the main thread has executed the anonymous procedure before returning.

Synchronization

So far, we've only looked at single threads running in parallel to the main thread. We haven't had to worry too much about coordinating things between threads. As you can imagine, however, such a thing is pretty important.

Threads can share data and when they do, there is a danger of them trying to access that shared data at the same time, at different times, and at unpredictable times.

> Again, this is the reason that the VCL can't be made thread-safe. It shares data prolifically, and all the thread synchronization that would have to take place would make the VCL slow to a snail's pace.

Thus, we must have a way to allow for the safe reading and writing of shared data.

Synchronization Classes

When you do multi-threaded programming, you will very often have to share data between threads. In order to do that, you have to synchronize the running of those threads in order to safely access that common data. When you synchronize two threads, you are really asking that one thread be given access to the shared resource to the exclusion of all others. In other words, you are serializing access to that resource.

Therefore, you should endeavor to synchronize as little as possible, as any synchronization in effect defeats the parallel nature of threading. However, synchronization is necessary. Without careful and proper synchronization, your application can have unpredictable results and even end up in a frozen state. And that's bad.

Therefore, the Delphi RTL provides a number of different ways to synchronize threads, each with their own way of doing things and each with their own advantages and disadvantages. While there are no code examples here in the chapter for each of these synchronization types, the code in the book's repository does include an example application that uses each of these techniques to protect a common resource.

TCriticalSection

Probably the most basic synchronization technique is the critical section. A critical section provides an exclusive place for your code to run, where no other thread can intrude. You can `Enter` a critical section, run your code and then `Leave`. Other threads can still be running, but only one thread at a time can be inside of a critical section, and thus code within a critical section is thread-safe.

If Thread A enters a critical section and Thread B tries to enter, it will be blocked until Thread A leaves. Because other threads may be blocked when you enter a critical section, your critical sections should be short and to the point.

In addition, critical sections can be recursive – that is, if a thread is inside a critical section, it can actually enter that critical section again. Of course, this means that the thread must leave the thread the same exact number of times it enters.

Critical sections are part of the Win32/64 API, but of course, Delphi doesn't leave you high and dry – the RTL provides `TCriticalSection`, which is a nice encapsulation of a critical section. `TCriticalSection` is even cross-platform, functioning the same on all the platforms that Delphi supports. `TCriticalSection` can be found in the `System.SyncObjs` unit.

However, as a general notion, rather than as a specific implementation, there are a number of ways to provide protection to code running in the context of multiple threads. I can't recommend one over the other, as they all provide the same basic functionality but with different purposes.

TMonitor

The `TMonitor` class is another way to synchronize threads, operating in a very similar manner to `TCriticalSection`. `TMonitor` is declared in the `System` unit, and operates on the notion of a token object. You create an object – any object will do – and then pass that object to `TMonitor`. The token object can then be locked and unlocked in order to provide protection for code within the lock.

TInterlocked

We saw the use of `TInterlocked` above to safely increment a shared integer between threads without locking. It does a number of other functions in a thread-safe, lock-less manner, including incrementing and decrementing variables, adding to a variable, and safely exchanging the values of two variables. All of `TInterlocked`'s operations are atomic, meaning that they can be treated as a single operation for the purpose of multi-threading code.

Use `TInterlocked` for doing simple operations like incrementing or decrementing integers. You'll find that it is easier than using a critical section or some other synchronization techniques for simple math operations and certainly more performant than other locking techniques.

TMutex

A mutex is a construct that provides a MUTually EXclusive mechanism. Mutexes are designed to be like a baton in a relay race – only one process can have the baton at a time. Thus, only one thread can have access to the mutex at a given time, and so it can be used to protect code that needs to run in a thread-safe manner.

Mutexes are created with and then referred to by a specific name. They are also cross-process and can be used to protect resources between multiple applications. As a result they are slower than a critical section.

TEvent

`TEvent` is a class in the `System.SyncObjs` unit that allows you to signal a thread that an event has occurred. Often, you'll want a thread to either wait until something specific happens or execute until that something happens. Either way, a `TEvent` can be used to send that signal to either stop or start a thread executing. They don't force mutual exclusion; rather, they send signals to let threads know how they should behave.

As Martin Harvey points out in his excellent threading article[23], events are like a stoplight – they are either red or green, and they either make you stop or let you move ahead. An event is a marvelous way of letting a thread sleep and take no CPU at all, then be woken when a condition fires. It's a great way to write CPU-efficient, and cleanly designed, code.

For instance, you may have a set of threads that you want to run, and you want to know when they are all finished. You can pass a `TEvent` to each of the threads, and mark each thread as "green", and then when the thread is done, mark the `TEvent` as "red". You then can use the `TEvent.WaitForMultiple` call to check all the threads and know when they are all terminated. The code on BitBucket that accompanies this book contains a demo called `EventDemo.exe` that shows this very technique.

A `TEvent` can be named, like a `TMutex`, in which case it can be used to communicate between processes. However, for use within a single process, it's preferable to use events without a name (anonymous events).

TSpinLock

A spinlock is a thread synchronizer that operates on the notion that there is a certain amount of overhead to starting and stopping the execution of a given thread. Think of a car coming to a stoplight. It would be a certain amount of overhead if every time you came to a red stop light, you stopped and turned off your car.

---

[23]http://www.nickhodges.com/MultiThreadingInDelphi/toc.html

Then, when the light turns green, you'd have to start up your car again before proceeding. This is similar to the notion of a thread stopping at a critical section. A spinlock is a synchronization technique that would be the equivalent of leaving your car running at a stoplight – it lets the thread "spin" rather than actually come to a halt while the critical section of code is executed.

Delphi provides TSpinLock to encapsulate the notion of a spinlock. Spinlocks should be used in instances of very high concurrency when performance is critical – i.e., when the wait is likely to be very short, and the overhead of actually coming to a complete stop doesn't make sense. The "spinning" consumes CPU cycles, and thus can prevent other threads from running. Therefore, it should be used with care. Unless you have a very specific reason for using TSpinLock, I'd recommend leaving it alone.

TMultiReadExclusiveWriteSynchronizer

Wow, that's a mouthful. Let's call it TMREWS for short. TMREWS is another synchronization technique that should be used in a specific situation: when you expect that the given shared resources within it will be read from many more times than it will be written to. TMREWS will grant a lock as long as no one is trying to write to the protected resource. If you need to write to the resource, then TMREWS will block all reads until the writing is done. If you need to read the resource, any number of threads can do so as long as no one is trying to write to the resource. For that reason, TMREWS implements the following interface, which provides all the functionality that you need from TMREWS. You should prefer the use of the interface over a reference to the class itself:

```
type
  IReadWriteSync = interface
    ['{7B108C52-1D8F-4CDB-9CDF-57E071193D3F}']
    procedure BeginRead;
    procedure EndRead;
    function BeginWrite: Boolean;
    procedure EndWrite;
  end;
```

As you can see, the interface allows you to choose whether you are going to read or write to the shared resource.
Remember, use TMREWS when reading is much more common that writing.

Abstracting the Notion of Synchronization

All of the above synchronization methods provide the same notion: that of locking and unlocking access to a block of code. Well, doesn't that make you think of something like this:

```
type
  ILockable = interface
  ['{FBDA6E23-E5F2-4CFD-8F23-75D3C36227E8}']
    procedure Lock;
    procedure Unlock;
  end;
```

We can use this interface to write classes that lock code using the various techniques described above. For instance, here is an implementation of ILockable that uses a critical section for locking:

```
type

  TCriticalSectionLocker = class(TInterfacedObject, ILockable)
  private
    FCS: TCriticalSection;
    FCurrentlyInside: Boolean;
  public
    constructor Create;
    destructor Destroy; override;
    procedure Lock;
    procedure Unlock;
  end;

constructor TCriticalSectionLocker.Create;
begin
  FCS := TCriticalSection.Create;
end;

destructor TCriticalSectionLocker.Destroy;
begin
  if FCurrentlyInside then
  begin
    FCS.Leave;
  end;
  FCS.Free;
  inherited;
end;

procedure TCriticalSectionLocker.Lock;
begin
  FCS.Enter;
  FCurrentlyInside := True;
end;

procedure TCriticalSectionLocker.Unlock;
begin
  FCurrentlyInside := False;
  FCS.Leave;
end;
```

Let's build an app that uses a number of these thread synchronization techniques and the ILockable interface. First, let's build a form that looks like this:

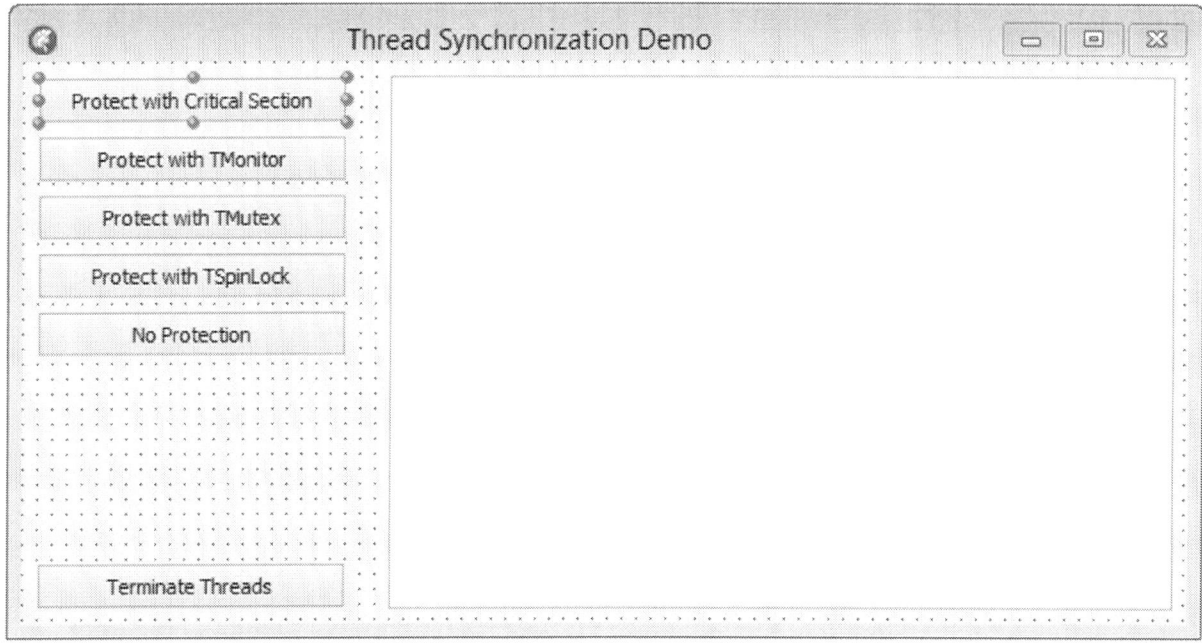

Second, let's declare a thread that will do the work of incrementing a simple integer. We'll create a number of these threads to compete over the integer value, and thus use the ILockable implementations to protect that integer. Here's the thread declaration:

```
type
  TIncrementerThread = class(TThread)
  private
    FLock: ILockable;
    FMemo: TMemo;
  protected
    procedure Execute; override;
  public
    constructor Create(aLock: ILockable; aMemo: TMemo);
  end;

constructor TIncrementerThread.Create(aLock: ILockable; aMemo: TMemo);
begin
  inherited Create(False);
  FreeOnTerminate := True;
  FLock := aLock;
  FMemo := aMemo;
end;

procedure TIncrementerThread.Execute;
begin
  i := 0;
  while not Terminated do
  begin
    FLock.Lock;
    try
      i := i + 1;    // i is a global variable
      Synchronize(procedure
```

```
            begin
              FMemo.Lines.Add(i.ToString);
            end);
      Sleep(1000);
    finally
      FLock.Unlock;
    end;
  end;
end;
```

TIncrementerThread takes an ILockable value as a parameter and stores it for later use. It also takes a TMemo for reporting on what it is up to. Naturally, the work gets done in the Execute method. Here, it calls Lock, writes to the shared integer, and then reports out what the current value is. It will do this until Terminated is set to True.

Now, Double click on the first button – the critical section one – and add the following code:

```
procedure TForm51.Button1Click(Sender: TObject);
begin
  FCSLocker := TCriticalSectionLocker.Create;
  CreateThreads(FCSLocker);
end;
```

The CreateThreads method is declared as follows:

```
procedure TForm51.CreateThreads(aLocker: ILockable);
var
  i: Integer;
begin
  Memo1.Clear;
  for i := 0 to MaxThreads - 1 do
  begin
    ThreadArray[i] := TIncrementerThread.Create(aLocker, Memo1);
  end;
end;
```

This code obviously creates as many threads as MaxThread is set to (I've set it to four, but you can experiment with that number). The threads don't start suspended, so they immediately start counting up and placing the count in the memo, one a second, thanks to the Sleep call.

If you run the application and press the first button, you should see something like this:

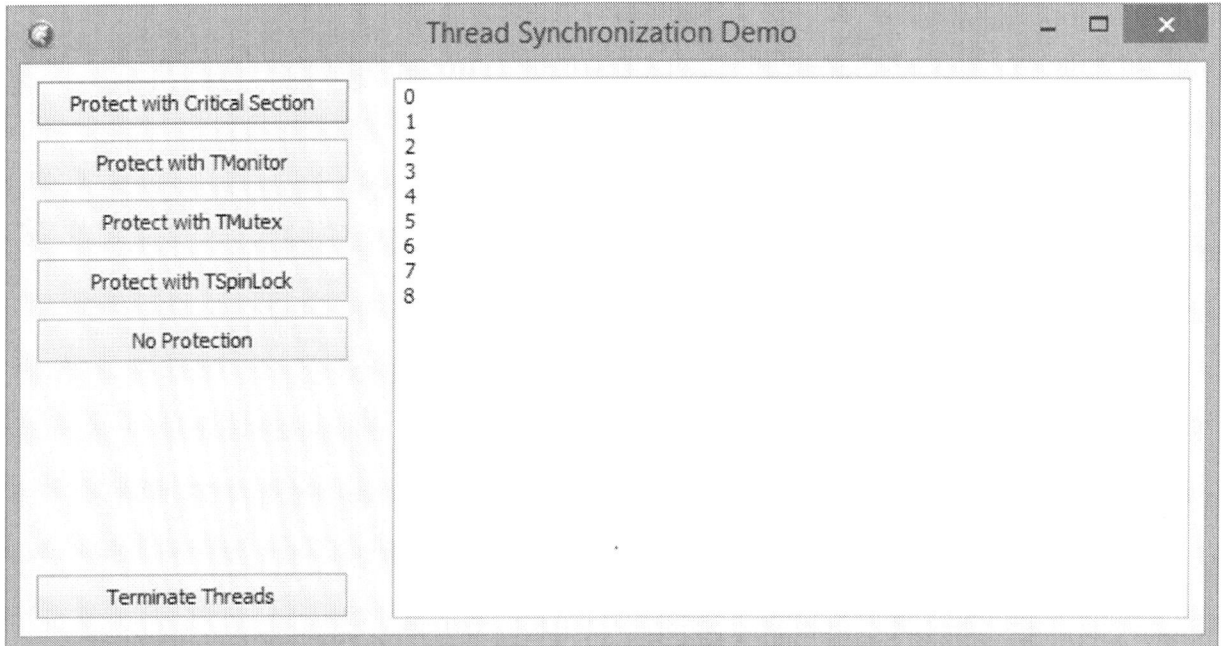

Because access to the integer is controlled, you should see the numbers show in order in the memo. The application should perform exactly the same for the other three synchronization techniques. You can see the rest of the code for the application on BitBucket. (See the Appendix for more information.)

The interesting part comes when you try to increment the integer without any protection. The last button uses TNoLocker to "protect" the shared integer:

```
type
  TNoLocker = class(TInterfacedObject, ILockable)
  public
    procedure Lock;
    procedure Unlock;
  end;

procedure TNoLocker.Lock;
begin
  // Do Nothing
end;

procedure TNoLocker.Unlock;
begin
  // Do Nothing
end;
```

Press the "No Protection" button and you'll see that the value is, well, a bit wacky. There's no predicting how it will look on your system, but on mine it looked like this (though it's different almost every time....):

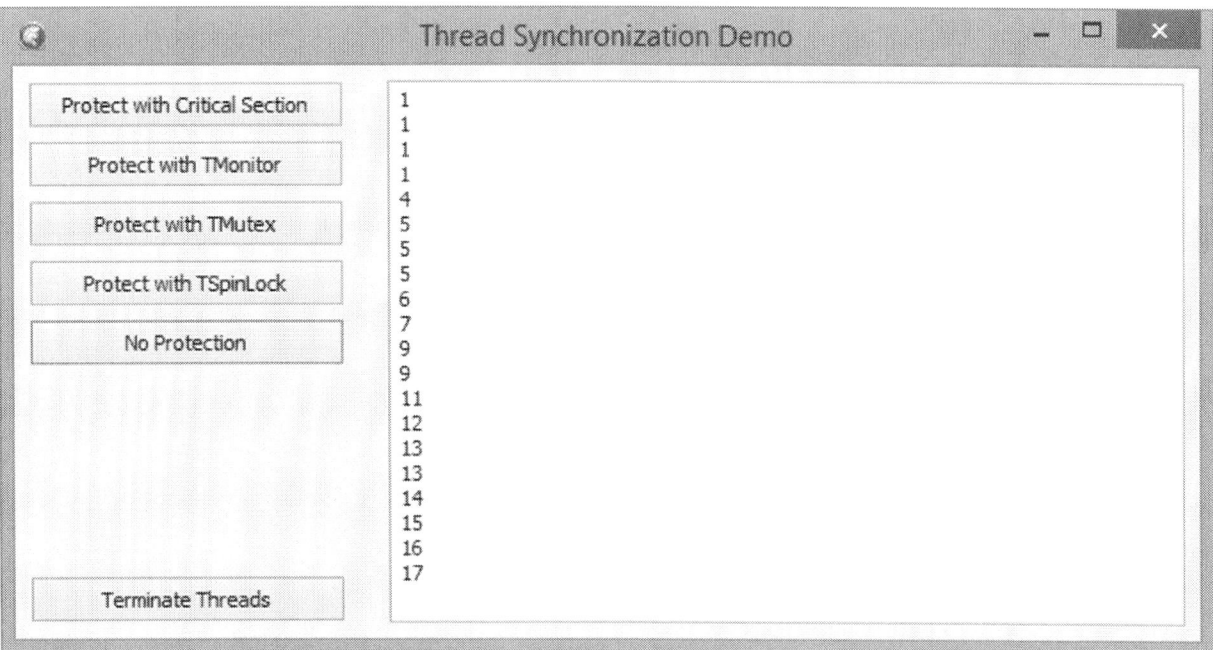

One other thing before we move on – there's a button in the bottom left with the caption "Terminate Threads". It's OnClick event is as follows:

```
procedure TForm51.Button2Click(Sender: TObject);
var
  i: Integer;
begin
  for i := 0 to MaxThreads - 1 do
  begin
    ThreadArray[i].Terminate;
  end;
end;
```

This is simple – it merely calls Terminate on all the threads. It is illustrative of how Terminate works, though. Run the app, press any of the buttons to start the threads rolling, and then press the "Terminate Threads" button. You'll notice that it stops the counting, but not immediately. It runs for a few more numbers before stopping. Remember, calling Terminate on a thread merely sets the internal FTerminated flag to True. At that point, the thread may still have work ongoing, and that work is finished before the thread actually stops.

TThread.WaitFor

The continuation of execution mentioned in the previous section emphasizes an important point: secondary threads – that is, threads created by the primary thread – are "on their own." They run until they are terminated. You can, as we've seen, set them to terminate themselves, but often they use a while not Terminated block and will run until terminated.

However, the main thread – that is, the thread that your Application object is running in – may terminate, and that will immediately end all secondary threads. But that's not always desirable; some of those secondary threads may still have work to do. They may need to write a file to disk or save data to a database or perform some other "clean up" functionality.

What to do? Well, a good threading citizen will ensure that all of their secondary threads are properly terminated. And when I say "properly," I mean that you should ensure the threads don't leave needed work undone. How do you do that?

Well, you politely ask any secondary threads to finish up and terminate themselves. We've seen one way to do that – via a call to Terminate. However, once you call Terminate – say in the destructor of a form – you still need to make sure that you wait for the thread to finish. That's where WaitFor comes in. You can call WaitFor to, well, wait for the terminated thread to finish up before you continue on closing down your application and its main thread. For instance:

```
MyThread.Terminate;
MyThread.WaitFor;
```

will allow your application to gracefully end MyThread by waiting for it to finish up. If you are writing the destructor for a class that uses threads that need terminating, this is the pattern you should use to ensure that things are all cleaned up properly.

You need to be a bit careful, though, as WaitFor may wait forever if the thread in question has deadlocked or otherwise hung. If that is a concern, you can use the Windows API WaitForSingleObject to wait on the thread with a timeout value set.

The Perils of Multi-threading

I warned you in the introduction that multi-threaded programming was tricky and fraught with peril. Here are a couple of bad things that can happen:

You can find yourself in a "race condition." Earlier, we talked about how to protect your variables with synchronization techniques. You must properly use these techniques, or you can have multiple threads racing each other to be the one that gets to a variable or resource first. Because the thread scheduling system of the operating system can switch threading contexts at any time, you can't predict which thread will win the race – and if you aren't careful, you may not even be aware that the race is happening. I think that we can all agree that unpredictability is not a good thing in your application. The solution? Properly protect your variables and resources with synchronization techniques.

Threads can become deadlocked. That is, sometimes a thread is waiting for another thread to finish doing something. But if Thread A is locked waiting for Thread B to get done, and Thread B is waiting for thread A to get done, then you have a deadlock. Neither thread will become free because each is waiting for the other to make a move. The solution? Don't hold one resource and then ask to hold another. Don't nest your locks, one inside another. In other words, make sure your locks are short, sweet, and singular in nature. If that is not possible, always ensure that your locks are acquired in a clear, well-defined order. For instance, locks should be released in the reverse order that they were acquired. Or put another way, "Don't cross the streams" (for you Ghostbusters fans out there...)

Threads can be starved. If you have multiple threads in your system and you prioritize some threads more than others, the threads with lower priority might end up getting little or no processing time, and thus they never complete their job. Thread starvation occurs when a greedy thread holds on to resources and doesn't let the other threads have processor time or access to a shared resource. The solution, of course, is to never create a greedy thread; ensure that your thread plays nice with others and doesn't hog resources.

Conclusion

We have taken a look at the basics of threads. We've seen how you can create descendants of TThread to perform specific tasks in a separate thread. We've seen the proper way to manage the lifetime of threads and how to protect shared data between threads. And we've looked at some of the potholes that you can fall into if you aren't careful when doing multi-threading.

The next natural step in multi-threading is parallelism. In the next two chapters we'll look at a new library in Delphi that allows you to very easily take advantage of the multiple cores in your computer.

Parallel Programming

Parallel Programming Library

Introduced in Delphi XE7, the Parallel Programming Library (PPL) is found in the System.Threading.pas unit. It is a further abstraction of the notion of multi-threading and contains three main abstractions that enable you to write multi-threaded code and take advantage of the multiple cores in your device, whether it be a laptop, a desktop, or a phone.

- TTask allows you to run discrete chunks of code in a separate thread quickly and easily.
- TFuture allows you to delay the retrieval of a given value until it is needed.
- The parallel for loop splits a loop into separate TTasks and enables each iteration to run as its own task. We'll cover TParallel.For into its own chapter.

The PPL is, by the way, completely cross-platform. You'll also note that there isn't a single {$IFDEF} in the unit. That is because it is a nice, clean abstraction of lower-level libraries. In fact, once you start using the PPL, you'll find that you probably don't need to use TThread much anymore because the library will enable you to do most of your threading work for you. Aren't abstractions cool?

Tasks

Remember this code from the threading and parallel coding introduction?

```
Stopwatch := TStopwatch.StartNew;
Total := PrimesBelow(200000);
ElapsedSeconds := StopWatch.Elapsed.TotalSeconds;
WriteLn('There are ', Total, ' primes under 100,000');
WriteLn('It took ', ElapsedSeconds, ' seconds to calculate that') ;
ReadLn;
```

The above code is not run in a background thread nor is it in any way parallelized. Run it in a console application and it will report nothing until the calculations are done. Put that code in a VCL application – replacing the WriteLn calls with calls writing to a TMemo –– and the application will be non-responsive until the CPU gets done cranking out all those prime numbers. But the PPL provides a simple way to make a VCL application responsive during the CPU-intensive calculations like the code above.

I'll dispense with the steps about dropping components, etc., and just say: Make a VCL application that looks like this:

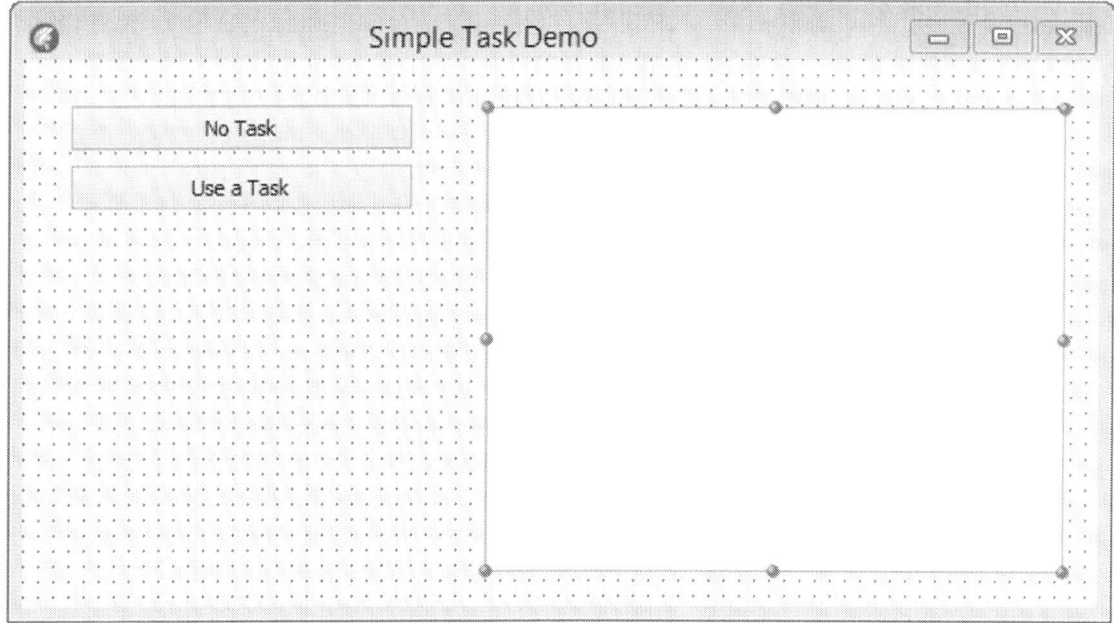

That's a `TMemo`, in case you were wondering.

Double click on the first button and add the following code:

```
procedure TSimpleTaskForm.Button1Click(Sender: TObject);
var
  Stopwatch: TStopWatch;
  Total: Integer;
  ElapsedSeconds: Double;
begin
  Stopwatch := TStopwatch.StartNew;
    Total := PrimesBelow(200000);
    ElapsedSeconds := StopWatch.Elapsed.TotalSeconds;
    Memo1.Lines.Add(Format('There are  %d primes under 200,000', [Total]));
    Memo1.Lines.Add(Format('It took %:2f seconds to calculate that', [ElapsedSeconds]));
end;
```

This code simply runs our slow procedure, measures how long it takes, and reports that information out to a `TMemo`. Pretty easy. Run the program and press the button and the application will do what you expect – except while it is calculating, the window won't respond. Try to move it and nothing happens until after the calculation is done. This is not good. And don't even think about trying `Application.ProcessMessages`. The PPL, however, has a simple solution to this problem – `TTask`.

Double click the second button and add this code:

```
procedure TSimpleTaskForm.Button2Click(Sender: TObject);
begin

  TTask.Run(procedure
            var
              Stopwatch: TStopWatch;
              Total: Integer;
              ElapsedSeconds: Double;
            begin
              Stopwatch := TStopwatch.StartNew;
              Total := PrimesBelow(200000);
              ElapsedSeconds := StopWatch.Elapsed.TotalSeconds;
              TThread.Synchronize(nil, procedure
                                       begin
                                         Memo1.Lines.Add(Format('There are  %d' +
                                                          'primes under 200,000',
                                                          [Total]));
                                         Memo1.Lines.Add(Format('It took %:2f seconds' +
                                                          ' to calculate that',
                                                          [ElapsedSeconds]));

                                       end);
            end
            );

end;
```

This code is more complex than the code from the first button, but if you run the app, press the second button, and try to move the form while the calculations are going in, it actually moves. That is because the code is being run inside the context of a TTask. You'll note that the code doesn't run any faster – it's the same code only running on a different thread – but because it is running on a different thread, the application is responsive to input.

Note, too, that this is technically one line of code: TTask.Run with a single parameter of an anonymous method running our slow code, with a TStopwatch timing it. It then writes the results out to the memo. But because we are not running in the context of the main thread (more on that in a minute), we need to Synchronize the output of the information to the TMemo. We do that with a TThread.Synchronize call. Note, too, that all the variables are now variables of the anonymous method itself. Again, this is a single line of code.

So what is going on here? In the PPL, a task is a discrete chunk of code. Think of it as a parallel procedure – a procedure run in the context of a thread. That thread is produced and managed by an internal Thread Pool that the PPL maintains. This thread pool will come more into play in a minute when we have multiple tasks running at the same time.The Thread Pool is "self-tuning" in that it automatically takes into account the number of cores that your CPU has, as well as the current burden on those cores. It creates threads as needed, trying to maximize the capabilities of your machine. When the system is free, it creates more threads, and when the system starts to get busy, it will try to get the work done as fast as possible to free up those threads.

 The PPL will allow you to provide your own TThreadPool, but in the vast majority of cases, this isn't necessary and the default Thread Pool will be sufficient. We won't be covering the ability to provide your own thread pool in this book.

The real fun starts when multiple tasks are run together and the Thread Pool can really go to town and take advantage of multiple cores while keeping your application responsive.

Again, create a VCL application that looks like this:

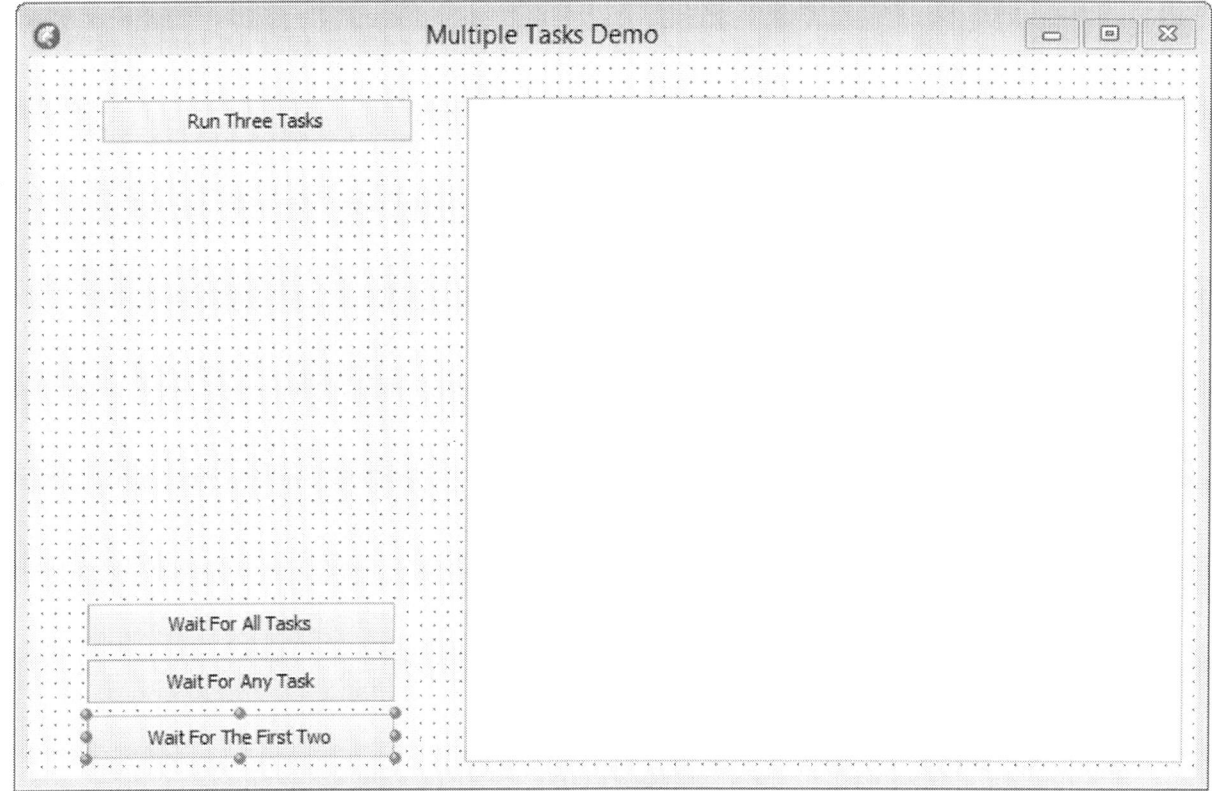

First, to the private section of the form's code, add the following array declaration:

```
AllTasks: array[0..2] of ITask;
```

This array will hold the three tasks we are going to create. Notice that it is an array of ITask. The call to TTask.Run will return an instance of this interface that references its task. We can store this for later use in an array. We'll see why in a minute.

To the top button, we'll add the following event handler:

```
procedure TMultipleTasksDemoForm.Button3Click(Sender: TObject);
begin
  AllTasks[0] := TTask.Run(procedure
                           begin
                             PrimesBelow(200000);
                             TThread.Synchronize(TThread.Current,
                                                 procedure
                                                 begin
                                                   Memo1.Lines.Add('200000 is done');
                                                 end);
                           end);

  AllTasks[1] := TTask.Run(procedure
                           begin
                             PrimesBelow(250000);
                             TThread.Synchronize(TThread.Current,
                                                 procedure
                                                 begin
                                                   Memo1.Lines.Add('250000 is done');
                                                 end);
                           end);

  AllTasks[2] := TTask.Run(procedure
                           begin
                             PrimesBelow(300000);
                             TThread.Synchronize(TThread.Current,
                                                 procedure
                                                 begin
                                                   Memo1.Lines.Add('300000 is done');
                                                 end);
                           end);
end;
```

These three tasks are basically the same, with the exception of how many primes they calculate. First, they calculate the primes, and then they simply report that they are done. Nothing much to it. Again, the output to the TMemo is done in a call to TThread.Synchronize because we are operating in a multi-threaded environment.

Now for the interesting part. When you have multiple tasks running – as we will when we top button – you might want to know when some or all of those tasks are complete. So TTask has two methods - WaitForAll and WaitForAny - that block until respectively all or one of the tasks in the array are complete, or until the given timeout is reached. They are declared as follows:

```
class function WaitForAll(const Tasks: array of ITask): Boolean; overload; static;
class function WaitForAll(const Tasks: array of ITask; Timeout: LongWord): Boolean; overload; static;
class function WaitForAll(const Tasks: array of ITask; const Timeout: TTimeSpan): Boolean; overload; static;
class function WaitForAny(const Tasks: array of ITask): Integer; overload; static;
class function WaitForAny(const Tasks: array of ITask; Timeout: LongWord): Integer; overload; static;
class function WaitForAny(const Tasks: array of ITask; const Timeout: TTimeSpan): Integer; overload; static;
```

All of the overloads take an array of ITask as their first parameter. You don't have to wait forever – you can supply a Timeout parameter that will limit your wait if you like.

So, let's see how these guys work. Here are the event handlers for the two lower buttons:

```
procedure TMultipleTasksDemoForm.Button4Click(Sender: TObject);
begin
  TTask.Run(procedure
            begin
              TTask.WaitForAll(AllTasks);
              TThread.Synchronize(nil,
                                  procedure
                                  begin
                                    Memo1.Lines.Add('All Done');
                                  end);
            end);
end;

procedure TMultipleTasksDemoForm.Button5Click(Sender: TObject);
begin
  TTask.Run(procedure
            begin
              TTask.WaitForAny(AllTasks);
              TThread.Synchronize(nil,
                                  procedure
                                  begin
                                    Memo1.Lines.Add('At least one is Done');
                                  end);
            end);
end;
```

As we press the top button, they are added to the array of tasks that we declared. Once they are started and on their way, we want to know when they are done. So then we can press the "Wait for All Tasks" button, and we'll get an output that looks like this:

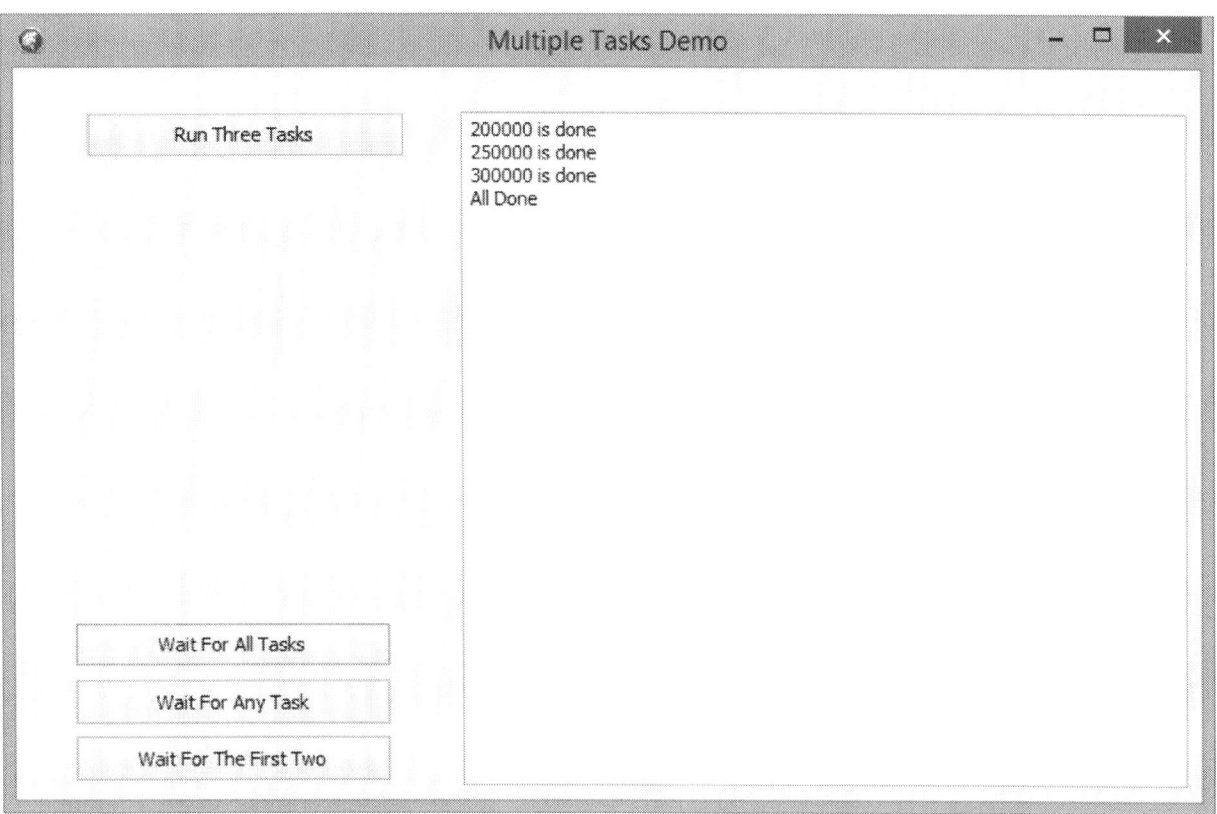

Pressing the "Wait For All Tasks" button calls the TTask.WaitForAll method, and takes our array of tasks as a parameter. You won't be surprised to discover that this call will wait for all of the tasks in the array to complete before continuing – hence we get the "All Done" at the end of the three tasks reporting that they are finished.

 Please note that during the entire execution cycle of this application, the form itself remains responsive and moveable.

The other button has "Wait for Any Task" on it. Press the top button to start the tasks, and then press the "Wait For Any Task" button, and you'll get the following result:

Notice that you get the "At least one is Done" message immediately after the first of the tasks is complete. It doesn't matter which one – as long as any task in the array completes, the call to WaitForAny will complete and then move on. The non-completed tasks still run and complete after the WaitForAny call returns.

One final example – let's add another button below the bottom two, set its caption to "Wait For The First Two," and add the following event handler to it:

```
procedure TMultipleTasksDemoForm.Button6Click(Sender: TObject);
begin
    TTask.Run(procedure
            var
              SomeTasks: array[0..1] of ITask;
            begin
              SomeTasks[0] := AllTasks[0];
              SomeTasks[1] := AllTasks[1];
              TTask.WaitForAll(SomeTasks);
              TThread.Synchronize(nil,
                              procedure
                              begin
                                Memo1.Lines.Add('The First Two are Done');
                              end);
            end);

end;
```

Now this code is a little different. It declares an array with two ITasks in it, puts the first two from AllTasks into it, and then calls WaitForAll on that "sub-array" of the main array. The output will then look like this:

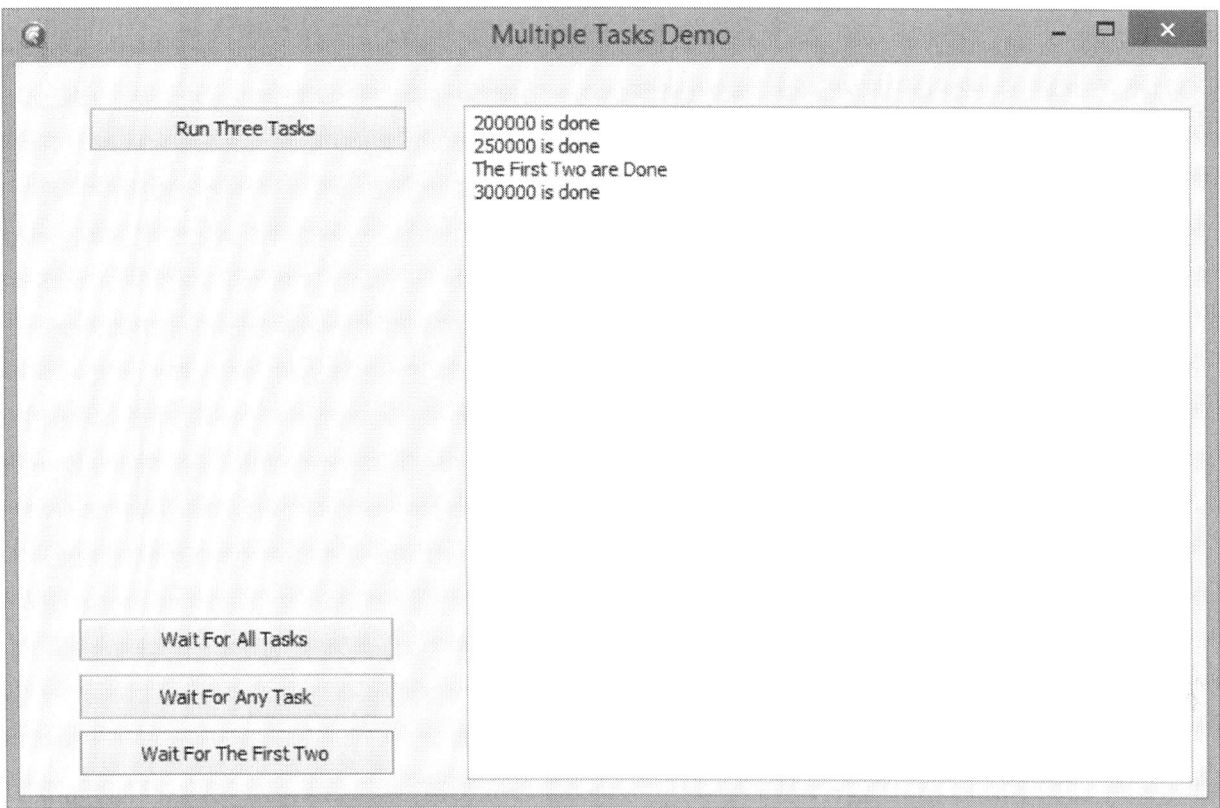

Notice that the call to "wait for" happened after the first two tasks completed. What an amazing coincidence that they happened to be the two that we placed in the "sub-array!"

Thus, you should be able to see that you can do what you want with regard to multiple tasks that become much easier to deal with than creating TThread descendants, and much easier to coordinate than multiple calls to TThread.Synchronize or TThread.Queue.

Futures

A Future is a specialized task that returns a value. Think of it as a parallel function – a function that runs in a thread and then returns a value. Futures can be declared and set on their way when you know that the calculation isn't needed right away and that the result can be retrieved at a later time. If you do happen to ask for the result before the future has finished, it will block until the result is ready.

Futures are implemented using generics and are parameterized by their return type. Thus

```
FutureInteger: IFuture<integer>;
```

is a IFuture variable that will return an integer value when you ask for it via FutureInteger.GetValue.

Basically, a Future allows you to return a result from a task. It is a "promise" to provide a value at some point in the future. If you have a value – say the number of prime numbers under a fixed threshold – to calculate that you know will take some time, and you want to do that calculation on a separate thread while maintaining the responsiveness of your application, you can do it in a Future.

Okay, let's look at how they work. Remember, Futures are just Tasks that return a value, so they can do all the things that Tasks do, in addition to returning values. We'll use the classic two-button, one memo application, and declare the following variables in the private section of the form:

```
Result200000: IFuture<integer>;
Result250000: IFuture<integer>;
Result300000: IFuture<integer>;
Futures: array[0..2] of ITask;
```

Then, we'll give the first button the following event handler:

```
procedure TFuturesDemoForm.Button1Click(Sender: TObject);
begin
  Result200000 := TTask.Future<integer>(function: integer
                                        begin
                                          Result := PrimesBelow(200000);
                                        end);
  Memo1.Lines.Add('200000 Started');
  Futures[0] := Result200000;

  Result250000 := TTask.Future<integer>(function: integer
                                        begin
                                          Result := PrimesBelow(250000);
                                        end);
  Memo1.Lines.Add('250000 Started');
  Futures[1] := Result250000;

  Result300000 := TTask.Future<integer>(function: integer
                                        begin
                                          Result := PrimesBelow(300000);
                                        end);
  Memo1.Lines.Add('300000 Started');
  Futures[2] := Result300000;

end;
```

Here are some things to note about the above code:

- It declares an IFuture<integer> for each of the three results we are going to calculate.
- Each Future writes out to the memo that it has started
- Each Future is stuffed into the array of Tasks. Note that the array can be one of the type ITask because IFuture augments the ITask interface.
- The result is three separate futures calculating values and an array that we can wait on.

So let's wait on that array. Attach the following event handler to our second button:

```
TFuture<integer>.WaitForAll(Futures);
Memo1.Lines.Add('Done Waiting.  This should appear with all the results.');
Memo1.Lines.Add('There are ' + Result200000.GetValue.ToString +  ' prime numbers under 200,000');
Memo1.Lines.Add('There are ' + Result250000.GetValue.ToString +  ' prime numbers under 250,000');
Memo1.Lines.Add('There are ' + Result300000.GetValue.ToString +  ' prime numbers under 300,000');
```

I shouldn't have to tell you what the call to `TTask.WaitForAll` does, but I will, just in case. It waits for all three of the Futures to be calculated. When they are, the call completes and then the code displays those values. It gets the values out of the `IFuture` by calling `GetValue` on the Future. Note that the first line of text appears at the exact same time as the following three lines. That is because we waited for all of the futures to finish before we continued on.

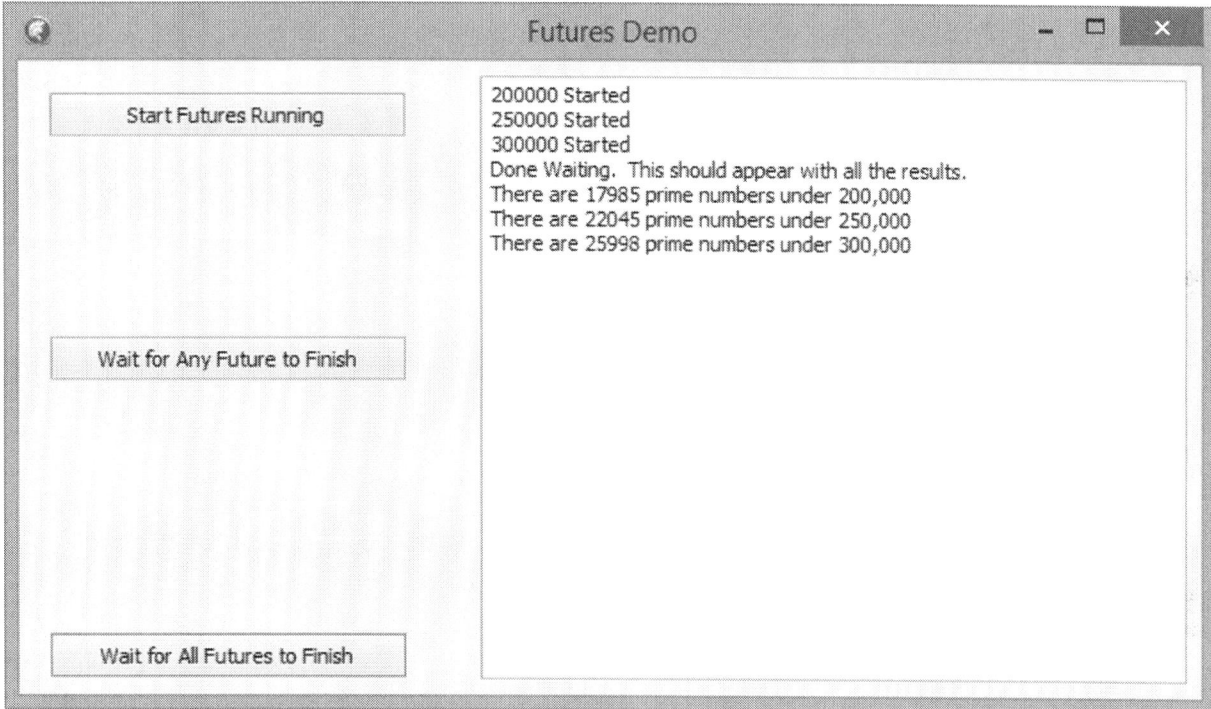

What if you don't want to wait for them all – how about we just wait for one, and let the rest finish as they will. Add another button in between the other two, and give it the following `OnClick` handler:

```
Memo1.Lines.Add('There are ' + Result200000.GetValue.ToString + ' prime numbers under 200,000');
Memo1.Lines.Add('Done Waiting. This should appear with the first result.');
Memo1.Lines.Add('There are ' + Result250000.GetValue.ToString + ' prime numbers under 250,000');
Memo1.Lines.Add('There are ' + Result300000.GetValue.ToString + ' prime numbers under 300,000');
```

Notice that you don't need to call a `WaitFor` method. Instead, you can just ask for the value via `GetValue`, and then the code will return control after each of the futures is calculated. Remember, the call to `GetValue` will block until the Future is calculated.

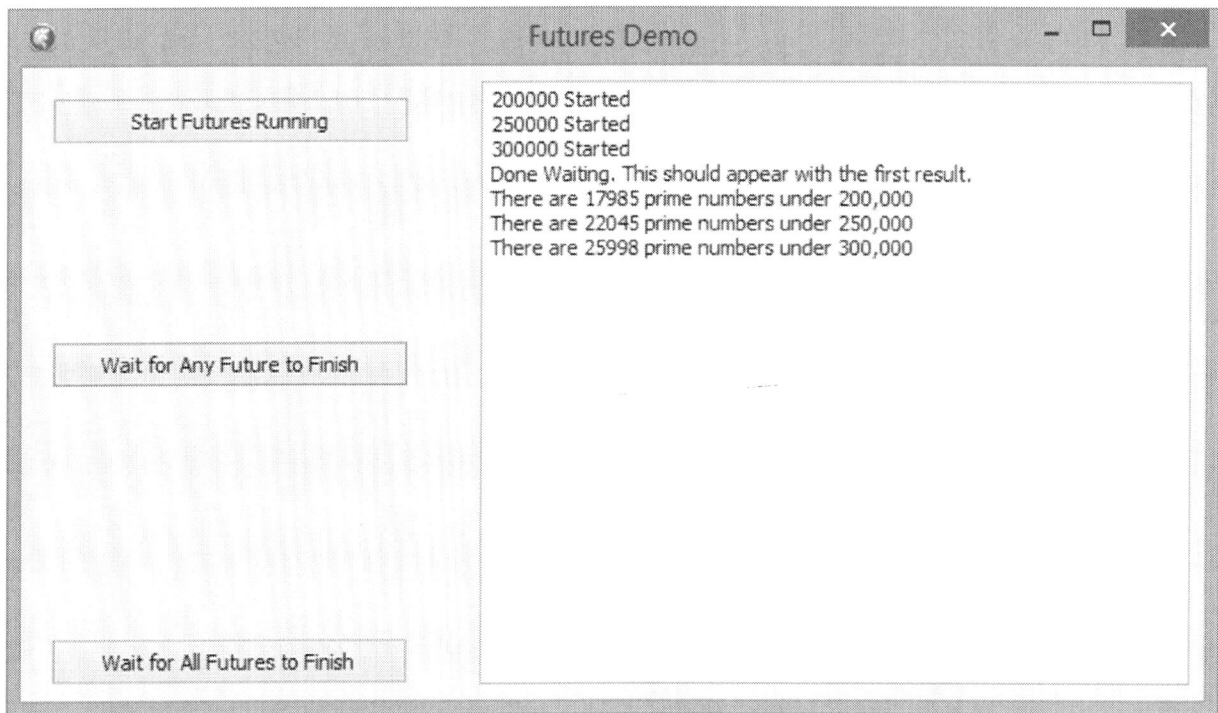

Thus, Futures are really no more than Tasks that return a value. In fact, they descend from ITask and TTask respectively.

Starting Tasks

One final simple demo before we move on. You can create tasks and have them not start right away. Let's take a quick look, using another two button, one memo VCL application.

First, in the private section of the form, add the following variable:

```
Task: ITask;
```

In the first button's OnClick event handler, put this code:

```
Task := TTask.Create(procedure
                var
                  Num: integer;
                begin
                  Num := PrimesBelow(200000);
                  TThread.Synchronize(nil,
                            procedure
                            begin
                              Memo1.Lines.Add('There are ' + Num.ToString() + ' primes below \
200000');
                            end);
                end);
```

This code should look familiar, but it's a bit different. Instead of calling `Run` on `TTask`, we merely call the constructor and assign the resulting value to the `Task` variable. It doesn't execute any of the code contained in the task; it merely creates the task. You can run the app and press the button and wait all you want – nothing will happen.

Instead, to get the task to execute, we press the second button, which has this in its `OnClick` event handler:

```
Task.Start;
```

Once you press the second button, the code will run, and the memo will be updated after a few seconds, pretty much like the very first demo in this chapter. Note that you can't do this kind of delayed start with an `IFuture`.

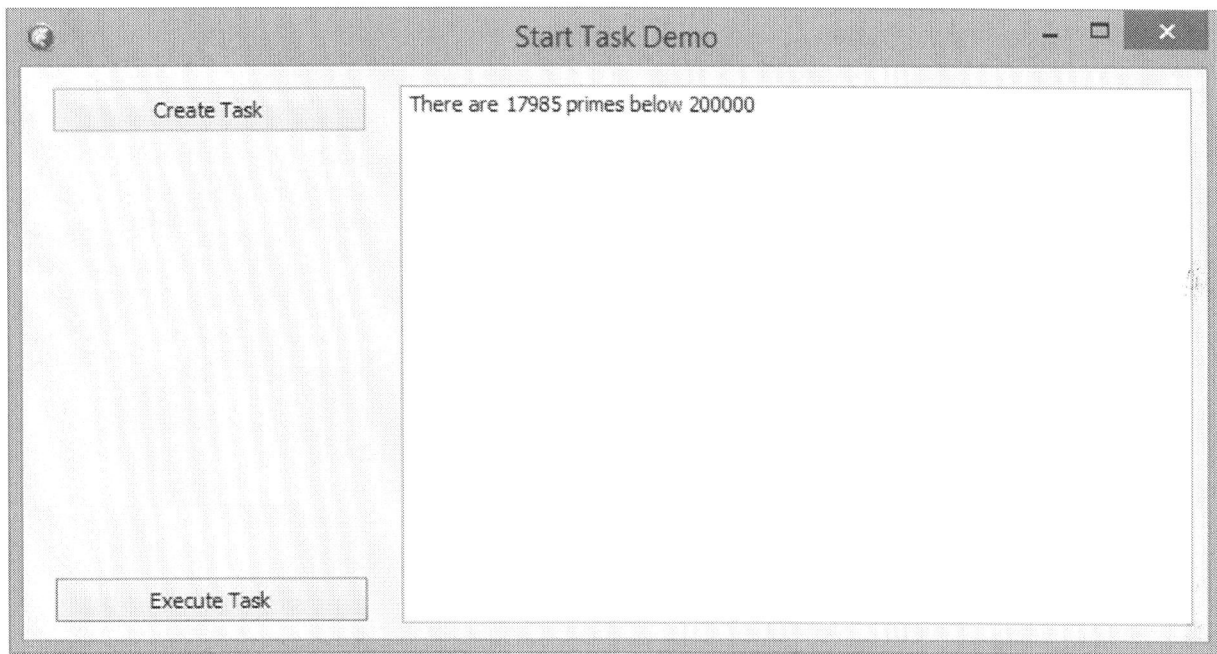

Handling Exceptions in Tasks

I am indebted to Robert Love's blog for this section. Please see the Bibliography for links to Robert's excellent blog and his posts on using `TTask`.

Now we have seen how Tasks and Futures can be used to make your applications performant and responsive. So far everything has been fine. But it is inevitable that something will go wrong and an exception will be raised. What should we do when an exception gets raised in a TTask?

Well, your natural tendency would be to just let the exception happen and have the default exception handling system deal with things.

We'll try this in our now classic three button/one memo form. Here's the implementation of an exception occurring and us just letting things flow like we normally would:

```
procedure TForm61.Button1Click(Sender: TObject);
begin

  TTask.Run(procedure
          var
            Stopwatch: TStopWatch;
            Total: Integer;
            ElapsedSeconds: Double;
          begin
            Stopwatch := TStopWatch.StartNew;
            // oops, something happened!
            raise Exception.Create('An error of some sort occurred in the task');
            Total := PrimesBelow(200000);
            ElapsedSeconds := StopWatch.Elapsed.TotalSeconds;
            TThread.Synchronize(nil, procedure
                                    begin
                                      Memo1.Lines.Add(Format('There are  %d primes under' +
                                                          ' 200,000', [Total]));
                                      Memo1.Lines.Add(Format('It took %:2f seconds to ' +
                                                          'calcluate that', [ElapsedSeconds]));

                                    end);
          end
          );

end;
```

Run this outside of the debugger, and push the button and.....nothing happens. (Note that if you run it in the debugger, the exception will be shown, but it won't propagate out to the main thread and thus won't be seen by the user.) Why is that? Well, the exception is raised in the context of the TTask, but it never leaves – it's trapped and never shown to the user. It's up to us to do that.

So we'll do it; we'll trap the exception in a try...finally block and raise it on the main thread:

```
procedure TForm61.Button2Click(Sender: TObject);
begin
  TTask.Run(procedure
          var
            Stopwatch: TStopWatch;
            Total: Integer;
            ElapsedSeconds: Double;
          begin
            try
              Stopwatch := TStopwatch.StartNew;
              // oops, something happened!
              raise ETaskException.Create('An error of some sort occurred in the task');
              Total := PrimesBelow(200000);
              ElapsedSeconds := StopWatch.Elapsed.TotalSeconds;
              TThread.Synchronize(nil, procedure
                                      begin
                                        Memo1.Lines.Add(Format('There are  %d primes under 200,000', [Tota\
l]));
                                        Memo1.Lines.Add(Format('It took %:2f seconds to calcluate that', [\
ElapsedSeconds]));
```

```
                                                end);
            except
              on e: ETaskException do
              begin
                TThread.Queue(TThread.CurrentThread,
                              procedure
                              begin
                                raise E;
                              end
                              );
              end
            end;
          end
          );
end;
```

Now let's run this, press the button (again, running outside of the debugger), and everything goes out of control. You get a series of ugly error messages.

Why? Well, this time, the variable E, which holds the exception, is actually freed before it gets to the main thread and thus you get some ugly messages and an access violation.

What to do? Well, TTask provides a way to get a hold of the exception that is raised and allows you to handle it yourself in a safe manner. This is done via a call to AcquireExceptionObject.

```
procedure TForm61.Button3Click(Sender: TObject);
var
  AcquiredException: Exception;
begin
  TTask.Run(procedure
            var
              Stopwatch: TStopWatch;
              Total: Integer;
              ElapsedSeconds: Double;
            begin
              try
                Stopwatch := TStopwatch.StartNew;
                // oops, something happened!
                raise ETaskException.Create('An error of some sort occurred in the task');
                Total := PrimesBelow(200000);
                ElapsedSeconds := StopWatch.Elapsed.TotalSeconds;
                TThread.Synchronize(nil, procedure
                                    begin
                                      Memo1.Lines.Add(Format('There are  %d primes' +
                                                             ' under 200,000', [Total]));
                                      Memo1.Lines.Add(Format('It took %:2f seconds' +
                                                             ' to calcluate that',
                                                             [ElapsedSeconds]));
                                    end);
              except
                on e: ETaskException do
                begin
                  AcquiredException := AcquireExceptionObject;
```

```
TThread.Queue(TThread.CurrentThread,
                    procedure
                    begin
                      raise AcquiredException;
                    end
                    );
        end
      end;
    end
    );
end;
```

We save off, via a local variable, the exception that is returned by the call to `AcquireExceptionObject`, and then we are able to safely raise that in a call to `TThread.Queue`. As you can imagine, exception propagation through a `TTask` is a complicated thing. The framework manages the handling of exceptions for you, and all you have to do is ask for a reference to the `Exception` and use it yourself. Press that third button, and the user will get the exception message as expected.

Stopping a Task

Sometimes a task can take a long time. What if you want to cancel it in the middle? Well, it's pretty easy, actually. Let's create a new VCL application and add two buttons and a memo (I know, this is getting boring, but it's a good, clean demo, and if it works, why not stick with it?).

Make the caption of the first button "Start Long Task" and the second's "Cancel." Then add a private variable to the form:

```
Task: ITask;
```

Double click on the first button and add this code:

```
procedure TForm62.Button1Click(Sender: TObject);
begin
  Task := TTask.Run(procedure
              var
                i: Integer;
              begin
                for i := 1 to 100000 do
                begin
                  Sleep(1000);
                  if TTask.CurrentTask.Status = TTaskStatus.Canceled then
                  begin
                    Exit;
                  end;
                  TThread.Queue(TThread.CurrentThread,
                          procedure
                          begin
                            Memo1.Lines.Add(i.ToString());
                          end );
                end;
              end
              ).Start;
end;
```

This code simply counts to 100,000, posting the current count to the memo every second (via a call to Sleep). But the interesting part comes after the Sleep call. The code checks to see if the current Task's status is set to TTaskStatus.Canceled. If it is, it exits the method. If not, it keeps rolling along.

How to cancel the thread? Simple. Just put the following code in the OnClick for the Cancel button:

```
procedure TForm62.Button2Click(Sender: TObject);
begin
  Task.Cancel;
end;
```

That's it. That sets the task to a canceled state, and if you press that button (after starting the task, of course), the task will come to a screeching halt. You can set the value while the task is running because the task is running on a background thread, and the call to TTask.Cancel is done on the main thread.

So that is how you can cancel a thread. I tell you, the PPL thinks of everything.

Summary

Futures and Tasks are a powerful means of completely utilizing your CPU without losing responsiveness in your application. And the best part is that they are really easy to use. None of the code that we've seen so far is that complicated – it's merely anonymous methods passed to methods of TTask. However, despite their easy syntax, there are still many potholes and other dangers inherent in their use. Care must be taken when using them. Despite the potential pitfalls, I encourage you start using TTask and IFuture<T> to parallelize your code.

In the next chapter, we'll look at the TParallel.For loop, which is the third way to speed up your code on multi-core machines.

Parallel For Loops

Introduction

For loops seem like the thing most people start with when talking about the PPL, but I've saved them for last, mainly because they are, well, not as easy and straight-forward as you might think. In fact, there's enough information here that I decided to split this topic into its own chapter.

The `for` loop is one of the most common constructs in programming: simple and powerful and to the point. The PPL provides a `TParallel.For` loop that can, when used properly, drastically increase the speed of your `for` loops by parallelizing their execution across multiple cores. It's fairly easy to convert a regular `for` loop into a parallel one, and it is also easy to make things worse by doing so. Here are some rules that you should follow when deciding whether to use `TParallel.For`.

- The steps in the body of the loop have to be completely independent of each other and designed in such a way that they don't need to be executed in any specific order. `TParallel.For` will split each iteration into a separate `TTask` and execute it on any available core in your processor. If your loop depends on a specific execution order, do not use the `TParallel.For` loop because it is highly likely that each iteration will not be completed in order.
- Do not write to shared resources inside the `for` loop's body: if you do that, chances are data will be corrupted. If you have to synchronize your code inside a `TParallel.For` loop, you lose most of the benefit of using it.

The reason that I've saved `TParallel.For` until last is that once you understand how Tasks work, understanding how `TParallel.For` works is a piece of cake. `TParallel.For` merely takes each iteration of the `For` loop and turns it into a `TTask` and places it in the Thread Pool. They then get executed like multiple `TTask` statements, as we saw in the last chapter.

Basics

Let's start with yet another simple VCL application – one with a button and a memo. Double click the button and add this code:

```
procedure TParallelForDemoForm.Button1Click(Sender: TObject);
begin
  Memo1.Clear;
  Memo1.Update;
  TParallel.&For(1, 10,
                 procedure (aIndex: integer)
                 begin
                   PrimesBelow(50000);
                   TThread.Queue(TThread.CurrentThread,
                              procedure
                              begin
                                Memo1.Lines.Add(aIndex.ToString());
                              end);
                 end);
end;
```

Run and press the button. My experience is that the first time you press the button, the loop performs in order. However, the second and subsequent times you press the button, the numbers all appear, but not in order:

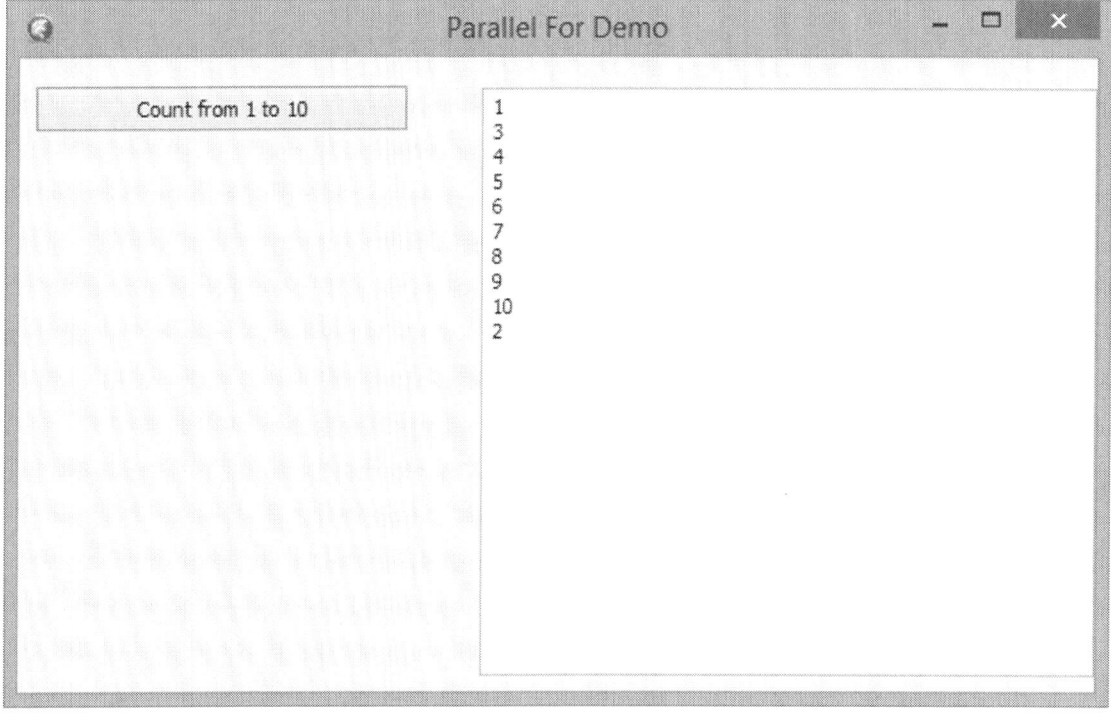

We've been using a prime number calculator to do our CPU-intensive activity. Here's an example:

```
function PrimesBelow(100000): integer;
var
  i: integer;
begin
  Result := 0;
  for i := 1 to 100000 do
  begin
    if SlowIsPrime(i) then
    begin
      Result := Result + 1;
    end;
  end;
end;
```

I bet we can use TParallel.For to speed that up:

```
function PrimesBelowParallel(aInteger: integer): integer;
var
  Temp: integer;
begin
  Temp := 0;
  TParallel.For(1, aInteger, procedure(aIndex: integer)
                             begin
                               if SlowIsPrime(aIndex) then
                               begin
                                 TInterlocked.Increment(Temp);
                               end;
                             end);
  Result := Temp;

end;
```

Here's the code that will show that the TParallel.For loop speeds up our code by about a factor of four on my machine which has four cores. Your mileage may vary depending upon the architecture of your CPU.

```
procedure TParallelForDemoForm.Button2Click(Sender: TObject);
var
  PrimeTotal: integer;
  TotalTime: integer;
  StopWatch: TStopWatch;
  S: string;
begin
  StopWatch := TStopWatch.StartNew;
  PrimeTotal := PrimesBelow(100000);
  StopWatch.Stop;
  TotalTime := StopWatch.ElapsedMilliseconds;
  S := Format('There are %d primes below 100,000.  It took %d milliseconds' +
              ' to figure that out.', [PrimeTotal, TotalTime]);
  Memo1.Lines.Add(S);

  Memo1.Lines.Add('');

  StopWatch := TStopWatch.StartNew;
```

```
PrimeTotal := PrimesBelowParallel(100000);
StopWatch.Stop;
TotalTime := StopWatch.ElapsedMilliseconds;
S := Format('There are %d primes below 100,000.  It took %d milliseconds' +
            ' to figure that out.', [PrimeTotal, TotalTime]);
Memo1.Lines.Add(S);

end;
```

Here's the output from my machine:

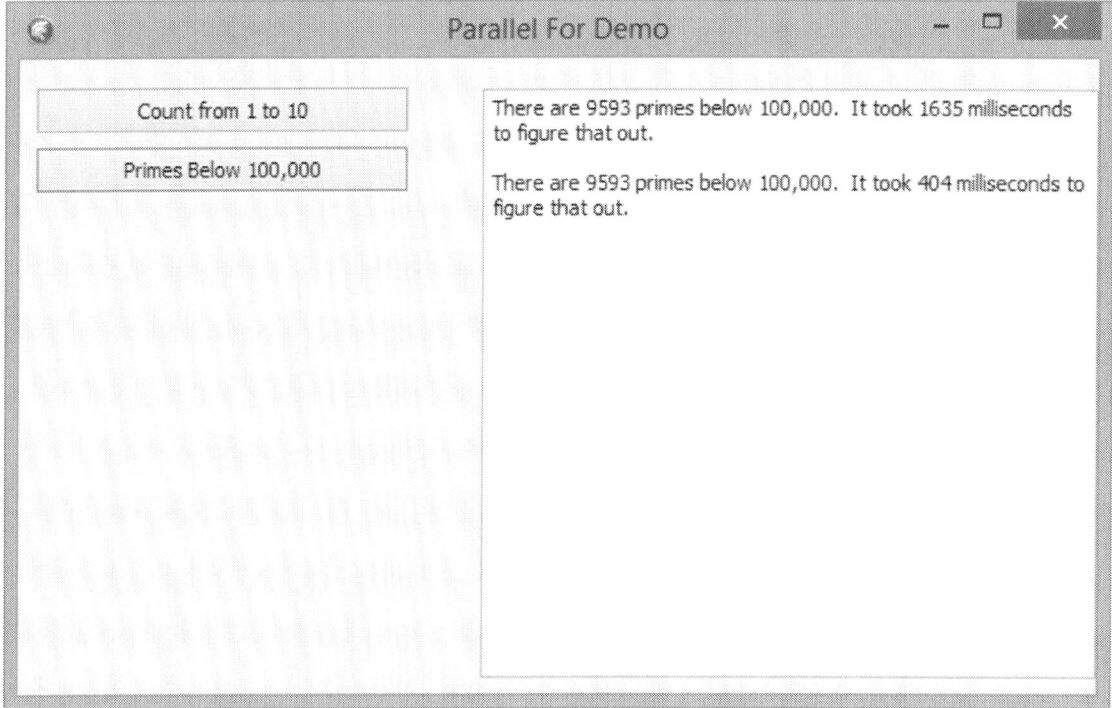

`TParallel.For` can drastically speed up your loops, usually by a factor of the number of cores that your computer has.

Making a Parallel Loop Responsive

Remember when I told you that this stuff was tricky? So far it hasn't been too bad. Well, it's about to get really tricky.

You might have noticed that the examples we've done for `TParallel.For` so far leave the application non-responsive. Try to move the window while the loop is spinning and you can't – it waits until the loop is done before moving the window.

The reason for this is that, while the contents of the loop are executed in different threads, the loop itself is blocked on the main one. The main thread is the one responsible for moving the window by processing the WM_SIZE message. However the main thread is blocked by the `TParallel.For` call, and so any messages will not be processed until the `TParallel.For` is completed.. You may be tempted to add in an

`Application.ProcessMessages` to the loop code, but resist that temptation: that call is not even remotely thread-safe and will have unpredictable results.

So what to do? Well, run the code in a separate thread. And what is the easiest way for us to do that? Why with `TTask.Run`, of course!

We'll add another button and give its `OnClick` the following code:

```
procedure TParallelForDemoForm.Button6Click(Sender: TObject);
var
  LoopResult: TParallel.TLoopResult;
begin
  Memo1.Clear;

  TTask.Run(
          procedure
          begin
            LoopResult :=  TParallel.&For(1, 30,
                                    procedure(aIndex: integer)
                                    begin
                                      PrimesBelow(50000);
                                      TThread.Queue(TThread.Current,
                                                procedure
                                                begin
                                                  Memo1.Lines.Add(aIndex.ToString());
                                                end);
                                    end);
            if LoopResult.Completed then
            begin
              Memo1.Lines.Add('The loop completed.')
            end;
          end);
end;
```

Yes, that is three anonymous methods nested within one another. The first is for the `TTask`, the second for the `TParallel.For` itself, and the third is for the `Thread.Queue` call. But if you run this app, and press the button, you can move the application around while it slowly counts to thirty (very likely out of order).

Note, too, that the call to `TParallel.For` is a function, returning the type `TParallel.TLoopResult`, a type nested inside of `TParallel`. It is declared as follows:

```
TLoopResult = record
private
  FCompleted: Boolean;
  FLowestBreakIteration: Variant;
public
  property Completed: Boolean read FCompleted;
  property LowestBreakIteration: Variant read FLowestBreakIteration;
end;
```

In the code above, we capture the result of the call to `TParallel.For` and then when the loop is over, we check to see if it completed. If it has, we say so in the memo.

Why are we always using `TThread.Queue` and not `TThread.Synchronize`? As noted in the last chapter, it's because `Synchronize` blocks on the main thread, which can cause problems when dealing with multiple threads on multiple cores.

Stopping a Parallel Loop

What if you get bored of waiting and want to stop a long-running parallel loop? Well, it's tricky, as I've said.

If you look at the Code Insight for `TParallel.For`, you'll notice a serious amount of overloads. I counted – there are 32 of them. So far, we've only used one which take "from" and "to" integers and a `TProc<integer>` as parameters. In order to have control over the stopping of the loop, we'll take a look specifically at this overload:

```
class function TParallel.&For(ALowInclusive, AHighInclusive: Integer; const AIteratorEvent: TProc<Integer, TLo\
opState>): TLoopResult; overload; static; inline;
```

Note that this takes an anonymous method with two parameters, where the second one is a `TLoopState` which is an internal class of `TParallel`. The variable of type `TLoopState` is passed to the anonymous method during each iteration for your use. It has three methods and three properties of interest:

```
public
  procedure Break;
  procedure Stop;
  function ShouldExit: Boolean;

  property Faulted: Boolean read GetFaulted;
  property Stopped: Boolean read GetStopped;
  property LowestBreakIteration: Variant read GetLowestBreakIteration;
```

The `Break` and `Stop` methods are the ones that allow you to notify the parallel loop that it should come to an end early.

The first thing to realize is that when you try to stop a parallel loop, there are already a number of iterations active and being run that will finish no matter when you decide to try to stop them. Remember, a given chunk of them are running at the same time – and thus a request to stop the loop will result in some processing continuing even after the request is made.

If you call `Break`, you are telling the loop to launch no more iterations from the moment that `Break` is called. If there are any iterations with higher index values than the one upon which `Break` is called, then they should shut themselves down as quickly as possible. Here's the crux: iterations that are *lower* than the iteration where `Break` is called are not affected and will still run. Remember, it's entirely possible that you call `Break` in iteration seven, while five and six have yet to be started. In that case, iterations five and six would be executed and finished, and any iterations greater than seven which had been launched would be finished as well.

`Stop` is different in that once it is called, no new iterations will be started, and all existing iterations will be completed as soon as possible.

Got that? I told you things got tricky.

So how does this work? Well, we need two new buttons – one to set the loop running, and one to stop it. But first, give the form a private field variable of type `ITask`:

```
ForLoopTask: ITask;
```

This will be the reference that we will check to see if the loop has been stopped. Then, in the first new button's `OnClick` event, put the following code:

```
procedure TParallelForDemoForm.Button3Click(Sender: TObject);
var
  LoopResult: TParallel.TLoopResult;
begin
  Memo1.Clear;
  Memo1.Update;
  ForLoopTask := TTask.Create(
    procedure
    begin
      LoopResult := TParallel.&For(1, 30,
        procedure (aIndex: integer; LoopState: TParallel.TLoopState)
        begin
          if (ForLoopTask.Status = TTaskStatus.Canceled) and (not LoopState.Stopped) then
          begin
            LoopState.Stop;
          end;
          if LoopState.Stopped then
          begin
            TThread.Queue(TThread.Current,
                          procedure
                          begin
                            Memo1.Lines.Add(aIndex.ToString +  ' has stopped early');
                          end);
            Exit;
          end;
          PrimesBelow(150000);
          TThread.Queue(TThread.Current,
                          procedure
                          begin
                            Memo1.Lines.Add(aIndex.ToString());
                          end
                          );
        end);
      if LoopResult.Completed then
      begin
        Memo1.Lines.Add('The Loop Completed')
      end else
      begin
        Memo1.Lines.Add('The loop stopped before the end')
      end;
    end
  );
  ForLoopTask.Start;
end;
```

and in the Cancel (Stop) button, we'll put this:

```
procedure TParallelForDemoForm.Button4Click(Sender: TObject);
begin
  if Assigned(ForLoopTask) then
  begin
    ForLoopTask.Cancel;
  end;
end;
```

We need something within the app to indicate that the loop should stop and the thing we use is the ForLoopTask status. When you press the Cancel button, it will call the Cancel method, marking the ITask itself as canceled, and as you'll see, we'll check that in the loop.

Okay, so the real meat of things is in the first button's OnClick. First up, we create a task. We pass it an anonymous method. That anonymous method consists entirely of a TParallel.For loop. That iterates from 1 to 30, each time executing another anonymous method that takes the iterator index and an instance of TLoopState as parameters. That anonymous method is divided into three chunks, and we'll take one at a time.

First:

```
if (ForLoopTask.Status = TTaskStatus.Canceled) and (not LoopState.Stopped) then
begin
  LoopState.Stop;
end;
```

This code checks the ForLoopTask.Status value to see if it is set to TTaskStatus.Canceled. It will be if we have pressed the Cancel button. If we aren't already stopped, then we call LoopState.Stop which signals the TParallel.For loop that it should stop creating new iterations and finish up any iterations that it has started.

The next chunk of code in the loop is this:

```
if LoopState.Stopped then
begin
  TThread.Queue(nil, procedure
                     begin
                       Memo1.Lines.Add(aIndex.ToString + ' has stopped early');
                     end);
  Exit;
end;
```

This code says "If this iteration is stopped, go ahead and say that it has stopped early and then exit the whole procedure". In other words, if Stop has been called, finish up as soon as possible.

Finally, if things get that far – that is, if things are not stopped, then the normal stuff occurs:

```
PrimesBelow50000;
TThread.Queue(nil, procedure
                   begin
                     Memo1.Lines.Add(aIndex.ToString());
                   end
```

Running this code leads to some unexpected results. To run it, press the first button and then the second one as quickly as you can. The output is really never the same twice, but it generally looks something like this:

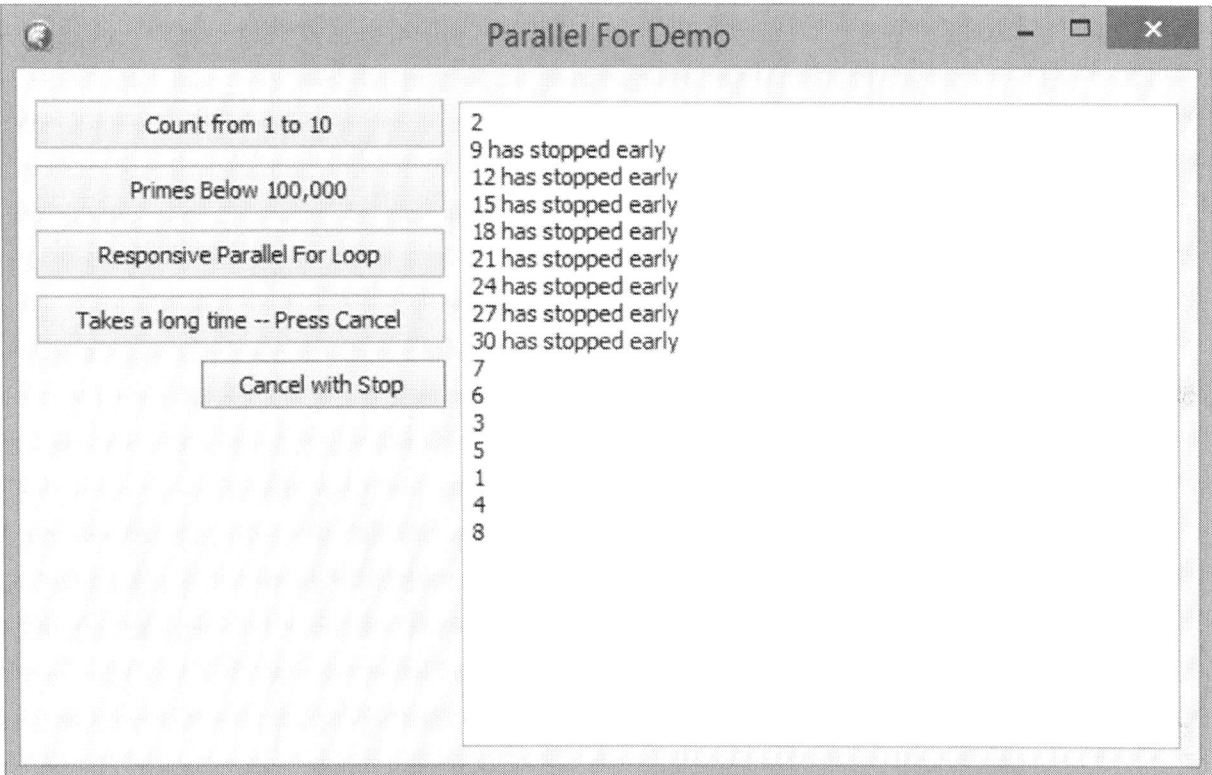

Now that output is interesting. Note that it reports out about one iteration being complete. Then, after I hit the Cancel button, it reports a bunch of iterations as having stopped early, including some of the very last ones. Finally, it reports a bunch more of completed iterations. Your outcomes will vary depending upon how quickly you press the Cancel button, but on this run, it started up a total of sixteen iterations out of thirty, stopped eight of them early, and completed eight.

Play around a bit with the time you allow the loop to run and see how it affects the output. See if you can figure out why different times between button pushes do different things.

I'll leave it as an exercise for the reader to change the line `LoopState.Stop;` to `LoopState.Break;` and see what happens. And what happens if you then check for `LoopState.ShouldExit` instead of `LoopState.Stopped`.

Strides

The last topic in this section will be about Strides. Strides allow you to group together sequential iterations onto the same thread. For instance, if you have ten iterations, and you set your `Stride` to two, the first two iterations will be attached to one thread, then the next two to the second thread, the next two to the third thread and so on.

You set the `Stride` for your `TParallel.For` loop by adding a parameter at the beginning of the parameter list. (As mentioned above, `TParallel.For` has a lot of overloads....) Stride can be any value less than the high value of your loop.

To more visually demonstrate how strides work, I've created a VCL version of a demo that was done originally by fellow Embarcadero MVP Danny Wind in his CodeRage 9 Video entitled *Parallel Programming Library: Create Responsive Object Pascal Apps*[24] Danny has kindly given me permission to adapt his code in my demo here.

This demo will draw squares on a paintbox in accordance with the number of strides we set for the parallel loop. The squares will be given a color for the thread that draws them, and we'll slow the drawing down a bit to see how the patterns emerge with different `Stride` settings.

To start, we'll create a simple VCL application with a button, a spinedit, a label, and a paintbox. It should look something like this:

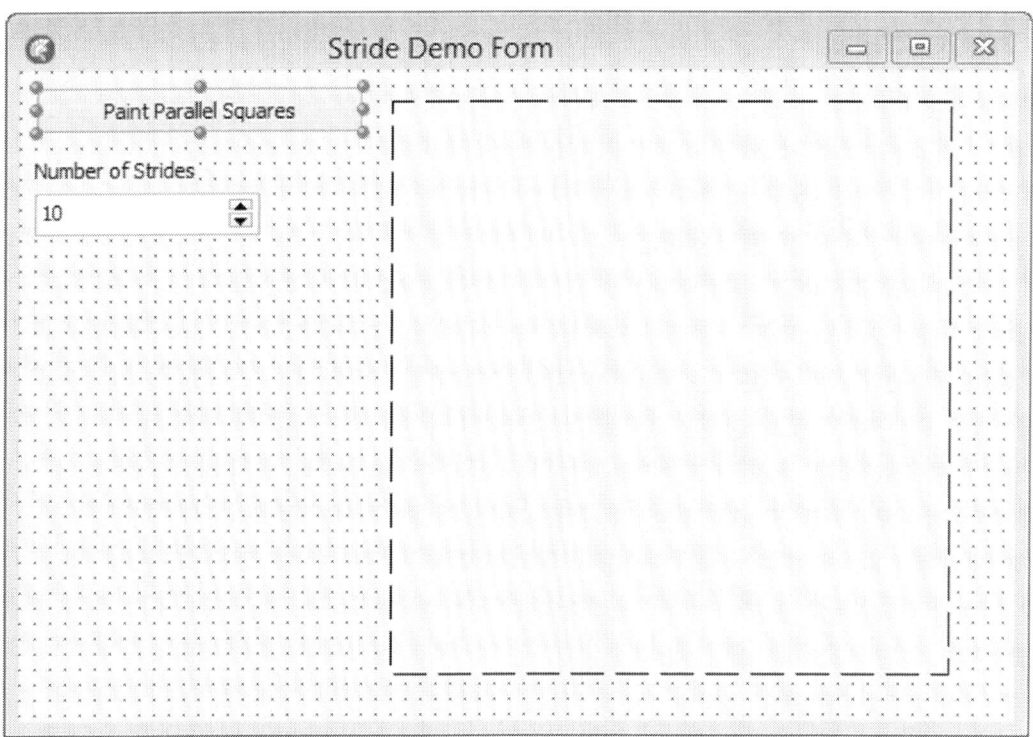

Set the `MaxValue` of the spinedit to 100 and the `MinValue` to 1. Make the paintbox exactly 300 by 300 pixels. Then, create the following method on the form:

---

[24]https://www.youtube.com/watch?v=rZfux4by0po

```
procedure TStrideDemoForm.ClearRectangle;
begin
  PaintBox1.Canvas.Brush.Color := Self.Color;
  PaintBox1.Canvas.Rectangle(0, 0, PaintBox1.Width, PaintBox1.Height);
end;
```

This will clear the paintbox after we get done painting on it, making sure it is ready for the tasks to do their thing.

We'll also set three constants:

```
const
  SquareSize = 30;
  SquaresPerRow = 10;
  TotalSquares = 100;
```

The paintbox will be divided into 100 squares, each 30 by 30 pixels, thus making 10 squares per row.

First, we'll create a method on the form that will draw a rectangle. This will be the iterator method (as opposed to anonymous methods that we've used so far) that we pass to the TParallel.For loop:

```
procedure TStrideDemoForm.PaintRectangle(aIndex: integer);
var
  LTop, LLeft: integer;
  LRed, LGreen, LBLue: Byte;
  LColor: TAlphaColor;
begin
    Sleep(100);
    LTop :=  (aIndex div SquaresPerRow) * SquareSize;
    LLeft := (aIndex mod SquaresPerRow) * SquareSize;

    LGreen := TThread.CurrentThread.ThreadID MOD High(Byte);
    LRed := (16 * LGreen) MOD High(Byte);
    LBlue := (4 * LGreen) MOD High(Byte);
    LColor := RGB(LRed, LGreen, LBlue);
    TThread.Queue(TThread.CurrentThread,
                     procedure
                     begin
                       Paintbox1.Canvas.Brush.Color := LColor;
                       Paintbox1.Canvas.Rectangle(LLeft, LTop, LLeft + SquareSize, LTop + SquareSize);
                     end);
end;
```

First, we'll sleep for 100 milliseconds. This will give us a chance to see the pattern of squares appearing. You can set this longer if you want to slow things down even more. Then, we calculate the top and left of the square. Remember, we are merely going to be given a number from 0 to 99. Then we generate a color based on the current thread that is being used to do the drawing. Finally, we simply set the brush color and draw a rectangle.

 At first, I forgot to use TThread.Queue to wrap up the VCL painting code and boy did that not work right. Blocks appeared in strange times, and not all blocks were drawn. Very frustrating. Then I remembered, "Ahh, yeah, you have to Queue that code because it is a call to the VCL" and things worked as they were supposed to.

Finally, let's do the actual loop: Double click on the button and give it the following handler code:

```
procedure TStrideDemoForm.Button1Click(Sender: TObject);
begin
  ClearRectangle;
  TTask.Run(procedure
            begin
              TParallel.For(SpinEdit1.Value, 0, TotalSquares - 1, PaintRectangle)
            end)
end;
```

Notice that we have a task wrapping the parallel code so that it operates within its own thread, ensuring that the application remains responsive when doing the work of painting squares. The `Stride` parameter is determined by the `Value` of the spinedit, and the code that gets called for each iteration is the method on the form, `PaintRectangle`.

Now the fun starts. This is actually a pretty cool demo. Run it, and press the button with the stride set to 10. You'll see the rectangles move across the paintbox at about the same rate, with each row a different color. Depending on how many cores you have, you'll see all ten rows in different colors, each row having been painted together.

You can get some interesting patterns if you set the `Stride` property to different values. For instance, set the `Stride` property to 11, and you'll see an interesting pattern get painted. Here's what it looked like on my machine with the `Stride` set to 11.

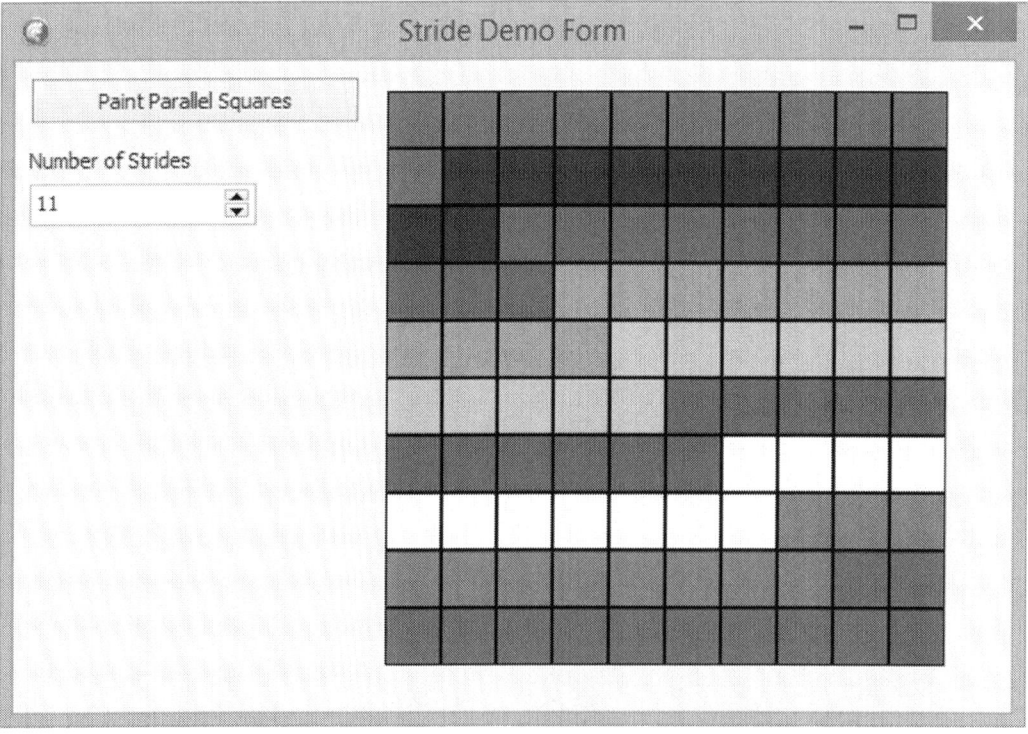

Notice the one lone square in the lower right corner, the "leftover" one after the 99 squares painted by the `Stride` value of 11. Try 12 and 13. You should see the pattern evolve. Try 50, or 99. They make for some interesting outcomes. What happens if you set the stride to 100?

Some Final Thoughts on Concurrent and Parallel Programming

Here are a few pointers to consider that can help you avoid the pitfalls of parallel programming:

- *Parallel programming will not always improve performance.* Sometimes, if you aren't careful, it can actually slow things down due to excessive overhead, and if you aren't really careful, it can bring everything to a screeching halt via a deadlock.
- *Bugs in concurrent code are often very difficult to track down.* Threading bugs are often viewed as "one-offs" or "Ghosts in the machine" because they are often transient, intermittent, and difficult to reproduce. They can also be impossible to reproduce on some hardware, while instantly causing issues on other machines.
- *One good way to avoid difficulties in parallel programming is to closely follow the Single Responsibility Principle.* Code that does one thing will very often be stand-alone and decoupled, limiting the race conditions that can cause deadlocks.
- *Severely limit data sharing amongst your concurrent code.* This is a similar notion to the previous point. When different modules share data in concurrent code, deadlocks and race conditions are much more likely to occur. Protect all common code with critical sections or other similar locking tools that ensure that race conditions don't occur. Better yet, don't write any common code that needs to be locked.
- *Keep concurrent and parallel code small.* If you have code in a `TTask` or a `TParallel.For` loop, keep it short and sweet and to the point. Don't let it "wander" as this makes it more likely that you'll start allowing it to mix with non-parallel code, and that could be bad.
- *Bottom Line*: Follow good coding practices, keep your concerns properly separated, and you can greatly reduce the dangers that may arise when writing parallel code.

Conclusion

Okay, so do you get the idea that parallel programming is hard and needs to be done with great care? I tried to scare you in the Introduction, but now that we've taken a look at things, and how the runtime library supports parallel programming to a pretty high degree, I hope that you aren't *too* afraid to wander into the world of multi-threaded programming, given that there are great rewards to be obtained by the intrepid developer who ventures into these waters. Just remember what Spider-Man's uncle said: "*With great power comes great responsibility*". That's just as true for developers as it is for superheroes.

Aspect-Oriented Programming

Introduction

When I first heard of Aspect Oriented Programming (AOP), I had just gotten to the point where Object Oriented Programming made sense to me. So my first reaction was "Oh, great, now I have to start all over again." Well, that wasn't really the case. AOP is really a complement to, and not a replacement for, Object Oriented programming.

AOP provides the ability to enhance an existing object framework by "sliding things in sideways" and providing cross-cutting functionality. It provides a way to separate out those cross-cutting concerns into their own hierarchy. Typical uses would be things like logging, security, and validation. These are concerns that would be difficult to insert into an inheritance hierarchy because they would have to be injected everywhere, even places where they were not wanted.

Instead, AOP utilizes features like attributes to insert features "on the side." For instance, you can build a logging framework and then place logging into any area of your class framework that you like via attributes.

If you've heard me speak or read almost anything I've written, you know that I'm a strong believer in decoupling -- that is, separating concerns in your code out into separate modules. Your code should be organized in such a way that each concern is only very loosely coupled with the other concerns it needs. Business logic should not be intertwined with the User Interface (UI).

These concerns, to as large a degree as possible, should not be tangled up with each other. Some of the concerns can be considered essential -- Business Logic, UIhandling, etc. -- and are normally called "core concerns," while others can be viewed as non-core: error handling, logging, minor UI control such as the cursor, etc. They are often said to be "cross-cutting concerns." They are also referred to as "system concerns." Note that I'm not saying that they aren't needed, but just that they aren't core concerns. These peripheral concerns are often called "aspects," and while they interact with the primary concerns of an application, it is best if they can be separated and decoupled.

Often, the inclusion of peripheral concerns means duplicating the code in many places. For instance, if you want to do logging, you usually have to write logging code all over the place. It means unnecessarily tangling up the logging code for peripheral concerns with primary concerns like your business logic. Such scattering of code makes for difficult maintainability and challenging testing. It also makes for repetition, causes code to grow unnecessarily and generally makes your code "unclean." Wouldn't it be better to have your logging code in one place and then be able to insert the logging with something simple like an attribute? That way you can make logging code changes in one place and not have to find it all over your code base when a change is needed. That's what AOP is all about.

> Most often, these concerns are called "cross-cutting concerns" because they don't fit into a single area of the application, but rather can cut across all sections of the application. For instance, if you want to implement security in your application, you wouldn't want to do it on an ad hoc, just-stick-it-in-where-you-need-it kind of way. Instead, you'd want to separate it out as a separate concern and then find a way to insert it into the

places it is needed without disturbing the existing code very much. You'd want to follow the Open/Closed Principle as much as possible.

Remember back in the Decorator Pattern chapter where I mentioned Aspect Oriented Programming? As we'll see, the Decorator Pattern will play a big role in AOP.

An Illustration

In order to illustrate and learn about AOP, we'll start from the bottom and work our way up.

For example, consider the following code:

```
function ChangeEmailAddress(aUserID: Integer; aNewEmail: string): Boolean;
var
  LUser: TUser;
begin
  Result := False;
  StartTransaction;
  Screen.Cursor := crWait;
  try try
    LUser := TUser.GetUserByID(aUserId);
    if LUser <> nil then
    begin
      LUser.UpdateEmail(aNewEmail);
    end else
    begin
      raise EUserNotFoundException.CreateFmt('User with id of %d not found.', [aUserId]);
    end;
    CommitTransaction;
  except
    RollbackTransaction;
    raise;
  end;
  finally
    Screen.Cursor := crNormal
  end;
  Result := True;
end;
```

In this code, you have a main concern, that of changing a user's email address. But tangled up in that code is also the concerns of a transaction, managing the screen cursor, and handling exceptions. Wouldn't it be nice if there were a way to separate these concerns out from the main concern? There is!

This is where Aspect Oriented Programming comes in. AOP allows you to untangle many of these secondary concerns from the primary concerns. It will allow you to "intercept" a method call and put in code at specific "point cuts" without affecting the functionality of the main method itself.

Typically, an AOP system will provide you with the following information at runtime:

- When you have entered a method
- When information about the parameters are passed to that method
- When you have exited from that method
- If the method is a function, the result of the method
- When an exception is raised.

You as an AOP developer can add code at entry and exit points and at the point where an exception is raised – these are often called "point cuts." The code you add is sometimes called "advice." Thus advice is "woven" into point cuts to create an aspect (those are fancy AOP terms, not mine…).

Thus, you can augment, change or even cancel the functionality of a given method from a class. For instance, if a specific method requires a certain level of security, you can intercept that method and check for the proper security level, canceling the method if the levels are not correct.

The Basics:

Before we get to doing actual AOP, we need to learn about a few building blocks, namely the `TVirtual-MethodInterceptor` class, and the notion of interception in general.

TVirtualMethodInterceptor

`TVirtualMethodInterceptor` is a class in the `RTTI.pas` unit. It was introduced in Delphi XE, and you'll never guess what it does – it intercepts virtual methods. In doing so, it provides easy point cuts for you to "hook" a given virtual method and insert your own code into it. You can grab a hold of a given virtual method and then change its arguments, change the return value if it is a function, intercept exceptions and even raise new ones, and if you want, you can even completely replace the code itself. It's pretty powerful, eh?

To demonstrate its use, we'll first need a class that has interceptable methods. Here is such a class:

```
type
  TVMIDemo = class(TObject)
    procedure DoSomething; virtual;
    procedure RaiseException; virtual;
  end;
```

This class obviously has two methods. The methods are implemented as follows:

```
procedure TVMIDemo.DoSomething;
begin
  WriteLn('Doing something');
end;

procedure TVMIDemo.RaiseException;
begin
  raise Exception.Create('Raised on purpose.');
end;
```

We'll use TVirtualMethodInterceptor to take control of both methods. Note that any method that is visible via RTTI can be intercepted. For the first, we'll simply show where the point cuts are and how they can be accessed. In the second, we'll raise an exception and show how you can control that process.

TVirtualMethodInterceptor has three events of interest: OnBefore, OnAfter, and OnException. In order to provide the additional functionality, you need to provide event handlers for these events. The OnBefore event fires, well, right before the "normal" code of the method is to execute. The OnAfter event fires at the end of the method, and the OnException fires if TVirtualMethodInterceptor runs across an exception.

Providing simple handlers to merely declare these events happening might look like the following:

```
procedure DoBefore(Instance: TObject; Method: TRttiMethod;
  const Args: TArray<TValue>; out DoInvoke: Boolean; out Result: TValue);
begin
  Writeln('Before: ', Method.Name);
end;

procedure DoAfter(Instance: TObject; Method: TRttiMethod; const Args: TArray<TValue>; var Result: TValue);
begin
  Writeln('After: ', Method.Name);
end;

procedure DoException(Instance: TObject; Method: TRttiMethod;
  const Args: TArray<TValue>; out RaiseException: Boolean;
  TheException: Exception; out Result: TValue);
var
  Str: string;
begin
  Str := Format('An exception occurred in %s with the message: %s', [Method.Name, TheException.Message]);
  WriteLn(Str);
  RaiseException := False;
  Result := False;
end;
```

OnBefore and OnAfter merely write out to the console that they are happening. Note, however, that they use the TRttiMethod.Name property to declare exactly which method is being intercepted, illustrating that the Method parameter has all the information about the method available to you. The OnException event handler is a bit more complex, as it provides a message about the Exception and then actually suppresses it by setting RaiseException to False.

Note the signatures of the method declarations. Through the parameters passed in to each, you have access to virtually (sorry) the entire method call itself, including the method name, arguments, and the result value. In the OnBefore method, you can even decide whether to invoke the method at all.

This given implementation is a very simple example, but it illustrates well the principle behind interception.

The interesting work gets done in the `Main` function of the simple console application. Here it is:

```
procedure Main;
var
  VMI: TVirtualMethodInterceptor;
  VMIDemo: TVMIDemo;
begin
  VMIDemo := TVMIDemo.Create;

  VMI := TVirtualMethodInterceptor.Create(TVMIDemo);
  try
    VMI.OnBefore := DoBefore;
    VMI.OnAfter := DoAfter;
    VMI.OnException := DoException;

    VMI.Proxify(VMIDemo);

    VMIDemo.DoSomething;
    VMIDemo.RaiseException;

    Writeln('class: ', VMIDemo.ClassName);
    Writeln('parent class: ', VMIDemo.ClassParent.ClassName);
  finally
    VMI.Free;
    VMIDemo.Free;
  end;
end;
```

The first thing the code does is to create an instance of `TVMIDemo`. In order to intercept methods, we must have a valid instance of a class to intercept.

Then the code creates a `TVirtualMethodInterceptor`, taking as a parameter in the constructor the type of the class that we want to intercept. From there, it assigns the three event handlers above to the events on the instance of `TVirtualMethodInterceptor`.

Then, the rubber hits the road. `VMI` "proxifies" the instance of `VMIDemo`, taking as a parameter that very instance. So, at this point, `VMI` knows the type that is going to be intercepted and "proxified", and it has an instance of that type. The process of proxification is to do the actual intercepting. Once `Proxify` is called on the instance, that instance is "hooked". That is, the methods have been intercepted and the `OnBegin`, `OnAfter`, and `OnException` events are part of the reference, along with the event handlers attached to them.

In this case, that means that `VMIDemo` isn't really itself anymore. Instead, it is a proxy for the methods attached to the events of the `TVirtualMethodInterceptor`.

The code then goes on to call the two methods of `TVMIDemo`, and then output some basic information about the `VMIDemo` class to prove what class was getting called.

Thus, the output looks like the following:

```
C:\Users\Nick\Google Drive\EKON2014\AOP\Code\VMIDemo\Debug\Win32\Vi...  —  □  ×
Before: DoSomething
Doing something
After: DoSomething
Before: RaiseException
An exception occurred in RaiseException with the message: Raised on purpose.
After: RaiseException
class: TVMIDemo
parent class: TVMIDemo
```

Note if you run the application in the debugger, you will see the IDE's version of the raised exception appear. Note, too, that the exception did not stop the flow of the application.

And that, in a very simple example, is the notion of virtual method interception. From here, we can move on to the more general notion of interception found in the Spring For Delphi Framework.

IInterception

The Spring for Delphi Framework has many features. One of the newest is the IInterceptor interface and the supporting code to create a proxy for a class, using the TVirtualMethodInterceptor as the underlying engine. It also supports interface proxies which are done using the TVirtualInterface class internally. As we saw above, interception is a critical part of doing AOP. We need the ability to grab a hold of a class or interface – i.e. intercept it – and add behavior at critical points. This is what the TVirtualMethodInterceptor class does. However, it seems to me a bit clumsy to use.

Enter IInterceptor in the Spring Framework. You aren't going to believe this, but this interface is used to intercept a class that you provide, allowing you to easily add code to the point cuts it provides. IInterceptor is simple – declared as follows:

```
IInterceptor = interface
  ['{B33137BC-AAEE-40D7-86F3-BD6A65F4F7C7}']
  procedure Intercept(const invocation: IInvocation);
end;
```

Of course, the important part is the IInvocation parameter, which gets passed to you when you do the intercepting, and which looks like this:

```
IInvocation = interface
  ['{A307FB1B-CA96-4B20-84FE-A71B286F0924}']
  function GetArguments: TArray<TValue>;
  function GetMethod: TRttiMethod;
  function GetResult: TValue;
  function GetTarget: TValue;
  procedure SetResult(const value: TValue);

  procedure Proceed;

  property Arguments: TArray<TValue> read GetArguments;
  property Method: TRttiMethod read GetMethod;
  property Result: TValue read GetResult write SetResult;
  property Target: TValue read GetTarget;
end;
```

When you implement IInterceptor, your implementation automatically gets an instance of IInvocation based on the type that you've "proxified". It in turn contains all the information about the methods of your class that is being called. You get the arguments passed to the method, the TRttiMethod instance of the method itself, the Result if the method is a function, and the Target, which is is the proxied instance itself.

And of course, you get the very interestingly named Proceed method. Proceed lets you, well, proceed with the code of the method. You can call it anytime you like, and it will execute the method.

Thus, to create an Aspect, you implement the Intercept method of IInterceptor, writing whatever code you want before and after your call to Proceed. You have Point Cuts to add your Advice to any method of any interface you choose to "proxify".

Let's take a look at a simple example:

First, we need a class to intercept:

```
TClassToIntercept = class
  procedure InterceptedMethod; virtual;
end;

procedure TClassToIntercept.InterceptedMethod;
begin
  WriteLn('Calling InterceptedMethod');
end;
```

This is a mindless class – you can see that it doesn't do anything other than output to the console – but it will be intercepted and we'll add some simple Aspects to it to illustrate the basic idea of using interception to do AOP.

In order to intercept it, we'll create a class called TInterceptor that implements IInterceptor:

```
TInterceptor = class(TInterfacedObject, IInterceptor)
  procedure Intercept(const invocation: IInvocation);
end;

procedure TInterceptor.Intercept(const Invocation: IInvocation);
begin
  WriteLn('Before Method call named: ', Invocation.Method.Name);
  try
    Invocation.Proceed;
  except
    on E: Exception do
    begin
      WriteLn('Method threw an exception: ' + E.Message);
    end;
  end;
  WriteLn('After Method Call named: ', Invocation.Method.Name);
end;
```

Note that this code simply outputs to the console the location of the point cuts where we add the `Writeln` calls. The code calls `Invocation.Proceed`, and that's when `TClassToIntercept.InterceptedMethod` will actually be called. The result, then, will be three lines of text in the console window.

Now of course, you are probably wondering how this all gets "hooked up" and runs? It happens in the `Main` function that gets called by the console application:

```
procedure Main;
var
  Interceptor: IInterceptor;
  InterceptedClass: TClassToIntercept;
begin
  Interceptor := TInterceptor.Create;
  InterceptedClass := TProxyGenerator.CreateClassProxy<TClassToIntercept>([Interceptor]);
  InterceptedClass.InterceptedMethod;
end;
```

Okay, here's where everything happens. First, we create an instance of our `TInterceptor` class and assign it to an interface variable of type `IInterceptor`. Then, we create a proxy of `TClassToIntercept` using a class method of `TProxyGenerator`. We do that by using the `TProxyGenerator` to create a proxy class, passing as a parameterized type the type of the class that we are proxy-ing. Finally we pass in our `Interceptor` instance. (Note that the `Interceptor` class is passed as an array, meaning that you can pass more than one interceptor to the proxy. We'll see an example of this below.)

Once the call to `CreateClassProxy` does its thing, we have a valid, proxified reference to `Intercepted-Class`, an instance of `TClassToIntercept` with our Aspects attached. This means we can call its methods as expected. And when we do, we get the intercepted call, not the "regular" one. Thus, our output is as follows:

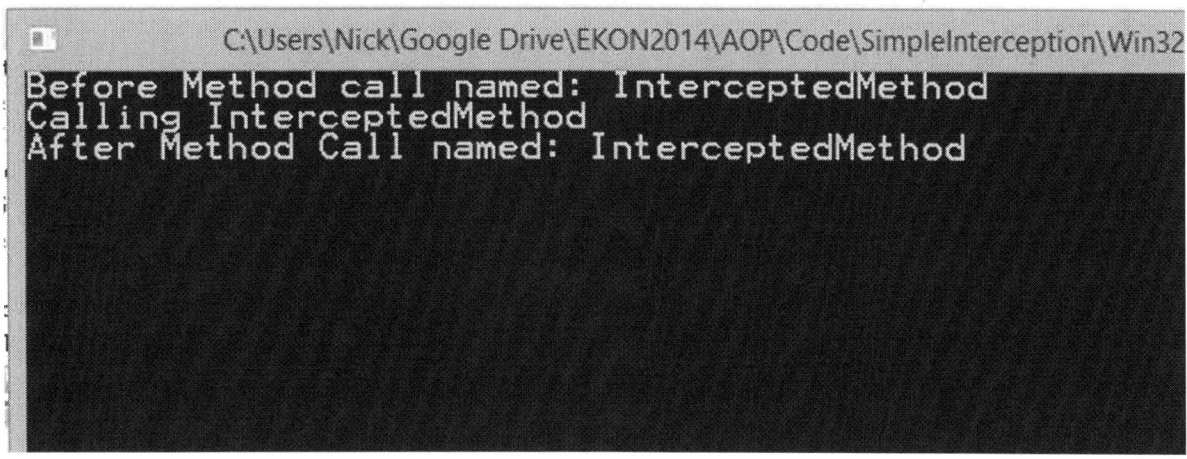

One more minor thing to note at this point: the Aspect code knows the name of the method being intercepted because it takes advantage of IInvocation's Method property. Remember, when you implement IInterceptor, you know almost everything there is to know about the class in question via the IInvocation interface that is passed to you.

At this point, it's my hope that you are noticing that what Interception is doing is really an implementation of the Decorator Pattern. The intercepted class is really being decorated by the proxy class. You should notice the similarity between the code from the Decorator Pattern chapter and the code in TInterceptor.Intercept method above.

But that is, again, a really simple example. Let's take a look at something a bit more practical.

A More Useful Example

Okay, let's take the next step and have these aspects actually do something useful.

Sometimes there are methods that you want only authorized people to call. One could imagine, for instance, a class that manages and reports on employee salaries, but that had methods that would require authorization to actually execute, such as one that would change a salary.

Consider the following code:

```
TSalaryChanger = class
  procedure ChangeSalary(const aNewSalary: Integer); virtual;
end;

procedure TSalaryChanger.ChangeSalary(const aNewSalary: Integer);
begin
  WriteLn('You changed the salary to ', aNewSalary);
end;
```

Here's a class that changes people's salaries. Obviously there would need to be some security around its use in an application – after all, we can't have anyone going around changing salaries willy-nilly, now, can we?

Let's intercept this class and make sure only people with the special password can actually execute this code.

```
TSalaryChangerInterceptor = class(TInterfacedObject, IInterceptor)
  procedure Intercept(const Invoker: IInvocation);
end;

procedure TSalaryChangerInterceptor.Intercept(const Invoker: IInvocation);
var
  LPassword: string;
begin
  if SameText(Invoker.Method.Name, 'ChangeSalary') then
  begin
    Write('Please enter the password to change the salary: ');
    ReadLn(LPassword);

    if LPassword = 'codingindelphi' then
    begin
      Invoker.Proceed;
    end else
    begin
      Writeln('Sorry, you are not authorized to change salaries');
    end;
  end;
end;
```

Here, we have created a class called TSalaryChangerInterceptor, which implements the IInterceptor interface. Thus, it has a single method, Intercept, which has the parameter Invoker of type IInvocation. First, it checks to see if we are calling the ChangeSalary method. (Remember, we know all about the class being intercepted including the method name.) If such is the case, the point cut will ask the user for the password. If the correct password is entered, then the call is made to Invoker.Proceed. If not, you get a message denying access. Note that it is not even required to call Invoker.Proceed, allowing you to completely ignore the method if you want to for whatever reason. You can also call it whenever you like, under any circumstances that you like. In our case, we are calling it only if the user is able to enter the correct password.

Now, we can have a method that tries to change the salary that looks like the following.

```
ISalaryChanger = interface(IInvokable)
['{9BD8D6E6-EC69-4FBA-9BD3-13BD958CDBC2}']
    procedure ChangeSalary(const aNewSalary: Integer);
end;

procedure TryToChangeSalary(aNewSalary: integer);
var
  SalaryInterceptor: IInterceptor;
  Proxy: ISalaryChanger;
  SalaryChanger: ISalaryChanger;
begin
  SalaryInterceptor := TSalaryChangerInterceptor.Create;
  SalaryChanger := TSalaryChanger.Create;
  Proxy :=   TProxyGenerator.CreateInterfaceProxyWithTarget<ISalaryChanger>(SalaryChanger, [SalaryInterceptor]\
);
  Proxy.ChangeSalary(aNewSalary);
end;
```

This is basically the same code that we saw above – we have a generator that creates a proxified version of our class, and we can call the methods on that proxified class, and the Aspect code will be executed as expected.

Thus, you can get an output like this:

Multiple interceptors

I am sure that you remember when I said that the parameter you pass to `CreateClassProxy` was an array of interceptors. For instance, we can add the following interceptor to our example above:

```
TMinSalaryChangerInterceptor = class(TInterfacedObject, IInterceptor)
  procedure Intercept(const Invoker: IInvocation);
end;

procedure TMinSalaryChangerInterceptor.Intercept(const Invoker: IInvocation);
begin
  if Invoker.Arguments[0].AsInteger < 25000 then
  begin
    WriteLn('No one should earn so little!');
  end else
  begin
    Invoker.Proceed;
  end;
end;
```

This interceptor won't let you set the salary less than $25,000. You can easily include it in the process by adding it to the array parameter in `CreateClassProxy`:

```
Proxy := TGeneratorProxy.CreateClassProxy<TSalaryChanger>([SalaryInterceptor, MinSalaryInterceptor]);
```

The interceptors are called in the order that they get passed. Thus, with that added, and an attempt to change the salary to $20,000, you'll see the following:

```
C:\Users\Nick\Google Drive\EKON2014\AOP\Code\SalaryChanger\Win32\Debug\SalaryChangerDemo.exe
Please enter the password to change the salary: codingindelphi
No one should earn so little!
```

AOP in a Single Place

In the previous example, we were able to inject code into our methods via interception. However, the code would still have to be scattered around your classes, complicating your code and making it harder to maintain. AOP is supposed to be about the exact opposite, right? There has to be a better way.

The way that AOP becomes really powerful is when you can declare its functionality in just one place, but then easily distribute the functionality throughout your code with simple attributes. In this way, you can disentangle your Aspects, place them in their own classes, and then apply their power in a relatively unobtrusive way. Because they are implemented via attributes, it's also easy to turn them off if need be by merely commenting out one line of code.

This is going to happen in an interesting and unexpected way – via the Spring4D Container. Don't worry, I'll explain everything.

First, let's declare an interface:

```
ISalaryChanger = interface(IInvokable)
['{9BD8D6E6-EC69-4FBA-9BD3-13BD958CDBC2}']
  procedure ChangeSalary(const aNewSalary: Integer);
end;
```

That will be what we end up using when we want to get the functionality of protecting a change to the salary. It has the single method ChangeSalary that we'll use to do the work. Note, too, that it enhances the IInvokable interface.

> IInvokable is merely the IInterface interface with {$M+} attached to is. In other words, it has RTTI attached to it and those interfaces that enhance it.

Next, we'll declare an interceptor (This is actually identical to the one in the previous example):

```
TSalaryChangerInterceptor = class(TInterfacedObject, IInterceptor)
  procedure Intercept(const Invoker: IInvocation);
end;

procedure TSalaryChangerInterceptor.Intercept(const Invoker: IInvocation);
var
  LPassword: string;
begin
  if SameText(Invoker.Method.Name, 'ChangeSalary') then
  begin
    Write('Please enter the password to change the salary: ');
    ReadLn(LPassword);

    if LPassword = 'mcid' then
    begin
      Invoker.Proceed;
    end else
    begin
      Writeln('Sorry, you are not authorized to change salaries');
    end;
  end;
end;
```

This is the "wrapper" that we'll put around the actual functionality of changing the salary. It checks to see if our input matches our very complicated password, and if it does, it calls `Invoker.Proceed` to actually run the code that we've wrapped up with this Interceptor. If the password doesn't match, it gives a failure message. Notice, again, that you aren't even obligated to call the `Proceed` method if the logic of your Aspect dictates as much.

Finally, we'll actually declare our salary changer class:

```
TSalaryChanger = class(TInterfacedObject, ISalaryChanger)
  procedure ChangeSalary(const aNewSalary: Integer); virtual;
end;

procedure TSalaryChanger.ChangeSalary(const aNewSalary: Integer);
begin
  WriteLn('You changed the salary to ', aNewSalary);
end;
```

In our previous example, we manually created a `TProxyGenerator` to proxify the `TSalaryChanger` class. Even with the interception code, this required us to do that every time we wanted to include the Aspect in our code. We don't want to do that. We want to write the code once, and then easily apply that code in the places throughout our code base. And we can do that with some new features of the Spring4D container. Let's take a look.

First, we'll create a unit called `uRegister.pas` that we'll use to register our classes with the Spring4D container. In it, we'll put the following:

```
procedure RegisterWithContainer(aContainer: TContainer);
begin
  aContainer.RegisterType<IInterceptor, TSalaryChangerInterceptor>('SalaryChangerInterface');
  aContainer.RegisterType<TSalaryChanger>.InterceptedBy('SalaryChangerInterface');
end;
```

Let's look at the first line. It simply registers `TSalaryChangerInterceptor` as implementing the `IInterceptor` interface. It's a bit different from what you are familiar with if you read about it in *"Coding in Delphi"*. The first line is equivalent to (and a simplification of):

```
aContainer.RegisterType<TSalaryChangerIntercepter>.Implements<IInterceptor>('SalaryChangerInterface');
```

Instead, it merely takes the two types in question as parameterized types, rather than having the second call to `Implements`, and identifies that relationship by the name `SalaryChangerInterface`.

The second line is the really interesting new feature of the Spring4D Container. It registers the `TSalaryChanger` class as being intercepted by the class registration named `SalaryChangerInterface`. This single line of code is the one that will proxify `TSalaryChanger`. Thus, in registering the relationship between the class to be proxified and the class doing the proxification, you are able to, in a single place, declare that relationship. You can do this for as many classes as you like in the single location where you register your classes and interfaces with the Spring4D Container.

Thus, we can pull it all together in the `Main` procedure:

```
procedure Main;
var
  SalaryChanger: ISalaryChanger;
  LContainer: TContainer;
begin
  LContainer := TContainer.Create;
  try
    RegisterWithContainer(LContainer);
    LContainer.Build;
    SalaryChanger := LContainer.Resolve<ISalaryChanger>;
    SalaryChanger.ChangeSalary(75000);
  finally
    LContainer.Free;
  end;
end;
```

AOP via Attributes

That's all well and good – now we can place our Aspects anywhere with a single declaration in our Container registration section. But that isn't nearly as cool as tagging the actual class with an attribute. Attributes are local to the class being proxified and thus can be easily added or removed as desired or needed.

 If you aren't familiar with Attributes and how to create them, I'll refer you back to my previous book *Coding in Delphi* which has a whole chapter on the subject.

The first step to using attributes is to stop using the `InterceptedBy` method. So we can just comment that out in our example:

```
aContainer.RegisterType<TSalaryChanger>;  //.InterceptedBy('SalaryChangerInterface');
```

Next, we go to the class that is going to be proxified and add the `Interceptor` attribute, passing as a parameter the name of the registered Interceptor.

```
[Interceptor('SalaryChangerInterface')]
TSalaryChanger = class(TInterfacedObject, ISalaryChanger)
   procedure ChangeSalary(const aNewSalary: Integer); virtual;
end;
```

Note that for the compiler to recognize the `Interceptor` attribute, the `Spring.Container.Common` unit must be added to the uses clause of the unit where it is used. That is the unit that declares `InterceptorAttribute`. If you are running into trouble, and the attributes don't appear to be working as you like, remember to add that unit, because if you don't, the compiler will quietly give you a warning:

```
[dcc32 Warning] uSalaryChangerAttributeDemo.pas(25): W1025 Unsupported language feature: 'custom attribute'
```

and unless you notice it, you won't get any other signal that something is wrong.

 You can promote that warning to an error in your project compiler settings. I'd recommend doing so, because I can tell you from personal experience that it's easy (and very frustrating) to miss that warning and spend a lot of time wondering why things aren't working.

So now, you've basically replaced the call to the Spring4D Container with an attribute. And it works! Run the code, and when you try to change the salary, you are asked for a password. Enter the correct one, and you can make the requested salary change, and enter the wrong password and you are denied.

Now, anywhere you want to give the Advice of the `SalaryChanger` Aspect, you simply add the attribute and you are done. You can, for instance, create an aspect that logs the entry and exit of any method, call it the `TLoggingAspect`, register an interceptor for it, and then you can add logging to any method with an attribute. No more gumming up the works of your main methods with logging code – a simple attribute will do the trick.

Conclusion

Sadly, it's really easy to let your code concerns get scattered all over your code base and tangled up with your important, "real" code. However, with a little bit of work using Aspect-oriented Programming, interception, and the Spring4D container,you can wrangle that code into its own corral and easily place it in the exact places it is needed, either via interception or with attributes. In that way, you can separate peripheral concerns from the main body of your code. And if there is one thing we Delphi developers need to do it is to separate out our concerns.

Component Writing

Introduction

Okay, this chapter is a bit out of step with the rest of the book. It's about writing VCL components. It's about code, sure, but it's also about the VCL, about the IDE, and thus it doesn't exactly fit in with the rest of things. But my friend and fellow Delphi community member Bob Dawson suggested that there had been a lot of water under the bridge since TSmiley first appeared. It has also been a while since component development had been given a thorough going over, as far as I can tell.

I suppose this may be "old hat" to some folks, but here it is. I won't pretend to cover all of component building – I recommend Ray Konopka's book *Developing Custom Delphi 3 Components*[25] for that. This chapter will just cover good old TSmiley and the lessons found therein.

TSmiley – A Brief History

If I had a dollar for every time I've been teased about TSmiley, I could finance my own startup. I'm pretty sure that I'll never live it down.

TSmiley, for those of you that don't know or haven't heard (is that anyone?) it may be the very first third-party VCL component ever. I built it for the first time way back in the fall of 1994 when I was on the original Delphi 1 beta. The VCL was brand new and in development, and the notion of building a component in Pascal was so cool, I couldn't resist.

> Remember, those were the days when the only "components" were VBX controls, used in Visual Basic, but written in C++. Remember when Delphi actually could consume VBX controls? Remember how cool it was to write components in the same language you programmed in?

I couldn't wait to write components, and of course, half the battle is coming up with an idea – not always easy. Windows95 was brand new at that time, and so was MineSweeper. Remember the old school Minesweeper version, with the little smiley face up there? It was a fun game.

---

[25]https://www.amazon.com/gp/yourstore/home/?ie=UTF8&camp=1789&creative=390957&linkCode=ur2&tag=nickhodgeshomepa&linkId=TMT4IIAHYRZ2PPIV

Minesweeper – I lost this one and smiley is sad.

I used to play on the smallest size to see how fast I could clear the board. Anyhow – I thought it was cool that it has this little smiley on there that would make faces at you if you lost, etc. So I decided to build a Delphi-based version of this little control.

I built the thing with two purposes in mind: to learn how to build components and to create something that others could learn from. It started out as a descendant of TImage (made sense at the time — trust me) and I did a few things like override protected methods that fire events, trap and handle Windows messages, etc. I even figured out how to build a property editor for it.

I posted it on the Compuserve forums (remember those?), and the next thing I know, Charlie Calvert, David I, and the Borland gang were all using it in Delphi demos all over the world. It became a pretty good running joke (to this day, Xavier Pacheco still teases me about it. Let it go, X…) and I sort of ran with it. I had a press release, I said things like, "The usefulness of TSmiley cannot be measured," and I generally rode that handy little component to fame and glory. Okay, maybe not much fame and glory, but it was fun, and I do believe that folks learned a thing or two from it. I mean, the thing was basically useless (though I did have people tell me that they used it in production apps…) but it did show some interesting ways to build components.

 If you want to take a trip down memory lane, a very early version of the TSmiley page is available on the Wayback machine[26], as is a copy of the "press release[27]" that I wrote.

---

[26]http://web.archive.org/web/19990220044534/www.icss.net/~nhodges/smiley.htm
[27]http://web.archive.org/web/19990210172731/www.icss.net/~nhodges/SmileyRelease.htm

I took a look recently at the original code, and as you might imagine, it was really, really embarrassing. So I've updated it to be much, much cleaner, and to use more modern coding techniques. You can find the current version of `TSmiley` on BitBucket[28].

So let's take a look.

Start from Scratch

Runtime Functionality

So I thought the way to go here would be to start from scratch and build `TSmiley` from the ground up. So, to get things started, let's create a package and call it `Smiley.bpl` by naming the main package file `Smiley.dpk`. I won't go into packages any more than to say that they are specialized DLL's that can hold Delphi classes and components. (I'm guessing that you know what a Delphi package is by now...)

The `Smiley.bpl` will hold all the runtime code for `TSmiley` and nothing but runtime code. Later, we'll create another package to hold all the design-time code, and that design-time package will `require` the runtime package. We'll discuss why when that time comes.

To make things official, right click on the package and select "Options" and then select the "Description" item in the treeview on the right. From there, select "Runtime only" in the "Usage Options" group box. This will tell the compiler to make the package a runtime package – that is, one that can't be installed into the IDE but can be used by applications and other packages at runtime.

Next, add a new unit to the package and name it `uSmiley.pas` To that unit, add the following `uses` clause in the `interface` section:

```
uses
    Classes
  , Graphics
  , Controls
  ;
```

and in the `implementation` section add the following:

```
uses
    TypInfo
  , SysUtils
  ;
```

Those are the units that we'll end up using.

And to get things really started, let's declare `TSmiley`:

---

[28]https://bitbucket.org/NickHodges/nickdemocode/src/af47c608363c097156cb3688215e530f3c391727/TSmiley/?at=default

```
TSmiley = class(TGraphicControl)

end;
```

There it is. TSmiley is a descendant of TGraphicControl. TGraphicControl descends from TControl, which in turn descends from TComponent.

TComponent is the base class for – surprise! – all components. TComponent includes enough code to support a non-visual component. It contains a number of different types of plumbing code, but at it's very core, it provides the ability to give a component a Name, to be owned by other components, as well as the streaming needed to persist itself in a DFM file.

TControl adds the notion of size and location to TComponent, as well as mouse messages, visibility, color, a font, and hints, among other features.

If your component requires mouse or keyboard input, or the ability to contain other controls, you should use TWinControl. The TWinControl also descends from TControl, and is a proper window in the WinAPI sense: it has a window handle and participates in the window messaging system.

TGraphicControl augments TControl with one thing: a TCanvas and thus the ability to be drawn on. That's why TSmiley descends from it, because all we are going to do is draw on the component, and TGraphicControl is the lowest class in the VCL hierarchy that allows for drawing. TSmiley is nothing but bitmaps drawn on the screen, and thus is a natural fit for TGraphicControl.

Okay, now we have some house-keeping to do first. In the uSmiley unit, declare the following enumeration:

```
type
  TMood = (smHappy, smSad, smShades, smTongue, smIndifferent, smOoh, smFrazzled, smOutCold, smWink);
```

This enumeration represents the nine different "moods" that TSmiley can take on. In actuality, they represent nine different bitmaps. Now, I'm not going to ask you to draw your own bitmaps, but instead, I'll point you to the bitmaps that come with TSmiley on BitBucket. The link is here:

http://bit.ly/TSmileyGraphics

Download the bitmaps, and put them in a sub-directory called "graphics" under the directory where you are saving TSmiley. You should have nine bitmaps as a result. In order to make those bitmaps useful to TSmiley, we have to include them as Windows resources. We do that by simply adding them to the project via the Project Manager:

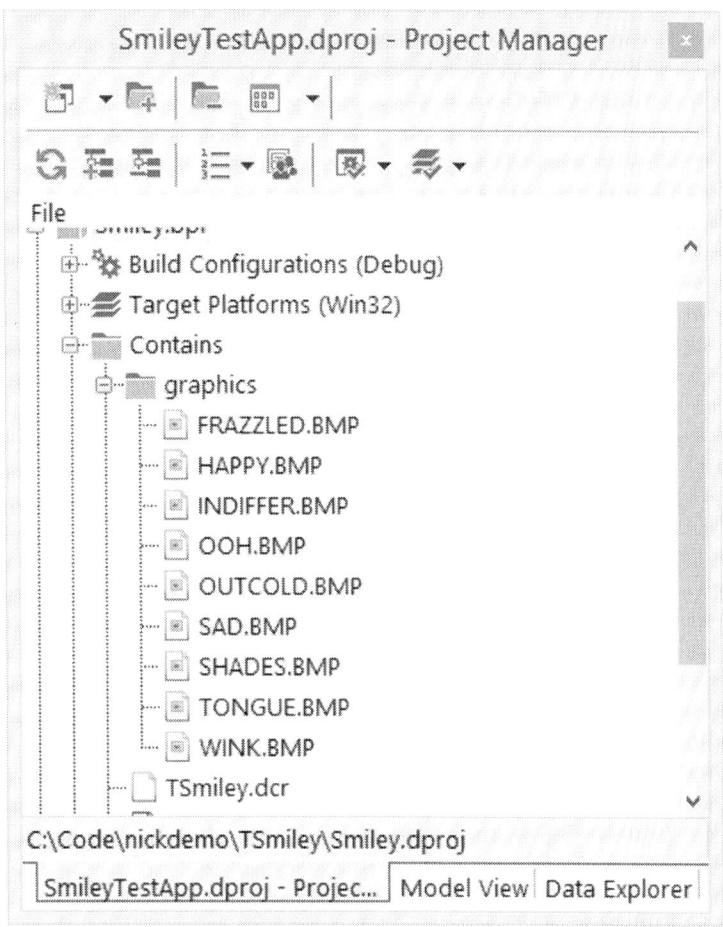

Next, create a new unit, call it uSmileyConsts.pas and make it look like this:

```
unit uSmileyConsts;

interface

resourcestring
  strHappy       = 'Happy';
  strSad         = 'Sad';
  strShades      = 'Shades';
  strTongue      = 'Tongue';
  strIndifferent = 'Indifferent';
  strOoh         = 'Ooh';
  strFrazzled    = 'Frazzled';
  strOutCold     = 'OutCold';
  strWink        = 'Wink';

  strHappyDesc       = 'Everything is really awesome with TSmiley';
  strSadDesc         = 'Something has upset TSmiley';
  strShadesDesc      = 'TSmiley is feeling pretty dang cool';
  strTongueDesc      = 'TSmiley is feeling quite smug indeed';
  strIndifferentDesc = 'TSmiley couldn''t care less';
  strOohDesc         = 'TSmiley is impressed and intrigued';
```

```
  strFrazzledDesc        = 'TSmiley is pretty frazzled';
  strOutColdDesc         = 'Someone has hit TSmiley in the head with a blunt instrument of some sort';
  strWinkDesc            = 'TSmiley is feeling pretty coy';

const
  HintStringTemplate = '%s|%s';
  MaxHeight = 26;
  MaxWidth = 26;

implementation

end.
```

This unit contains nothing but constants, specifically the strings for the short hint and the long hint for each of the different moods that TSmiley will show. I like to keep my constants in a separate unit so as not to clutter up my code. Note that they are declared as resourcestring making it easier to translate TSmiley's hints into another language other than English.

Next up, let's create an array that makes those strings easy to access based on the TMood enumeration:

```
type
  TMoodStrings: array [TMood] of string = (strHappy, strSad, strShades, strTongue,
                                           strIndifferent, strOoh, strFrazzled,
                                           strOutCold, strWink);
```

That should go into the uSmiley.pas unit. And oh, let's put uSmileyConsts in the uses clause of uSmiley.pas.

Let's do the same for the long descriptions:

```
type
  TMoodDescriptions: array [TMood] of string = (strHappyDesc, strSadDesc, strShadesDesc,
                                                strTongueDesc, strIndifferentDesc, strOohDesc,
                                                strFrazzledDesc, strOutColdDesc, strWinkDesc);
```

That should get most of the preliminary, house-keeping type stuff out of the way. Now we are ready to start giving some functionality to our pal TSmiley.

The first thing we'll do is to provide a constructor and a destructor for TSmiley and get things initialized and properly cleaned up. The constructor will override the TComponent constructor as follows:

```
public
  constructor Create(AOwner: TComponent); override;
```

The constructor will initialize things for TSmiley, but first we'll need some things to initialize.

Here's a new declaration for TSmiley that will get things rolling:

```
TSmiley = class(TGraphicControl)
private
  FMood: TMood;
  FFace: TBitmap;
  procedure SetBitmap;
  procedure SetSmileyHint;
  procedure SetupSmiley;
public
  constructor Create(aOwner: TComponent); override;
  destructor Destroy; override;
  class procedure GetMoodBitmap(aBitmap: TBitmap; aMood: TMood);
end;


constructor TSmiley.Create(aOwner: TComponent);
begin
  inherited Create(AOwner);
  FMood := smHappy;
  FFace := TBitmap.Create;
  Self.Height := MaxHeight;
  Self.Width := MaxWidth;
  SetupSmiley;
end;
```

First, we call the inherited `constructor`, passing the owner to the parent component. The owner of a component is responsible for holding on to a reference to the component and destroying it if the owner itself is destroyed.

Next, we set the initial mood – stored in `FMood` – to the happy face. Then, we create a `TBitmap`, stored in `FFace`, to hold the actual bitmap that will be displayed. Then, we set the `Height` and `Width` of the component. Later, we'll ensure that no one can size the component to something other than its default size.

There's one other thing to do: call `SetupSmiley`. Here's the declaration for it:

```
procedure TSmiley.SetupSmiley;
begin
  SetBitmap;
  SetSmileyHint;
end;
```

It in turn calls two methods, which are declared below:

```
procedure TSmiley.SetBitmap;
begin
  GetMoodBitmap(FFace, FMood);
  Invalidate;
end;

procedure TSmiley.SetSmileyHint;
begin
  Hint := Format(HintStringTemplate, [TMoodStrings[FMood], TMoodDescriptions[FMood]]);
end;
```

SetBitmap in turn calls GetMoodBitmap which is a class method:

```
class procedure GetMoodBitmap(aBitmap: TBitmap; aMood: TMood);
```

A class method is a method that can be called both on the class itself as well as on an instance of the class. In this way, we provide sort of a "TSmiley API" by letting the class get a specific bitmap on request without having to create an instance of TSmiley. We'll be adding a couple of other items to the API in a bit. Here is its implementation:

```
class procedure TSmiley.GetMoodBitmap(aBitmap: TBitmap; aMood: TMood);
var
  TempName: string;
begin
  if aBitmap = nil then
  begin
    raise ESmileyException.Create('You can''t pass a nil bitmap to TSmiley.GetMoodBitmap');
  end;
  begin
    TempName := UpperCase(GetEnumName(TypeInfo(TMood), Ord(aMood)));
    aBitmap.LoadFromResourceName(hInstance, TempName);
  end;
end;
```

This is an interesting bit of code. First, it uses a Guard clause to refuse to accept a nil bitmap. Then, it grabs the name of the mood enumeration value using a call to GetEnumName, which is found in the TypInfo unit. Once it does that, it it uses the TBitmap.LoadFromResourceName method to load the correct bitmap out of the resources of the executable.

SetBitmap uses FFace and fills it with the bitmap that corresponds to the FMood field, whose initial value is smHappy. Thus, TSmiley starts out happy by default. It then calls Invalidate, which tells the component that it needs to be repainted. We'll get to the painting in a minute.

SetSmileyHint does exactly what its name implies – it sets both the long and short hints for TSmiley. Delphi handles hints by using a single string for both the long and short hints. They are separated by a "pipe" character (|), with the short hint coming first and the long hint following. The short hint is displayed when the mouse hovers over the component if its ShowHint property is set to true.

And of course, after all that setup, we want to make sure that we clean up after ourselves, so we declare a destructor as follows:

```
destructor TSmiley.Destroy;
begin
  FFace.Free;
  inherited Destroy;
end;
```

This merely calls `Free` on the bitmap object and then calls the inherited destructor. Not much to explain, other than it is always important to clean up after yourself.

Okay, we are close to having something that actually will work. We have one last thing to do before we can have the minimum up and running, and that is to implement a `Paint` method.

So now our `TSmiley` declaration looks like this:

```
TSmiley = class(TGraphicControl)
private
  FMood: TMood;
  FFace: TBitmap;
  procedure SetBitmap;
  procedure SetSmileyHint;
  procedure SetupSmiley;
protected
  procedure Paint; override;
public
  constructor Create(aOwner: TComponent); override;
  destructor Destroy; override;
  class procedure GetMoodBitmap(aBitmap: TBitmap; aMood: TMood);
end;
```

Notice the addition of the `Paint` method in the `protected` section of the class declaration. Also notice that it is overridden, because it is `virtual` in `TGraphicControl`. Here's the implementation:

```
procedure TSmiley.Paint;
begin
  inherited;
  Canvas.Draw(0, 0, FFace);
end;
```

First it calls the inherited method, even though `TGraphicControl.Paint` doesn't do anything. I think it is a good habit to call `inherited` unless you have a really good reason not to. Next, it simply draws the bitmap on the canvas in the upper left corner. All the bitmaps are 26x26, and so it will fit perfectly with the control which is fixed at that same height.

At this point, we have the functionality – but not the infrastructure – for actually painting a bitmap on the component at runtime. We'll continue on providing runtime functionality before we turn our attention to the design-time aspects of the control.

Right now, `TSmiley`'s mood is stuck on `smHappy`. Let's allow for that mood to change by providing a property called `Mood`. Our declaration will now look like this:

```
TSmiley = class(TGraphicControl)
private
  FMood: TMood;
  FFace: TBitmap;
  procedure SetBitmap;
  procedure SetMood(aNewMood: TMood)
  procedure SetSmileyHint;
  procedure SetupSmiley;
protected
  procedure Paint; override;
public
  constructor Create(aOwner: TComponent); override;
  destructor Destroy; override;
  class procedure GetMoodBitmap(aBitmap: TBitmap; aMood: TMood);
published
  property Mood: TMood read FMood write SetMood;
end;
```

The property reads the internal field when its value is requested, but when we want to set a new value, it uses SetMood, which is declared as follows:

```
procedure TSmiley.SetMood(aNewMood: TMood);
begin
  FMood := aNewMood;
  SetupSmiley;
end;
```

You should be able to figure out what this does – it changes the internal field and calls SetupSmiley which you've seen before. This code allows you to change the mood both at runtime and design-time. It works at design-time because the property is published, meaning it will show up in the Object Inspector via runtime type information (RTTI) as well as being streamed to and from the DFM file. Since the property is an enumeration, you can select any of its values at design-time. Later in the chapter, we'll create a property editor for Mood that allows you to choose a new mood visually.

Okay, so we can change the mood programmatically and in the Object Inspector. We've seen how to override the Paint method to paint whatever we want on a TGraphicControl. But there's more functionality that we can provide. How about we let you set a face for TSmiley that will appear when you click on the component? Yeah, that's a good idea, right? Okay, let's do it.

First, we need to declare a few new things:

```
TSmiley = class(TGraphicControl)
private
  FMood: TMood;
  FOldMood: TMood;
  FClicking: Boolean;
  FClickMood: TMood;
  FFace: TBitmap;
  procedure SetBitmap;
  procedure SetMood(aNewMood: TMood)
  procedure SetSmileyHint;
  procedure SetClickMood(const Value: TMood);
  procedure SetupSmiley;
protected
  procedure Paint; override;
  procedure MouseDown(Button: TMouseButton; Shift: TShiftState; X, Y: Integer); override;
  procedure MouseUp(Button: TMouseButton; Shift: TShiftState; X, Y: Integer); override;
public
  constructor Create(aOwner: TComponent); override;
  destructor Destroy; override;
  class procedure GetMoodBitmap(aBitmap: TBitmap; aMood: TMood);
published
  property Mood: TMood read FMood write SetMood;
  property ClickMood: TMood read FClickMood write SetClickMood;
end;
```

Note the new fields that will allow us to assign a value to the mood that will be shown when the component is clicked, as well as one that will keep track of the old field. FClicking will keep track of the fact that the component is being clicked on. We have also added a ClickMood property in the published section that will allow you to set the ClickMood property in the Object Inspector (and later with a visual property editor).

In addition, we've overridden two more methods, this time from TControl, that get fired when the mouse goes down on the control and when it goes back up. These are the events that will fire when we click on TSmiley and they'll handle painting the "click face" for the component.

 The original TSmiley changed the mood when clicked by capturing the WM_LBUTTONDOWN and WM_LBUTTONUP messages. This worked, but it was a bit of a wasted effort as TControl already provides two virtual methods that are fired by those messages. Simply overriding them is a more efficient and proper way to provide the functionality.

Those two methods are implemented as follows:

```
procedure TSmiley.MouseDown(Button: TMouseButton; Shift: TShiftState; X, Y: Integer);
begin
  inherited MouseDown(Button, Shift, X, Y);
  FOldMood := Mood;
  FClicking := True;
  SetMood(ClickMood);
end;

procedure TSmiley.MouseUp(Button: TMouseButton; Shift: TShiftState; X, Y: Integer);
begin
  inherited MouseUp(Button, Shift, X, Y);
  SetMood(FOldMood);
  FClicking := False;
end;
```

The code is pretty straight-forward. The component first calls inherited, then keeps track of its "old" mood, displays the ClickMood when the mouse goes down, and restores the old mood when the mouse goes back up. Along the way, it sets the FClicking field to True and then False again. We'll see why it does that in a minute.

Okay, so now TSmiley can change his face if you click on him, and you can change his mood as desired. But what if you want to do something when his mood does change? The VCL has a notion of events, and we can create an event when TSmiley's mood changes.

If we want to "fire" an event whenever the Mood property changes, we'll want to know what that new mood is. Thus, we'll need to declare our own event type:

```
type
  TMoodChangeEvent = procedure(Sender: TObject; NewMood: TMood) of object;
```

This event follows the typical VCL pattern by having Sender as the first parameter. This will be the object that itself fires the event. The second parameter will pass the new mood that is being set. This way you can write code in an event handler to execute when the mood changes. This is done as follows:

```
TSmiley = class(TGraphicControl)
private
  FMood: TMood;
  FOldMood: TMood;
  FClicking: Boolean;
  FClickMood: TMood;
  FOnMoodChange: TMoodChange;
  FFace: TBitmap;
  procedure SetBitmap;
  procedure SetMood(NewMood: TMood)
  procedure SetSmileyHint;
  procedure SetupSmiley;
protected
  procedure DoMoodChange; virtual;
  procedure Paint; override;
  procedure MouseDown(Button: TMouseButton; Shift: TShiftState; X, Y: Integer); override;
  procedure MouseUp(Button: TMouseButton; Shift: TShiftState; X, Y: Integer); override;
public
```

```
  constructor Create(aOwner: TComponent); override;
  destructor Destroy; override;
  class procedure GetMoodBitmap(aBitmap: TBitmap; aMood: TMood);
published
  property Mood: TMood read FMood write SetMood;
  property ClickMood: TMood read FClickMood write SetClickMood;
  property OnMoodChange: TMoodChangeEvent read FOnMoodChange write FOnMoodChange;
end;
```

Note that we've added a field value FOnMoodChange which is of type TMoodChangeEvent to hold a reference to the event handler that a user will add. We've declared a property OnMoodChange as published, to put the event in the Object Inspector and allow users to add that event handler at design-time.

We've also declared a method called DoMoodChange which is declared as follows:

```
procedure TSmiley.DoMoodChange;
begin
  if Assigned(FOnMoodChange) and (not FClicking) then
  begin
    FOnMoodChange(Self, FMood);
  end;
end;
```

Again, this is standard VCL code. If there is an event handler assigned to FOnMoodChange, then we call the code that the user has attached. There's one more caveat – we can't be in the "Clicking" mode. Remember when we set FClicking to True when the mouse went down? We don't want the OnMoodChange event firing as a result of the mood changes that takes place with the click. Otherwise, we're happy to run the user's code by calling the event, passing in Self and the new mood being set.

There's one more change to make it all work. We need to actually call DoMoodChange when the mood changes. To do that, we'll add it to the SetMood method:

```
procedure TSmiley.SetMood(aNewMood: TMood);
begin
  FMood := aNewMood;
  DoMoodChange;
  SetupSmiley;
end;
```

Now when the Mood property is changed, the OnMoodChange event is fired.

 It is a good practice to have your events fired in a stand alone, virtual method. That way, you allow descendant components to easily augment the behavior if desired. If you have an event called OnMoodChange, it's good to have a DoMoodChange method that is virtual and does nothing more than fire the event.

Remember the API stuff I mentioned before? Well, here are the other two API class methods and their implementations. I don't think they require any discussion as they are pretty self-explanatory.

```
public
  class function GetMoodName(aMood: TMood): string;
  class function GetMoodDescription(aMood: TMood): string;

  class function TSmiley.GetMoodDescription(aMood: TMood): string;
  begin
    Result := TMoodDescriptions[aMood];
  end;

  class function TSmiley.GetMoodName(aMood: TMood): string;
  begin
    Result := TMoodStrings[aMood];
  end;
```

TSmiley's bitmaps are all fixed in size, and so we'd like TSmiley to be fixed in size as well. In order to do that, we can override the ConstrainedResize method found in TControl. This method is called whenever the control is resized, and it lets you set the minimum and maximum size that the control can be set to. Thus, we'll just use the four var parameters it provides and constrain TSmiley to one fixed size:

```
procedure TSmiley.ConstrainedResize(var MinWidth, MinHeight, MaxWidth, MaxHeight: Integer);
begin
  MinWidth := cMaxWidth;
  MaxWidth := cMaxWidth;
  MinHeight := cMaxHeight;
  MaxHeight := cMaxHeight;
end;
```

We have one more public method to do – the Increment method. Increment is declared as follows:

```
procedure TSmiley.Increment;
begin
  if FMood = High(TMood) then
  begin
    FMood := Low(TMood)
  end else
  begin
    Inc(FMood);
  end;
  SetMood(FMood);
end;
```

All it does is move the Mood property to the next mood in the enumeration. If it reaches the end, it rolls around back to the beginning. Nothing important, but it just shows another way to change the Mood property in code. At the end, it calls SetMood to ensure that the new graphic is drawn and the OnMoodChange event is fired.

One further thing that we should do. TComponent, TControl, and TGraphicControl all have events that aren't published. They aren't published in order to give component creators more control over what events show up in the Object Inspector. But we'd like TSmiley to be able to handle a number of these events, so we add the following to the published section of our declaration:

```
property OnClick;
property OnContextPopup;
property OnDblClick;
property OnDragDrop;
property OnDragOver;
property OnEndDock;
property OnEndDrag;
property OnGesture;
property OnMouseActivate;
property OnMouseDown;
property OnMouseMove;
property OnMouseUp;
property OnMouseEnter;
property OnMouseLeave;
property OnStartDock;
property OnStartDrag;
```

Now, `TSmiley` will allow the user to provide any event handlers for those events that they want.

So that is all the runtime code. You could, if you wanted, create a `TSmiley` in code like follows (assuming you are writing this code in a method of a `TForm`):

```
MySmiley := TSmiley.Create(Self);
MySmiley.Parent := Self;
```

and the good old happy faced `TSmiley` will appear. Simple as pie.

However, that's not really how it should work. You want to be able to drag-n-drop the component from the Tool Palette. Well, that's where the design-time package comes in.

Design-time Functionality

Okay, so that's the runtime stuff. We put it all in a runtime package. Now it is time to take a look at the design-time side of things.

First, create a new package, and call it `dclSmiley.bpl` "dcl" is a long-time Delphi convention that stands for "Design-time Component Library".

Registering TSmiley

First thing to do for a design-time package is to set its `Requires` clause. In this case, we require the following other packages:

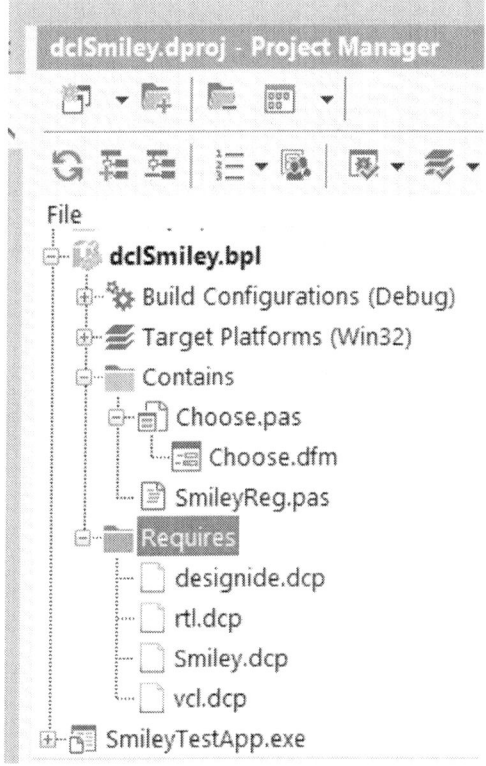

Next, add a new unit to the package and call it `SmileyReg.pas`. Make it look like this:

```
unit SmileyReg;

interface

uses
  Classes,
  uSmiley,
  Choose,
  DesignEditors,
  DesignIntf;

procedure Register;

implementation

procedure Register;
begin
  RegisterComponents('Custom', [TSmiley]);
  RegisterPropertyEditor(TypeInfo(TMood), TSmiley, '', TMoodProperty);
end;

end.
```

There are two things going on here. First, we declare a method in the interface section called `Register`. And believe it or not, that method name is case sensitive because of the need to work with C++Builder. The procedure does two things. First, it registers TSmiley with the IDE, and then it registers a Property Editor for the TMood property of the TSmiley component.

The call to RegisterComponents is quite simple. The first parameter is a string which names the tab in the Tool Palette under which the passed components will be registered. The second parameter is an open array of class types of components that will be registered.

A registered component is installed into the Tool Palette and available at design-time. You can drag-n-drop it onto a form and then set its properties via the Object Inspector.

In the case of the code above, we do that for TSmiley. When the design-time package is registered with the IDE, the IDE will automatically call the Register method and install the components listed therein. It will install the Property Editors registered there as well.

In order to give TSmiley a proper bitmap in the Tool Palette, you need to include in the project a *.DCR file that contains a single bitmap. A *.DCR file is a renamed *.RES file that contains a single bitmap resource that will be displayed in the Tool Palette. The TSmiley project has a DCR file included with it.

Building a Property Editor

Let's build a Property Editor for the TSmiley.Mood property. A property editor is a special kind of component that is installed into the Object Inspector and allows you to edit a given property type. You already use property editors – for instance, if you press the little button with an ellipse in it next to a Color property, a window will pop up allowing you to pick a color with your mouse. When you choose an enumeration in the Object Inspector, you are using a property editor for enumerations.

To create the form for our Mood property editor, take the following steps:

1. Create a new VCL form in the dclSmiley.bpl package. Call it TChooseDlg. Name the unit "frmChoose".
2. Drop a button on the form and set its Caption to "Ok".
3. Drop a TListView on the form. Right click on it and select "Column Editor".
4. Add two columns with the captions of "Smiley Type" and "Description".
5. Drop a TImageList on the form. Name it "SmileyImageList".

The form should end up looking something like this:

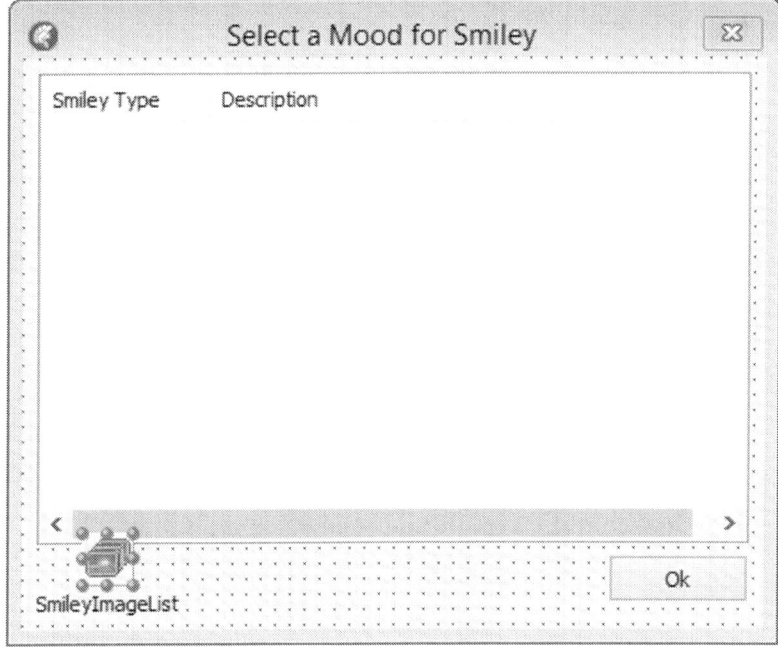

Now for some code. First, double click on the form and add the following to the OnCreate event handler:

```
procedure TChooseDlg.FormCreate(Sender: TObject);
begin
  FillUpListView;
  SetConstraints;
end;
```

This handler has two method calls. Those methods are declared below:

```
procedure TChooseDlg.SetConstraints;
begin
  Constraints.MinHeight := Height;
  Constraints.MinWidth := Width;
end;

procedure TChooseDlg.FillUpListView;
var
  TempItem: TListItem;
  i: integer;
  TempName: string;
  TempDescription: string;
begin
  PopulateImageList;
  for i := Ord( low(TMood)) to Ord( high(TMood)) do
  begin
    TempItem := SmileyListView.Items.Add;
    TempName := TSmiley.GetMoodName(TMood(i));
    TempItem.Caption := TempName;
```

```
      TempDescription := TSmiley.GetMoodDescription(TMood(i));
      TempItem.SubItems.Add(TempDescription);
      TempItem.ImageIndex := i;
      TempItem.Data := Pointer(i);
    end;
end;
```

`PopulateImageList` is declared as follows:

```
procedure TChooseDlg.PopulateImageList;
var
  TempMood: TMood;
  TempBitmap: TBitmap;
  TempName: string;
begin
  SmileyImageList.Height := MaxHeight;
  SmileyImageList.Width := MaxWidth;
  TempBitmap := TBitmap.Create;
  try
    for TempMood := Low(TMood) to High(TMood) do
    begin
      TempName := UpperCase(GetEnumName(TypeInfo(TMood), Ord(TempMood)));
      TSmiley.GetMoodBitmap(TempBitmap, TempMood);
      SmileyImageList.Add(TempBitmap, nil);
    end;
  finally
    TempBitmap.Free;
  end;
end;
```

`SetContraints` merely sets the minimum `Width` and `Height` of the dialog so a user can't shrink it down so small it can't function.

The `FillupListView` method is a bit more complex. It iterates over all the moods and creates a `TListItem` for each of them. It then adds the picture and the description to the listview. It keeps track of the index of each item so that you can choose one and have a reference after the `Ok` button is pressed. Basically it displays all the moods with their long descriptions and allows you to pick a mood.

The design is flexible in that if you choose to add another mood to `TSmiley`, you don't have to change the code in the dialog.

Adding the Dialog as a Property Editor

So far all we have done is create a simple dialog. What we need to do is to add the code to turn it into a property editor. Let's do that.

The first thing we need to do is to include two units in our uses clause: `DesignEditors` and `DesignIntf`. These are two units that only have any meaning in design-time packages. The `DesignIntf` unit contains all the interfaces you need to "talk" to the IDE, as well as `TBasePropertyEditor`. The `DesignEditors` unit contains all the code defining the standard property editors, starting with `TPropertyEditor`.

The standard property editor we are interested in is `TEnumPropertyEditor`. By default, this property editor provides a dropdown list of all the members of a given enumeration. However, we want to provide the `TChooseDlg` form that we created above as the property editor for the `TMood` property. This is done as follows:

```
TMoodProperty = class(TEnumProperty)
    function GetAttributes: TPropertyAttributes; override;
    procedure Edit; override;
  end;
```

We declare TMoodProperty which overrides two of the methods on TEnumProperty. The first is GetAttributes which is a function that returns TPropertyAttributes which is a set of TPropertyAttribute. We need to tell the IDE that our property editor is going to be a dialog box, so its implementation looks like this:

```
function TMoodProperty.GetAttributes: TPropertyAttributes;
begin
  Result := [paDialog];
end;
```

Pretty simple.

The other method, Edit is a bit more complicated. It is where we actually create the dialog and use it to choose a new mood.

```
procedure TMoodProperty.Edit;
var
  ChooseDlg: TChooseDlg;
begin
  ChooseDlg := TChooseDlg.Create(Application);
  try
    ChooseDlg.Mood := TMood(GetOrdValue);
    ChooseDlg.ShowModal;
    SetOrdValue(Ord(ChooseDlg.Mood));
  finally
    ChooseDlg.Free
  end;
end;
```

It's pretty straightforward. We create an instance of the dialog (passing Application as the owner), and then set the selected mood to the current value of the Mood property. That is done by using the GetOrdValue of the TPropertyEditor class itself. The dialog is then shown modally, and when it returns, its Mood property is used to set the new value via SetOrdValue, another method inherited from TPropertyEditor.

That's it for the property editor side of things.

 It's important to separate out the design-time code from the runtime code. The proper way to set up a component is to do as we have done - create two packages: one that holds only the runtime code, and a design-time package that requires the runtime package and provides all the design-time support for the component. This way, if your users decide to compile their application with packages, they don't have to carry along design-time code that need not be part of a regular application.

The property editor is registered as follows:

```
RegisterPropertyEditor(TypeInfo(TMood), TSmiley, '', TMoodProperty);
```

The call tells the IDE the `TypeInfo` for the type that the property editor will be used with, which component the editor should be registered against, and the property editor class that should be used to manage the property in the Object Inspector. The IDE then knows to provide the little button with an ellipse for the `TMood` property on `TSmiley`, and when pressed, we end up with the following:

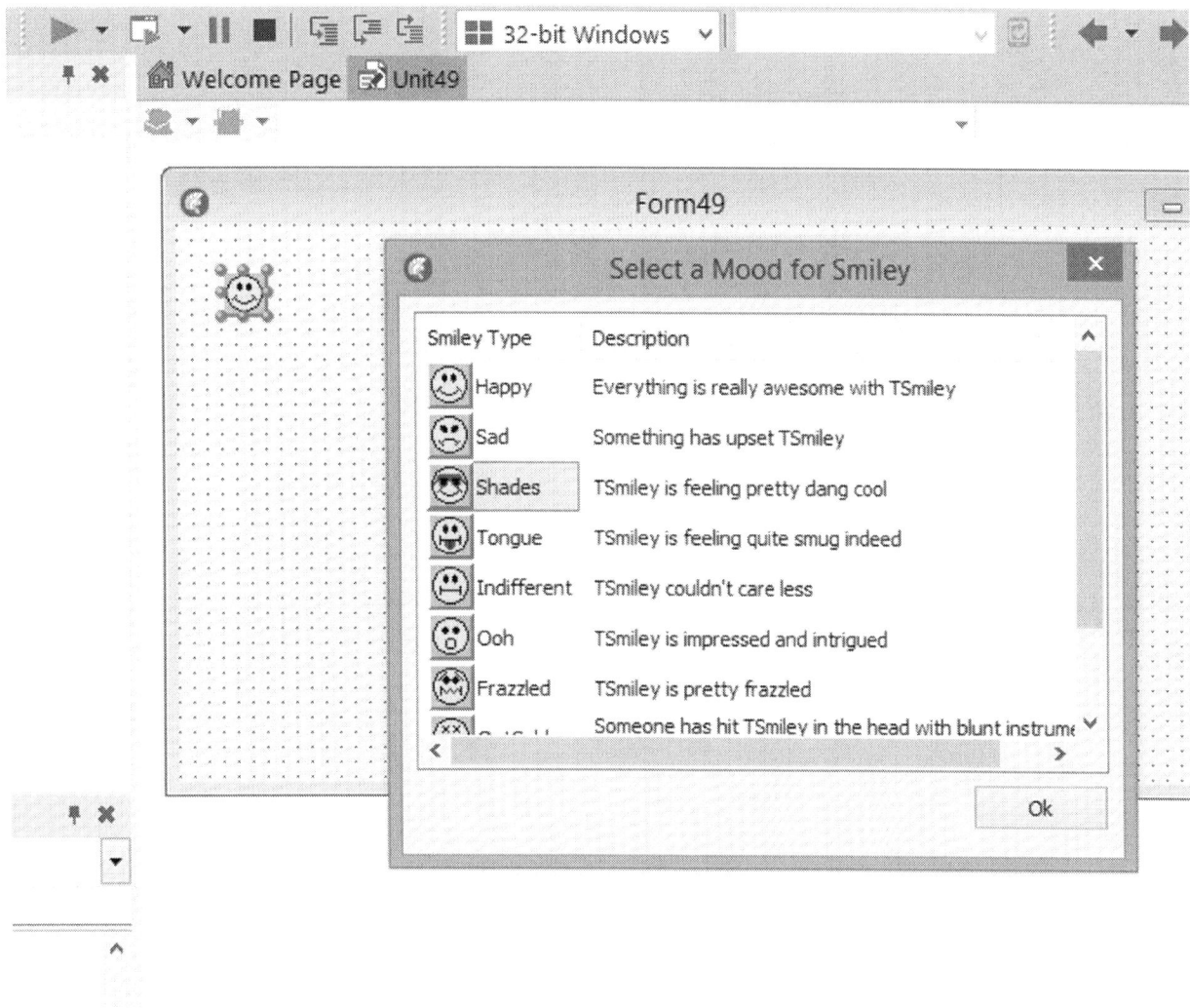

This makes for a much nicer user experience than merely choosing from a dropdown box.

A Demo App to Show It All Off

Testing your components can be a bit tricky. If they are buggy and you test them by installing them into the IDE and then dropping them on a form, they can bring the entire IDE down. Your component, when registered, is running in the IDE itself, and a rogue component can crash the IDE. Thus, the best way to test your component is to create it at runtime. That's what I've done, and you can find the test application as part of the code for TSmiley on BitBucket.

Here's a look at the application in action:

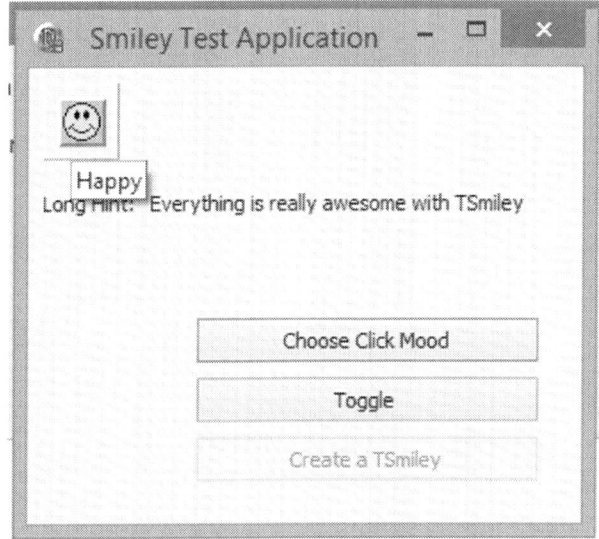

I won't go over the entire application here, but just point out how to create a component at runtime. Here's the code to do so:

```
MySmiley := TSmiley.Create(Panel1);

// Centers the TSmiley in the Panel
MySmiley.Left := Panel1.ClientRect.CenterPoint.X - (MySmiley.Width div 2);
MySmiley.Top := Panel1.ClientRect.CenterPoint.Y - (MySmiley.Height div 2);

MySmiley.Parent := Panel1;
```

The first thing of course is to call `Create`. In this case, we'll pass `Panel1` as the owner, since in the application places the smiley on a panel. The owner of a component is itself a component and is responsible for managing the lifetime of all the components that it owns. In this case, the panel will destroy the smiley when it is destroyed (The panel is owned by the form with will in turn destroy the panel when the form itself is freed).

We then have some code that centers the smiley on the panel. The final line is important – it sets the `Parent` to the panel as well. The `Parent` of a component is the place where the component will be painted. It's important when creating a component at runtime to set the `Parent` property, or your component will not appear anywhere. If you can't get your component to appear, make sure you've set its `Parent` property.

Conclusion

Well, there you have it: `TSmiley` explained. Component Development may be a bit of a lost art in the blogs and books. Again, I do recommend Ray Konopka's book. Don't be put off by the "Delphi 3" in the title – almost all of what is in there is still relevant. Components are really at the heart of Delphi's power, and knowing how to build them can greatly enhance your applications. Hopefully the "blast from the past" of `TSmiley` will help you remember what components can do.

Appendix A: Resources

Source Control

Most of the frameworks I recommend in the book are obtained via public source control repositories. Here are some links to get you started if you aren't familiar with Git, Mercurial, or Subversion.

Subversion

Subversion is the popular, server-based follow-on to CVS. A server-based source control system means that the repository is held centrally on a server, and clients make read and write requests to that central repository. Subversion has been popular for many years and remains so. However, I recommend that you use one of the distributed VCS's like Git or Mercurial when possible.

In any event, here are the particulars for Subversion:

- Download Subversion at: https://subversion.apache.org/[29]
- Documentation can be referenced at: https://subversion.apache.org/docs/[30]

Git

Git is a distributed version control system, originally written by Linus Torvalds to support Linux development.

- Git can be downloaded here: http://git-scm.com/downloads[31]
- A nice, step-by-step tutorial that teaches Git Basics: http://gitimmersion.com/[32]
- An excellent, online book teaching Git: http://git-scm.com/book/en/[33]

Mercurial

Mercurial (hg) is another popular distributed version control system.

- Mercurial can be downloaded here: http://mercurial.selenic.com/wiki/Download[34]
- A simple and well-done tutorial for Mercurial is hginit.com[35]. It's specifically designed for people moving to a distributed source control system from a server-based world.
- The Mercurial team has a nice tutorial: http://mercurial.selenic.com/wiki/Tutorial[36]

---

[29]https://subversion.apache.org/
[30]https://subversion.apache.org/docs/
[31]http://git-scm.com/downloads
[32]http://gitimmersion.com/
[33]http://git-scm.com/book/en/
[34]http://mercurial.selenic.com/wiki/Download
[35]http://hginit.com
[36]http://mercurial.selenic.com/wiki/Tutorial

Patterns

Resources for software design patterns are many. Here are a few that I found useful:

- Website: Delphi Patterns Blog[37]
- Website: http://sourcemaking.com/design_patterns[38]
- Book: Design Patterns: Elements of Reusable Object-Oriented Software by Gamma, Helm, Johnson, and Vlissides[39]
- Book: Head First Design Patterns by Freeman, Bates, Sierra, and Robson[40]

---

[37]http://delphipatterns.blog.com/

[38]http://sourcemaking.com/design_patterns

[39]http://www.amazon.com/gp/product/0201633612/ref=as_li_tl?ie=UTF8&camp=1789&creative=390957&creativeASIN=0201633612&linkCode=as2&tag=nickhodgeshomepa&linkId=762DLB7YLIWUSXDZ

[40]http://www.amazon.com/gp/product/0596007124/ref=as_li_tl?ie=UTF8&camp=1789&creative=390957&creativeASIN=0596007124&linkCode=as2&tag=nickhodgeshomepa&linkId=6WHBJGS6F7FPDBTK

Appendix B: Duck Typing

I originally had this as a chapter in the main part of the book. However, my reviewers came to the conclusion that while duck-typing is cool, it's not something to be too terribly encouraged in Delphi. But it is an interesting topic, and I had the chapter written. Therefore, as a compromise, I've put the chapter here in the Appendix. Read it with all of that in mind.

Introduction

If it looks like a duck, swims like a duck, and quacks like a duck, then it probably is a duck.

We've all read this quote. Its origin is somewhat unclear[41], but the point remains the same.

The phrase has made it into the computer science world as "duck typing" – the notion that semantics and situation will determine the way a given variable behaves. That is, an object will be utilized based on what it can do rather than what it is. This seems quite counter to Delphi's notion of strong-typing, but as you'll see, it can have its advantages.

Duck typing allows for an object to be passed to a method as long as that object supports what the method expects. In other words, if the method expects the object to have aMakeToast method, you can pass any class to it that has a `MakeToast` method, even if it isn't a toaster. The object can be of any type at all as long as it supports the `MakeToast` method. Now this might be a strange notion to us die-hard Delphi developers, but the Ruby folks and users of other dynamically-typed languages are doing all kinds of duck-typing, so there has to be something to it, right?

What is Going on Here?

So, how does this all work in Delphi, a strongly-typed language? Consider these simple types:

```
TDuck = class
  procedure Quack;
end;

TGoose = class
  procedure Honk;
end;
```

Normally, in Delphi, you have to pass a specific type to a method:

---

[41]http://en.wikipedia.org/wiki/Duck_test

```
procedure Quack(aDuck: TDuck);
begin
  aDuck.Quack;
end;
```

If you try to pass a `TGoose` to that function, the compiler will refuse to accept it.

The first step towards Duck Typing in Delphi would be interfaces. You can declare the following:

```
type
  IQuackable = interface
    function Quack;
  end;

procedure Quack(aQuacker: IQuackable);
begin
  aQuacker.Quack;
end;
```

In this case, you can use any class to implement the interface `IQuackable` and it will respond correctly when passed to the `Quack` procedure. However, that still requires that you implement the given interface to make a Goose "quackable" and you have to pass a class that implements that interface.

Wouldn't it be great if there were a way to make that connection automatically? Wouldn't it be nice if sometimes you could just pass anything that has a `Quack` method to a procedure and have it "just work"? Sure it would. Duck Typing will allow any class that has a `Quack` method to be passed to the procedure and have it work. How does that happen?

Well, in the Delphi community there are two main libraries that make that work: DSharp and DuckDuck-Delphi.

Duck Typing with DSharp

The DSharp Framework by Stefan Glienke contains a class that allows you to do duck typing on interfaces. (You can find out more about DSharp in Appendix A.) Let's take a look at that. Here's the declaration:

```
type
  Duck<T: IInterface> = record
  private
    FInstance: T;
    function GetInstance: TObject;
    procedure SetInstance(const Value: TObject);
  public
    class operator Implicit(const Value: TObject): Duck<T>;
    class operator Implicit(const Value: Duck<T>): T;

    property Instance: TObject read GetInstance write SetInstance;
  end;
```

The Duck type is a record that takes any interface as a parameterized type. It has two class operators and a single property. Basically, it does only one thing: become something else. The class operators are both of type Implicit, meaning you can "silently" turn any object into a Duck<T>, as well as turn any Duck<T> into an instance of type T (you can investigate the details of exactly how that happens yourself in the code. Suffice it to say it is very cleverly written.). That's really the essence of Duck Typing – the ability to, at runtime, morph one thing into another.

So let's see it in action. First, we'll declare an interface:

```
type
  IDrivable = interface(IInvokable)
    procedure Drive;
  end;
```

This obviously can be used for drive-able things. But you can drive a lot of different things. For instance, you can drive a car and you can drive a golf ball and you can drive a nail. Note that the interface augments IInvokable, providing needed RTTI on the resulting interface.

Next, let's declare an implementation of IDriveable, as well as a plain old Delphi object that has a Drive method:

```
  TCar = class(TInterfacedObject, IDriveable)
    procedure Drive;
  end;

  TGolfBall = class
    procedure Drive;
  end;
```

Note that TCar has a Drive method, as does TGolfBall, but that they are going to do two very different things:

```
procedure TCar.Drive;
begin
  WriteLn('Ease on down the road.');
end;

procedure TGolfBall.Drive;
begin
  Writeln('Swing and SMACK!');
end;
```

Now, here's where things get interesting. Let's write a simple procedure that takes an IDriveable as a parameter and – surprise! – drives things.

```
procedure DriveTheThing(aDriveable: IDriveable);
begin
  aDrivable.Drive;
end;
```

In the face of it, you should only be able to pass to this procedure a class that implements IDriveable, but hey, TGolfBall has a Drive method, and I want to be able to pass it to DriveTheThing as well. Well, I can – watch:

```
var
  Car: IDriveable;
  GolfBall: TGolfBall;
begin
  Car := TCar.Create;
  GolfBall := TGolfBall.Create;

  DriveTheThing(Car);
  DriveTheThing(Duck<IDriveable>(GolfBall));
  ReadLn;
end.
```

Here's where Duck<T> comes into play. It takes as a parameterized type the interface in question – here, IDriveable – and then takes as a regular parameter an instance of a class that has a Drive method.

I bet at this point you are wondering what happens if you try to pass an object to Duck<T> that has no Drive method. Let's find out.

```
TNotDriveable = class
  procedure SitThere;
end;

procedure TNotDriveable.SitThere;
begin
  WriteLn('Just sitting here.');
end;

var
  NotDriveable: TNotDriveable;
begin
  NotDriveable := TNotDriveable.Create;

  DriveTheThing(Duck<IDriveable>(NotDriveable));
  ReadLn;
end.
```

This code results in an ENotImplemented exception originating inside of Duck<T>. Duck<T> can obviously tell that there is no Drive method available and throws the exception.

Note that the compiler has no way of detecting this error, and as mentioned above you end up with a runtime error. Thus it is up to you to ensure at compile-time that the given class instance you pass to Duck<T> actually implements the properly named method. Note, too, that you must pass the exact signature of the method, or it will fail as well.

Duck Typing with DuckDuckDelphi

The DuckDuckDelphi framework was written by Jason Southwell, a longtime Delphi community member. It's a framework that takes advantage of the new powerful runtime Type Information (RTTI) in Delphi, allowing you to identify things for what they do and not necessarily for what they are. You can find out more about it and how to get it in Appendix A.

DuckDuckDelphi takes a different approach than DSharp. To use it, you simply add the Duck unit from the framework to your unit, and it automatically provides duck typing to any type in that unit. The Duck unit attaches an interface called Duck to every object by creating a class helper for TObject which in turn provides methods that allow you to call methods and set properties among other things.

Let's take a look at a "quack" demo again using DuckDuckDelphi.

First, as noted above, you first should place the Duck unit in your uses clause. Then, you can create a simple method like the following that will call a Quack' method on any object that you pass to it that has such a method:

```
procedure DoQuack(obj: TObject);
begin
  obj.duck.call('Quack');
end;
```

If you pass an object to this procedure that has a Quack method, then that method will be called. If there is no Quack method, nothing will happen.

In addition, you can use the can method to check to see if the object has a Quack method and act accordingly.

```
procedure ProtectedQuack(obj: TObject);
begin
  if obj.duck.can('Quack') then
  begin
    obj.duck.call('Quack')
  end else
  begin
    Writeln('Sorry, I can''t quack!');
  end;
end;
```

Let's create a few things that quack:

```pascal
unit uQuackingThings;

interface

type
  TDuck = class
    procedure Quack;
  end;

  TRubberDuck = class
    procedure Quack;
  end;

  TWAVFileOfADuck = class
    procedure Quack;
  end;

implementation

{ TWAVFileOfADuck }

procedure TWAVFileOfADuck.Quack;
begin
  WriteLn('<sound>Quack!</sound>');
end;

{ TRubberDuck }

procedure TRubberDuck.Quack;
begin
  WriteLn('Squeaky Quack!');
end;

{ TDuck }

procedure TDuck.Quack;
begin
  WriteLn('Quack');
end;

end.
```

And then let's hook it all up so that we can see how it works:

```
procedure DoIt;
var
  LDuck: TObject;
  LRubberDuck: TRubberDuck;
  LWaveFileDuck: TWAVFileOfADuck;
  LGoose: TGoose;
begin
  LDuck := TDuck.Create;
  LRubberDuck := TRubberDuck.Create;
  LWaveFileDuck := TWAVFileOfADuck.Create;
  LGoose := TGoose.Create;
  try
    DoQuack(LDuck);
    DoQuack(LRubberDuck);
    DoQuack(LWaveFileDuck);
    DoQuack(LGoose);

    WriteLn;

    ProtectedQuack(LDuck);
    ProtectedQuack(LRubberDuck);
    ProtectedQuack(LWaveFileDuck);
    ProtectedQuack(LGoose);

  finally
    LDuck.Free;
    LRubberDuck.Free;
    LWaveFileDuck.Free;
    LGoose.Free;
  end;

  ReadLn;
end;
```

All three of the classes that we created can "quack". We didn't have to use inheritance or any type-casting to coerce the types to quack. They have a Quack method and we can just call it.

TGoose is declared below. It's an example of a class that can't Quack. When it is called with DoQuack, nothing happens, but when it is called with ProtectedQuack, it reports that it can't quack.

```
type
  TGoose = class
    procedure Honk;
  end;

procedure TGoose.Honk;
begin
  WriteLn('Honk!');
end;
```

A call to DoIt results in the following output:

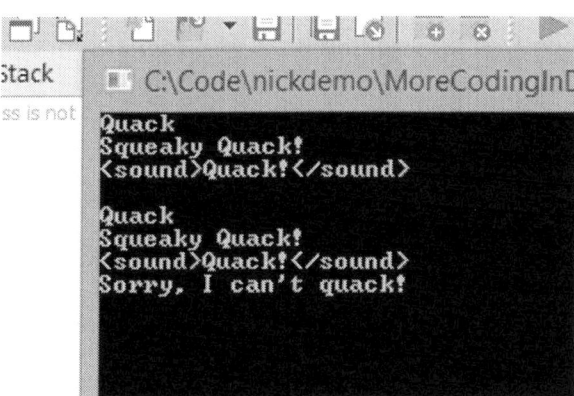

Note that in the first set of quacks, the goose is silent, but in the second one, it declares that it can't quack.

That's cool, but wait, there's more!

Let's add a property to TGoose:

```
type
  TGoose = class
  strict private
    FName: string;
  public
    procedure Honk;
    property Name: string read FName write FName;
  end;
```

And now, we can use duck typing to change the Name of anything with a Name property using the SetTo method:

```
procedure ChangeName(aObj: TObject; aName: string);
begin
  aObj.duck.setTo('Name', aName);
end;
```

Here's some code that calls it, with predictable results:

```
ChangeName(LGoose, 'Marvin');
WriteLn('The goose''s name is ', LGoose.Duck.get('Name').ToString);

LComponent := TComponent.Create(nil);
try
  ChangeName(LComponent, 'Jennifer');
  WriteLn('The component''s name is ', LComponent.Duck.get('name').ToString);
finally
  LComponent.Free;
end;
```

Note that once the name is set, it is retrieved via the IDuck.get method. I need to call the TValue.ToString method because WriteLn can't handle the TValue that IDuck returns. (For more information on TValue, see my previous book...) IDuck also has a has method that returns a Boolean if the given object has the property asked about.

The thing to note here is that these helper methods I'm using to do all the "work" all take a simple TObject as their parameter, but they all can have their Quack method called, or their Name property set. The code doesn't care what the real type passed to it is, it can still call methods and set properties.

But what if the method has parameters? No problem, IDuck can take arguments as a set of TValues:

```
procedure DoAddSix(aObj: TObject; aInteger: integer);
begin
  aObj.duck.call('AddSix', [aInteger]);
end;
```

Again, here's some simple code that has predictable results:

```
var
  LAdd6: TAddSix
begin
    LAdd6 := TAddSix.Create;
    try
      DoAddSix(LAdd6, 7);
    finally
      LAdd6.Free;
    end;
end;
```

It outputs:

Nice, eh?

Duck Typing in the VCL

Most of this book doesn't cover the VCL, but I'm going to build a VCL app here because it illustrates another aspect of DuckDuckDelphi pretty well. A VCL form normally has a lot of TComponents on it, and provides a great opportunity to illustrate the all method of IDuck.

To build the simple application, take the following steps:

1. Create a new VCL application.
2. Drop the following components on it: a TButton, a TCheckBox, a TRadioButton, a TPanel, and a TLabel.
3. Double-click on the button and add the following code: Self.duck.all.setTo('Caption', 'Hello');

Run the app, press the button, and all the components on the form that have the `Caption` property – that is, all of them – will get the caption "Hello". (I couldn't think of any other components that had a "Caption" property…) All with one line of code:

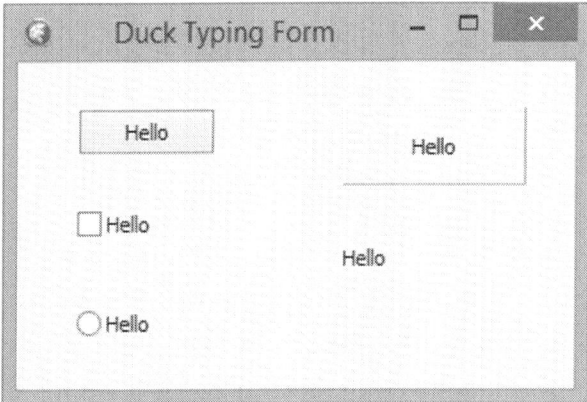

The `all` method can save you a lot of typing, eh?

Why Use Duck Typing?

Duck-typing is sort of an anathema to us strongly-typed Delphi programmers. So why would you use it?

- It can fill some gaps that you can't otherwise fill. For instance, it can allow you to provide Fake objects for unit testing which might otherwise be difficult to fake. Imagine a class that has a complex interface, doesn't implement an interface, is sealed, and thus can't easily be mocked. Duck-typing could allow you to more easily mock that object.
- It can make your code simpler. As we saw in the VCL app above, instead of iterating over all the components on the form, checking to see if their type is of `TComponent`, and then casting to be able to set the property, we can do all that with a single simple line of code.
- One argument in favor of duck-typing is that you can use unit testing to ensure that your classes are correctly typed when duck-typing is involved.

Problems with Duck Typing

Duck Typing is cool, but it has its problems as well.

- Delphi is strongly typed, and all the arguments in favor of strong typing are arguments against Duck Typing.
- Because duck-typing in Delphi requires late-binding, errors with Duck Typing will only reveal themselves at runtime, and folks argue – including me – that you want as many errors as possible to show up at compile time. This forces you to be more careful at design-time than you might be when using static-typing.

- If you are using Duck Typing, you have to be very careful about what you pass, and you have to know exactly what each parameter is capable of. For instance, you might want to call the `Run` method on a bunch of animals, all of whom can run. But be careful not to call `Clock.Run`, because you'll get a very different result than you were expecting. If `Clock.Run` does end up getting called without your knowledge, you probably have a hard to track down bug on your hands.
- If you need to write unit tests to verify and check your typing, aren't you giving up some of the productivity that you gain with dynamic typing? Not that I'm against writing unit tests, but maybe you end up writing more than you have to?
- One issue that could be a problem is performance. Duck-typing requires a lot of runtime support, particularly from the `RTTI` unit, which can degrade performance.

Conclusion

Duck-typing is a cool thing to be able to do in a strongly-typed language like Delphi. It gives you flexibility in situations where you might need it. It does have its dangers, though, so it should be used with care.

Appendix C: Stuff Nick Does When Coding

In this Appendix, I'm going to describe as many things as I can think of that I do when I code – habits, quirks, patterns, etc. I am making this section an Appendix rather than a regular chapter because I don't want to give the impression that this information is supposed to be taken with more than a grain of salt. Frankly, 90% of this is just my obsessive/compulsive behavior. In this Appendix, I've gathered up all the coding habits that I've developed over the years. I'm totally aware that you will likely disagree with much of what I write here. That's fine. Maybe you'll pick up a practice that you like. That's great. Maybe it will stimulate some thought into how you go about writing your code. That's great as well. Either way, thanks for indulging me.

Formatting Stuff

I'm not going to outline my entire formatting policy. I think that formatting is a personal thing and you should do it however you like as long as you are consistent with it. If you are on a team, create a policy for everyone.

I will say this about formatting, though: I'm absolutely fanatical about it. I format everything correctly immediately. I indent everything two spaces right away. I fanatically ensure that everything lines up correctly. I do this even with "throw away code". **Good, consistent formatting can reveal bugs and logic errors**. If your formatting doesn't look right, it could indicate a problem in your code. Keeping your code properly formatted is a solid habit that you should have, no matter what rules you follow.

An additional formatting rule I follow: Even though Object Pascal is case-insensitive, I always ensure that my names are properly cased. Always. I know that is a bit obsessive, but I do it.

Spacing

I always put spaces around = and := , as well as around all operators. I don't ever do this:

```
i:=SomeNumber+AnotherNumber;
```

vastly preferring this:

```
i := SomeNumber + AnotherNumber;
```

I always put a space after a comma and a semi-colon, but never before:

```
procedure DoSomething(aString: string; aInteger: integer);
  ...
DoSomething(SomeString, SomeInteger);
```

I always put a space after a colon, but not before:

```
var
  i: integer;
  s: string;
```

Begins and Ends

I always line up begins and ends. Every time. I always type

```
begin
  . . .
end;
```

and that never varies. begin always goes on its own line. I always make both lowercase. I don't put my begin on the same line as an if or any other lines:

```
if SomeBoolean then
begin
  . . .
end;
```

Also, I never, ever type begin without immediately typing the corresponding end. I always indent two spaces between the begin and the end and start coding there.

And probably the thing that will drive you all the most crazy: I put begin/end pairs around everything – even single lines of code:

```
if SomeBoolean then
begin
  EvenASingleLine;
end;
```

Why? Because I never want to make the mistake of forgetting to add the begin/end when it's needed.

```
if SomeBoolean then
  SingleLineOfCode;
```

can very easily become

```
if SomeBoolean then
  SingleLineOfCode;
  AnotherLineThatShouldBeInABegin;
```

and then you have a subtle bug that you might not see right away. If you put the begin\end pair in there at the very start, that will never happen. You'll always get:

```
if SomeBoolean then
begin
  SingleLineOfCode;
  AnotherLineThatShouldBeInABegin;
end;
```

Variable Prefixes

I use prefixes to denote what the scope of a variable is. I preface local variables with L, I put a lower-case a in front of all parameters, a lowercase c in front of constants, and an uppercase F in front of fields in a class. I know that's inconsistent, but that's what I do.

var Declarations

var always gets its own line, followed by the declarations. And every declaration gets its own line. I never type:

```
var
  This, That: string;
```

always

```
var
  This: string;
  That: string;
```

I do that because it makes it easier to hunt up any given declaration. This makes it hard to find things:

```
var
  i: integer
  This, That, Theother: integer;
  They, Them, Their: string;
  Widget: TWidget
```

as the names are within the declaration and not at the beginning of a line.

if statement

I always say that Object Pascal has two if statements – one with else and one without. if will either be:

```
if SomeBoolean then
begin
  ...
end;
```

or

```
if SomeBoolean then
begin
  ...
end else
begin
  ...
end;
```

with the end and the else always on the same line. That's the only two ways an if statement will be formatted.

Capitalization

I have absolutely no rhyme nor reason to what I do and don't capitalize. Variable names always start with a capital letter.

The following things I always capitalize:

```
Result
Boolean
Exit
Break (though I almost never use this one.....)
True
False
```

the following I always put in lower case:

```
integer
begin
end
if
for
while
repeat
until
then
do
var
const
to
else
procedure
function
constructor
destructor
finally
except
```

I'm sure there are others, but you should get the idea. I know, it makes little sense, but there you have it.

Coding Stuff

There are certain rules I always follow when I write code. Perhaps they are a bit quirky, but they are all designed to make my code clean, easy to read, and easy to maintain. I also maintain that these techniques help prevent bugs.

Asset Allocation

I never create anything without immediately seeing to its proper destruction. Immediately. Directly. I always end up with this:

```
MyWidget := TMyWidget.Create;
try

finally
  MyWidget.Free;
end;
```

before I actually do anything with `MyWidget`.

If I create something in a `constructor` I *immediately* destroy it in a `destructor`. Same thing for an `OnCreate` event – the object is immediately freed in the `OnDestroy` event. Immediately. If I call `GetMem`, I immediately call `FreeMem`. (Not that I use `GetMem\FreeMem` very much). I don't allocate or create anything without seeing to its proper disposal ***immediately***. Doing so prevents memory leaks.

Scope

I try to limit the scope of everything as much as possible. If a variable can be local, I make it local. If it can't be local, make it a `strict private` field. If I need a constant for a class, I put it in the `strict private` section of the class, rather than let it be stand-alone. If something can be placed in the `implementation` section, I put it there. `uses` clause entries should be placed in the `implementation` section unless they are needed in the `interface` section.

And global variables? Never, ever, ever. Ever. Never.

I always use `strict private` and `strict protected` over simply `private` and `protected`. The latter two allow for "friends" scoping within units, and that violates my "Limit scoping as much as possible" rule.

Why limit scope? Because the more limited in scope a variable is, the less likely it is to be misused and become out of control. It's vastly preferable to pass a variable to a method than it is to make it a field of a class. There's no telling what mischief a subsequent programmer might cause by allowing a variable to get out of proper scope and thus out of control.

Formatting Strings

I tend to prefer the use of the `Format` function over the use of string concatenation with the + symbol. I use `Format` because it allows for easy mixing of types when creating a string. It avoids things like:

```
Str := 'It can get ugly to add ' + aString + ' and a ' + aNumber.ToString + ' together'.
```

You have to watch your spaces, the typing is awkward, and it's just messy. This is far better:

```
Str := Format('It can get ugly to add %s and a %d together', [aString, aNumber]);
```

Spacing

I put one space between functions, procedures, and methods.

```
procedure One;
begin
  ...
end;

procedure Two;
begin
  ...
end;
```

I never, ever separate them with something like this:

```
//---------------------------------------------------------------
```

For some reason I just hate that. I'm not a C++ developer.

uses Clauses

Here's an uncommon thing I do – I stack my uses clauses vertically, and put the comma at the beginning of the line. I also put the resulting semi-colon on its own line. For example:

```
uses
      SysUtils
    , HTMLWriterUtils
    , Classes
    , Generics.Collections
    , HTMLWriterIntf
    , LoadSaveIntf
    ;
```

I do this for two reasons. First, it makes it really easy to comment out a given entry. Second, it makes it easy to cut a single entry for movement from the implementation section to the interface section if need be.

Also, I put the more broadly used unit names – like the VCL and System namespaces – first, and the more specific unit names, like my own units, later in the uses clause.

Identifiers

First, I'm a Delphi developer, so all my type identifiers begin with T. End of discussion about that.

I endeavor to make my identifiers meaningful. I don't care if they end up being long:

```
procedure ProcessWidgetWithSprocketHandlesAndFoobarKnobs;
```

is perfectly fine by me. If the identifier explains what it identifies, then you've given the readers of your code a step up on what your code does. If you are writing a class that deals with HTML, is there much doubt what the `CloseTheTag` procedure does?

I use Pascal case with my identifiers. Not camelCase, PascalCase. (The two are often confused.)

I can't stand the use of underscores and never use them anywhere. Does anyone like typing an underscore? Not me.

The only exception to the above it using `i`, `j`, etc., as a `for` loop counter. Everyone knows what that means.

Comments

I try to write code that "documents itself". If your code is clearly written, well refactored, and has good names, then you don't need comments to explain it. If you feel the need to add a comment to explain what is going on, a rewrite may be the better option.

I generally am against code commenting. As above, if you feel the need to comment, it usually indicates that you've failed to write good, clean code. I know this is controversial. Heck, I know people and organizations that require ***every routine*** to be commented. I won't rehash the entire debate here. I'll just say that I've had success with my "almost no comments" policy, and I think it's the right way to go.

> Note, I'm not against "triple slash" (`///`) comments that document your code as an API. Those kind of comments should be encouraged for framework code.

If I ever do feel the need to put comments in my code, I make sure that they are "why" comments and not "what" comments. Explaining why you did something is the only reason I can think of for commenting your code, though I still believe that code should "comment itself" as much as possible.

Say 'No' to Boolean Parameters

I mentioned earlier that I put a lowercase 'a' in front of my parameter names. Another thing I do is avoid Boolean parameters. For instance, what does this code mean?

```
ProcessWidgets(True);
```

Who knows? That Boolean parameter conveys no meaning at all. Instead, I prefer to declare an enumeration, even if it just has two members:

```
type
  TWidgetProcessorEnum = (UseLocalProcessor, UseRemoteProcessor);
```

and then my code can read like this:

```
ProcessWidgets(UseLocalProcessor);
```

which clearly conveys what is going on.

Nested Routines

Sure, the language allows them, but in general they are distracting, annoying, and ill-advised. I never use them. If you have a nested function, or worse, multiple nested functions, or even *worse* a nested function in a nested function (and yes, I have seen this....) you should consider that all these procedures really should be a class.

Conclusion

Okay, so that's some of the stuff I do when coding. Some of it is weird, some of it a little crazy, I know – but it's all done for a reason: To write better, easier to read, easier to maintain code. And that's what we are all trying to do, right?

Appendix D: Sources Used in Writing This Book

This is a partial list of resources that I used in writing this book. I'm sure that I referred to more sources than this, but this is my best effort at giving credit to those books and places on the web that helped me write this book.

Books

- *Parallel Programming with Microsoft.Net* by Colin Campbell, Ralph Johnson, Ade Miller, and Stephen Toub
- *Head First Design Patterns* by Eric Freeman and Elisabeth Freeman with Kathy Sierra and Bert Bates
- *Clean Code* by Robert C. Martin
- *Agile Principles, Patterns, and Practices in C#* by Robert C. Martin and Micah Martin
- *Delphi XE2 Foundations* by Chris Rolliston
- *Dependency Injection in .Net* by Mark Seemann
- *Delphi Cookbook* by Daniele Teti

Web Links

- Multi-threading in .NET: http://yoda.arachsys.com/csharp/threads/index.shtml
- Multithreading - The Delphi Way: http://www.nickhodges.com/MultiThreadingInDelphi/ToC.html
- http://robstechcorner.blogspot.com/2015/02/tpl-ttask-example-in-how-not-to-use.html
- http://robstechcorner.blogspot.com/2015/02/tpl-ttask-exception-management.html
- http://delphi.org/2015/02/parallel-for-loops/
- How Duck Typing Benefits C# Developers: http://haacked.com/archive/2007/08/19/why-duck-typing-matters-to-c-developers.aspx/
- Duck Typing in Wikipedia: http://en.wikipedia.org/wiki/Duck_typing
- Introduction to Concurrency:

  - http://www.cs.colorado.edu/~kena/classes/5828/s12/lectures/04-introconcurrency.pdf
- Aspect-Oriented Programming with the RealProxy Class by Bruno Sonnino: https://msdn.microsoft.com/en-us/magazine/dn574804.aspx
- Interface Segregation Principle: http://www.oodesign.com/interface-segregation-principle.html
- http://www.codeproject.com/Tips/766045/Interface-Segregation-Principle-ISP-of-SOLID-in-Cs
- Working with TMultiReadExclusiveWriteSynchronizer: http://edn.embarcadero.com/article/28258
- Encapsulation: You're Doing It Wrong: https://lostechies.com/derickbailey/2011/03/28/encapsulation-youre-doing-it-wrong/

- Poka-yoke Design: From Smell to Fragrance: http://blog.ploeh.dk/2011/05/24/Poka-yokeDesignFromSmelltoFragrance/
- http://grabbagoft.blogspot.com/2007/12/dealing-with-primitive-obsession.html
- http://www.javamex.com/tutorials/threads/deadlock.shtml
- Safe Thread Synchronization: https://msdn.microsoft.com/en-us/magazine/cc188793.aspx
- Aspect Oriented Programming (AOP) using AspectJ: http://www.luisrocha.net/2008_06_01_archive.html
- Exploring the Factory Design Pattern: https://msdn.microsoft.com/en-us/library/ee817667.aspx
- http://www.dofactory.com/net/abstract-factory-design-pattern
- http://www.dofactory.com/net/factory-method-design-pattern
- http://stackoverflow.com/questions/5847443/how-to-avoid-switch-case-in-a-factory-method-of-child-classes
- http://stackoverflow.com/questions/69849/factory-pattern-when-to-use-factory-methods

Videos

- Allen Bauer's PPL Talk: https://www.youtube.com/watch?v=4_PB5bnapXw#t=60
- Jim McKeeth on Parallel For loops: https://www.youtube.com/watch?v=uZ79t4bSM1w&t=1112
- Danny Wind's PPL Talk: https://www.youtube.com/watch?v=rZfux4by0po
- Mark Seemann on Encapsulation and SOLID: http://www.pluralsight.com/courses/encapsulation-solid
- How to really build an adapter: https://www.youtube.com/watch?v=tGtJ5U_eeIU#t=12

Printed in Great Britain
by Amazon